Louise Eleanor Shimer Hogan

A Study of a Child

Louise Eleanor Shimer Hogan

A Study of a Child

ISBN/EAN: 9783337219147

Printed in Europe, USA, Canada, Australia, Japan

Cover: Foto ©Suzi / pixelio.de

More available books at **www.hansebooks.com**

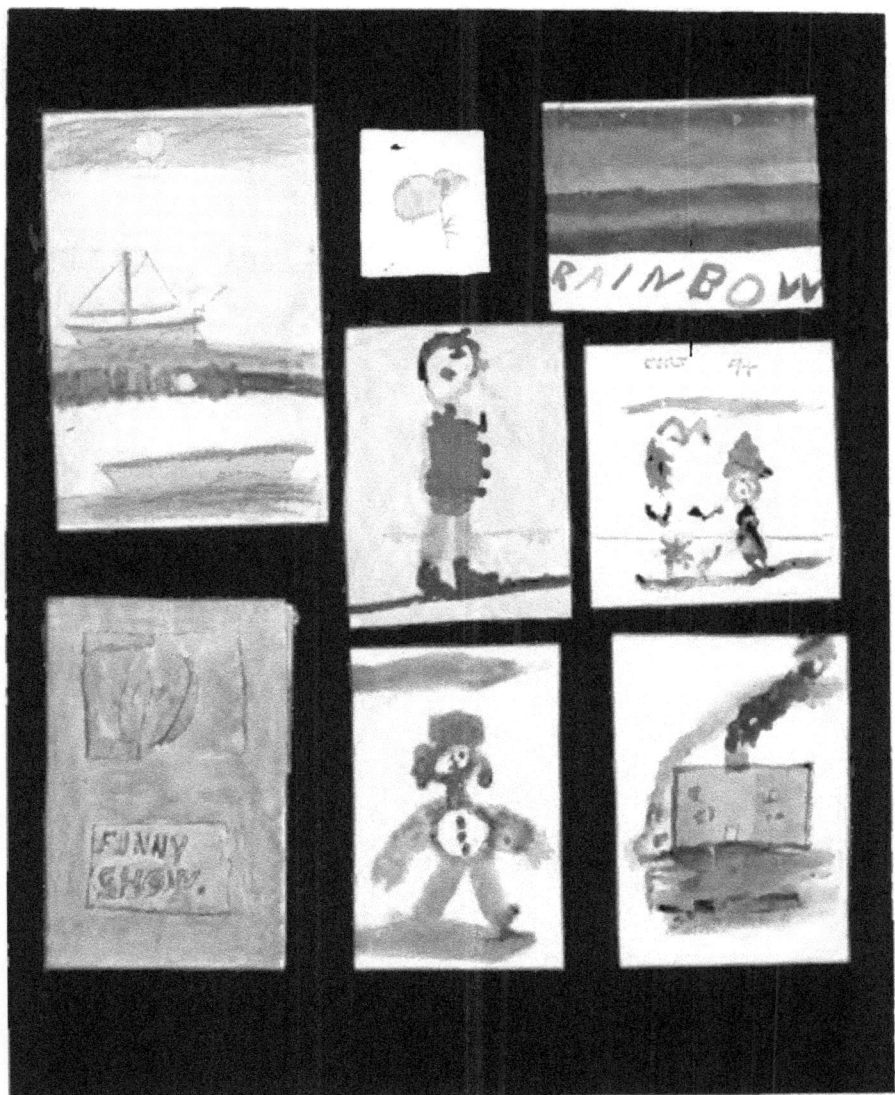

SPONTANEOUS EFFORTS WITH COLORS, 1891 TO 1898

A STUDY OF A CHILD

BY

LOUISE E. HOGAN

ILLUSTRATED WITH OVER 500 ORIGINAL DRAWINGS
BY THE CHILD

NEW YORK AND LONDON
HARPER & BROTHERS PUBLISHERS
1898

PREFACE

THE interest awakened in America and Europe by the child-study movement, the fascination that lies in the sayings and the doings of children, and especially the expressed desire of psychologists, physicians, and teachers for opportunity to study individual child records, both normal and abnormal, have led to the preparation of this book, with the hope of entertaining the general reader and of stimulating interest in practical methods for mental, moral, and physical development of the child in the nursery.

Professor Ladd, of Yale, says in a recent work (*Outlines of Descriptive Psychology*), that of six sources of psychology, one is "observation of the mental processes of infants and children. . . . as necessary to a better analysis of the mature mental processes of man and to the detection of hitherto concealed factors within them." Such understanding, he says, is indispensable to the understanding of human mental life as being, what it undoubtedly is, a development.

Dr. Arnold, of Rugby, whose stand for the principles of humanity in education is known throughout the world, declared boyhood to be an inferior state, a dangerous

time, when temptation is great and resistance exceed-
ingly small; and he said that the change from boyhood
to manhood should be hastened, for the growth of his
character and for the development of the love of unselfishness and fear of God. More in keeping, however, with accepted educational theories of to-day, John
Corbin says, in this connection, in his study of *School-
boy Life in England* that since Arnold's day many
experiments have been made in bringing up boys, and
many thoughtful men have written on the subject, and
in consequence we are more likely to respect the state
of boyhood and sympathize with it, to regard it as
necessary and beautiful rather than dangerous, and to
believe that the more fully a boy learns to be a boy,
the more thoroughly he will be a man when the time
comes. He adds, forcibly: "In its way, boyhood is as
little to be avoided as old age. Both were ordained by
the Power that no one has ever understood; they are
equally necessary for the fulness of life, and equally
beautiful."

The history of the child Harold is given exactly as
it was originally written, with but few additional ex-
planatory remarks concerning the course taken to produce the results recorded. This plan has been followed
as most likely to attract the attention of the general
reader whose aid in furnishing child-diaries is asked
for by scientists; yet the record, though unclassified,
will be of no less value to the student. As the results are obvious, the reader may draw his own conclusions.

A portion of the record and the introductory chapter
were sent to Dr. Preyer, and annotations to the manuscript, which are duly noted, were received in reply,

with several letters of singular charm, in one of which he says :

"Since fifteen years, when the first German edition of my book on *The Mind of the Infant* was published, I have wished that a lady, after having studied the work done, would let a child develop itself naturally and without continually interfering with mother-nature. I actually brought my boy up in this way, and he is always happy. The boy you have observed seems to have been educated in a similar way. I feel nearly sure we are sailing carefully, but with energy, in exactly the same direction. I think the wish I mentioned will soon be fulfilled by you to my heart's content. Mind you do not go too deep into psychology—controversies would spoil the effect of your observations, which in many cases may serve as a practical guide, without any commentary. When some years ago I was often asked to write a popular nursery psychology with my pedagogical rules, I always answered that such a manual must be written by a mother who has not intrusted her baby to nurses, but brought it up and thoroughly studied it lovingly herself, and I added that I would help any lady who would undertake the lengthy but very pleasant work."

The recent and much lamented death of Dr. Preyer adds special significance to these words, which illustrate so clearly the comprehensive character of the work to which his life was given.

While the gradual development of an infant during its first year may be of great interest to both scientist and mother, the quaint and fanciful tangents of a child's self-activity during the years following closely upon infancy are the most absorbing to the general reader, and for this reason the following selections have been made as illustrative of various stages of unconscious growth, and as not altogether of simply scientific interest.

LOUISE E. HOGAN.

NEW YORK, *June*, 1898.

CONTENTS

INTRODUCTION

PAGE

Reasons for Child-Study in the Home.......................... 1

CHAPTER I

Fragmentary First-Year Notes 15

CHAPTER II

Second Year—Covering Development of Language, and, Incidentally, the Cultivation of Obedience and Trust............ 22

CHAPTER III

Third Year—Language and Other Incidental Development Continued.. 76

CHAPTER IV

Fourth Year—Record of Spontaneous Development After the Child was Three Years Old, with Selections of Drawings and Cuttings, all Mental Pictures, Done as a Result of Self-Activity, and Accompanied by the Child's Explanations..... 140

CHAPTER V

Fifth Year — Record Continued — Nature Stories — Training Butterflies and White Mice — The Child's First Effort at Relating a Story.. 149

CONTENTS

CHAPTER VI

PAGE

Sixth Year — Number-Work—Composition—Fancy—The Story of Kitty—The Adventures of a Lady-Bug................ 167

CHAPTER VII

Seventh Year—Learning German, Writing, and Spelling through Play—A Bedtime Question Talk—Comparison Questions and Answers—The Child's Song to His Colors—Two Stories Told by the Child 181

CHAPTER VIII

Eighth Year—Efforts at Arithmetic—"A Story all Upsidedown" and "A Wonderful Dream" Told by the Child — Memory-Work — Conception of Fractions — Development in Drawing and Designing... 215

ILLUSTRATIONS

SPONTANEOUS EFFORTS WITH COLORS, 1891 TO 1898. . *Frontispiece*

NO DATE DRAWINGS . . . . *Facing p.* 94

NO DATE DRAWINGS . . . . " 108

NO DATE DRAWINGS . . . . " 120

1892 AND 1893 DRAWINGS AND CUTTINGS—THE CHILD'S
EARLIEST EFFORTS . . . . " 132

1893 DRAWINGS—THREE YEARS OLD . . . . . . " 134

1893 AND 1894 DRAWINGS. . . . . " 136

1894 CUTTINGS . . . . " 138

1893 DRAWINGS—ENGINES . . . . " 140

1893 DRAWINGS—BOATS, TROLLEYS, ETC. . . . " 142

1893 DRAWINGS—ENGINES—THREE YEARS OLD . . . " 144

1893 DRAWINGS—THREE YEARS OLD . . . . . . " 144

1893 DRAWINGS . . . . " 146

1893 DRAWINGS—THREE YEARS OLD . . . . . . " 148

1894 CUTTINGS AND 1893 AND 1894 PRINTED LETTER
WORK . . . . " 150

1894 CUTTINGS—FOUR YEARS OLD . . . . . . " 150

1894 CUTTINGS OF ENGINES . . . . " 152

1894 ENGINE AND CAR CUTTINGS—FOUR YEARS OLD . " 152

1894 DRAWINGS—FOUR YEARS OLD . . . . . . " 154

1894 DRAWINGS—FOUR YEARS OLD . . . . . . " 154

1894 DRAWINGS . . . . " 156

1894 DRAWINGS—FOUR YEARS OLD . . . . . . " 156

1894 DRAWINGS—FOUR YEARS OLD . . . . . . " 158

1894 DRAWINGS—FOUR YEARS OLD . . . . . . " 158

DINNER FOR TWO . . . . " 160

THE BUTTERFLY'S BATH . . . . " 162

THE BUTTERFLY ON THE CURTAIN . . . . Facing p. 164

1895 AND 1896 DRAWINGS . . . . " 166

1895 DRAWINGS . . . . " 168

1895 ENGINE DRAWINGS—FIVE YEARS OLD . . . . " 170

1895 DRAWINGS—FIVE YEARS OLD . . . . . . " 172

1895 DRAWINGS—FIVE YEARS OLD . . . . . . " 172

1895 DRAWINGS—FIVE YEARS OLD . . . . . . " 174

1895 DRAWINGS—FIVE YEARS OLD . . . . . . " 174

1895 BOAT DRAWINGS—FIVE YEARS OLD . . . . . " 176

1895 DRAWINGS—FIVE YEARS OLD . . . . . " 176

1895 DRAWINGS—FIVE YEARS OLD . . . . " 178

1895 CUTTINGS—FIVE YEARS OLD . . . . . . " 180

1896 DRAWINGS . . . . " 182

1896 DRAWINGS—SIX YEARS OLD . . . . . . " 184

1896 DRAWINGS—SIX YEARS OLD . . . . . " 186

1896 DRAWINGS—SIX YEARS OLD . . " 188

1896 DRAWINGS . . . . " 190

GRADED EFFORT AT WRITING — COMPOSITION AND
  EARLY EFFORTS AT NUMBERS . . . . . . " 192

1896 DRAWINGS—SIX YEARS OLD . . . . . . " 196

1896 CUTTINGS AND DRAWINGS—SIX YEARS OLD . " 200

1896 CUTTINGS—SIX YEARS OLD . . . . . " 204

EARLY CUTTINGS AND WRITINGS . . . . . " 208

1896 CUTTINGS AND DRAWINGS . . . . . . " 212

A LESSON IN ADDITION . . . . Page 215

A LESSON AND ITS RESULT: EARLY ATTEMPTS AT SUB-
  TRACTION, DIVISION, AND MULTIPLICATION . . . " 216

1897 DRAWINGS—SEVEN YEARS OLD . . . . . Facing p. 216

1897 DRAWINGS—SEVEN YEARS OLD . . . . . . " 216

1897 DRAWINGS . . . . " 218

1897 DRAWINGS—SEVEN YEARS OLD . . . . . . " 218

1897 AND 1898 DRAWINGS . . . . " 218

A STUDY OF A CHILD

A STUDY OF A CHILD

INTRODUCTION

REASONS FOR CHILD-STUDY IN THE HOME

PROFESSOR COMPAYRÉ says: "If childhood is the cradle of humanity, the study of childhood is the natural and necessary introduction to all future psychology."

Lowell says: "We were designed in the cradle, per-haps earlier, and it is in finding out this design and shaping ourselves to it that our years are spent wisely. It is the vain endeavor to make ourselves what we are not that has strewn history with so many broken pur-poses and lives left in the rough."

Dr. Harris, United States Commissioner of Education, says parents and teachers are *directly* concerned with the aggregation of facts of value gathered by child-students, and from which is being evolved a new edu-cation, which deals in explanations which are the key-note to infant development.

Perez says, in *The First Three Years of Childhood:* "The business of psychological educators is much more concerned with the habits that children may acquire, and with their wills, which are also developed by habitual

A   1

practice, than with the development of their moral conscience. The latter is the blossom which will be followed by fruit, but the former are the roots and branches."

Professor Sully says in his introduction to this work that the cardinal principle of modern educational theory is that systematic training should watch the spontaneous movements of the child's mind and adapt its processes to these. It is in the first three or four years of life that we have the key to the emotional and moral nature of the young. He says, "if the study be deferred to school-life, it will never be full or exact. The artificial character of even the brightest school surroundings offers too serious an obstacle to the free play of childish likings." He says, further, that nothing, perhaps, has been more misunderstood than childhood; that few have the disposition to seriously endeavor to think themselves into the situation and circumstances of the child, casting aside their own adult habits of mind and trying to become themselves for the moment as little children, and that the man to whom children will reveal themselves is not he who is wont to look on them as a nuisance or a bore, but he who finds them an amusement and a delight, who likes nothing better than to cast aside now and again the heavy armor of serious business and indulge in a good childish romp. He suggests the father as an observer, because his masculine intelligence will be less exposed to the risk of taking too sentimental and eulogistic a view of the baby mind; but he says the father cannot, however, hope to accomplish the task alone. His restricted leisure compels him to call in the mother as collaborateur, and "the mother's enthusiasm and patient, brooding watchfulness are need-

2

ed quite as much as the father's keen, analytic vision. The mother should note under the guidance of the father, he taking due care to test and verify. In this way we may look for something like a complete record of infant life."

In his recent work, *Studies of Childhood*, he says that the greatest desideratum to-day for practical results in child-study is the study of individual children as they may be approached in the nursery; that environment, heredity, and methods of education should all be noted in relation to the child in question if the record is to be of the greatest value. In view of the fact that children as well as their environments differ very widely, he says we need to know much more about these variations; that there is no substitute for the careful, methodical, study of the individual child, and that the co-operation of the mother is indispensable, as the knowledge of others never equals that of the mother. He predicts that women will become valuable laborers in this new field of investigation if they will only acquire a genuine scientific interest in babyhood and a fair amount of scientific training. He indicates the necessity of careful training in observation, because a child is very quick to see whether he is being observed, and as soon as he suspects that you are specially interested in his talk he is apt to try to produce an effect. This wish to say something startling or wonderful will, it is obvious, detract from the value of the utterance.

Stanley Hall also points out that child-study is especially the woman's province of work, that all teaching, especially of the very young, must always be a work of love to be really effective, and that child-study should be so directed as to instruct concerning child-nature and awaken child-love. He also says the love of childhood and youth has always been one of the strongest incentives to high thoughts and noble deeds, and, quite apart from its results, the study of children is good in itself, enriches parenthood, and brings the adult and the child nearer together.

To sum up authorities, the late Dr. Preyer, whose work in child-study is known all over the world, says, in *Infant Mind:* "But, after all, the observation in mental development in the earliest years naturally falls to the mother more than to any other person; that other persons also, teachers, both male and female, fathers, older brothers and sisters, are to be induced to consider the importance of the facts in this field, which has, indeed, been lying open for hundreds of years, but has been little trodden, and is therefore a new field."

He continues: "Although the little child shows himself to the observer always without the least dissimulation, still there is great danger with the anthropomorphic tendency of most people in their way of looking at things, that more will be attributed to the child than actually belongs to him." He says, "new comprehensive diaries concerning the actions of children are urgently to be desired, and they should contain nothing but well-established facts, no hypotheses, and no repetition of the statements of others."

Following such suggestions as these, I began seven years ago to observe systematically a healthy, happy, and intelligent child, endeavoring to keep constantly in view the fact that he was but one of many, and taking no liberty of expression whatever beyond recording facts. The record was taken at intervals under exceptionally favorable circumstances, for he was trained under what might be called the Pestalozzian principle of letting alone, with unconscious supervision in a carefully guarded environment which supplied a great number of centres of interest that were full of indirect suggestion. Preyer says in one of his works: "The more numerous the sounds of interest imitated, the quicker the child will learn to talk;" he noted later, however, in one of the letters, before mentioned, "but their then mental development may thus be disturbed." It was for fear of such disturbance that no formal teaching of any kind was allowed until the end of the sixth year, but all questions were carefully answered, and effort was made to see that the answers were clearly understood. Servants were instructed to refer the child to his parents for answers to all questions they did not themselves comprehend, and sufficient supervision was given to see that these directions were followed. All baby-talk was forbidden, and great care was taken to enunciate distinctly. Surroundings were carefully planned to meet growing needs from the moment he began to notice things. The record is therefore one of spontaneous development of self-activity produced as a result: (1) of suggestion, based upon a carefully considered environment; (2) of accurate and sympathetic explanation, given only when asked for; and (3) of carefully graded steps that were taken one at a time. (Dr. Preyer's annotation here was "Quite true.") Edward Gardiner Howe says: "Restraint upon the part of the parent or teacher is a necessity to prevent giving more information than can be absorbed." He also says: "There is no subject so profound but its central truth can be taught to very small children, and a child can be led to any height if the steps are made short

5

enough." (Dr. Preyer here added, "This is not the case.")

The results recorded illustrate, however, very clearly the practicability of Froebel's theory of inducing and guiding in the nursery a self-activity which eventually will develop power, cultivate observation and memory, produce accuracy, teach a child to think—in short, develop every faculty a child may possess, and enable it to educate itself easily by giving it a *technic,* so to speak, and a desire for study which will continue through a lifetime if it is not dulled by routine method during the period following nursery life, after which time only must instruction become formal. This method of training also affords the parent an opportunity of discovering inherent weaknesses and removing them by encouraging and sympathetic influences; for, as Mrs. Felix Adler sympathetically says: "In the case of children, they are sure to distress and discourage us, but we must not make the mistake of overlooking the light parts that balance the dark shadows. We must expect to find inconsistencies, curious incongruities, paradoxes in the character. If we study both good and evil traits, the good ones will enable us to eradicate the evil ones." It is a well-established fact that a child learns through playing and by having opportunity to let nature assert itself spontaneously and without restraint, under watchful supervision —of which, however, it must be unconscious—yet how commonly we see nurses, and even parents, endeavoring to attract the attention of an infant, perhaps with the idea of amusing, when most probably its only requirement at the time is *to be let alone to do what pleases it.* (Dr. Preyer here added "Yes," and underscored the phrase). Instead of being quietly placed where the child may reach it, a ball will be shaken to and fro, or up and down so rapidly that the babe's eyes are unable to follow it; hands will be clapped so loud that the child becomes frightened; the nurse will keep up an eternal jogging on the knee of the body of the child, with some curious notion of the necessity for constant movement as a pacifier. Some persons go so far even as to toss baby up and down as if he were a ball, while the poor little atom of humanity wants only to be let alone to find out for himself what all the curious things mean with which he finds himself surrounded. If the persons whose business it is to take care of infants would, instead of amusing themselves at the expense of the child's nerves, practise sufficient self-restraint to watch the efforts of a four-months'-old child when it is trying to touch a ball or any object within its reach and line of vision, as the one observed did when three and one-half months' old, the immense possibility would be evident at once of training a child to self-entertainment by simply letting him alone to find out about things and do for himself. (Dr. Preyer wrote in this connection: " Yes, this is quite true. Need not be verified. Even the shaking of the cradle, of the baby in the nurse's arms, I strictly forbid, on account of the disturbance of the blood circulation of the brain.") A study of the record of the child observed should be sufficient to convince the most incredulous mother of the fact that she may save herself much care and worry and do much better for her child by shaping with a compelling hand the environment of her nursery from the very beginning of its life, for it is at this time that a correct habit of body may be laid with very little effort, and it is also the time when many a child's life develops an impulse in the opposite direction difficult to overcome in later years.

If during the first six months a regular regime has been established in regard to hours of feeding, sleep, bathing, and letting alone, the mother will, by this time, have leisure to consider the needs of the awakening mind. Regularity in nursery routine, with its result showing in the serenity of the child, will give opportunity for study as to how best to meet the new requirements, and also to take records of daily development for reference as to future guidance and study. Compayré says the better the child's health and the better he is fed, the more activity he has to dispense and the more active will be his motor faculty; and inasmuch as physical care favors intellectual growth from the very first, that mothers shall provide *intelligently* for physical needs and beware of *restraining* this motor faculty, if it is not too great. Nervous children *must* be restrained, Preyer added. This restraint, however, must be wisely exercised, or not at all.

Children are proverbially good when they are busy, but constant diversion is necessary to keep them so, because the child-mind is not capable of fixed attention for more than a few minutes at a time. Herein lies the value of the principle of suggestion in environment. It is possible and very easy for a mother who has any comprehension of Froebel's inner meaning to prepare each day in a very few minutes, after her child has gone to sleep, a suggestive environment that will relieve her almost entirely during the following hours of any care beyond the physical, and even this may, if necessary, under proper direction and supervision, be delegated to a faithful servant. It is in the constant supervision

8

with wise and gentle guidance that the necessary work for the mother lies, not in the actual labor involved, which may be regulated according to circumstances.

The usual attitude of the parent not versed in child-study is sceptical and antagonistic to reform. A very frequent excuse offered by such a parent for the careless training of children, and the consequent arrest of their physical, mental, and moral development, is that there are too many other duties pressing upon them to allow of sufficient attention to these things. I have frequently heard mothers and teachers say, in a tone of scepticism, that child-study is productive of no practical good; that children have done well enough heretofore, and that they will do so again. One of the greatest results to be hoped from child-study is to show just such parents and teachers how much easier it is to develop good than evil in *all* children, and that letting "well enough" alone will never yield the greatest development of character, the true aim of education. The practical application of child-study must begin in the nursery and continue through the kindergarten and primary school, which must all be in touch one with the other.

Susan Blow says, pertinently, that notwithstanding all that has been said and written about conforming to the different stages of natural development, we still make knowledge an idol, and continue to fill the child's mind with foreign material, under the gratuitous assumption that at a later age he will be able, through some magic transubstantiation, to make it a vital part of his own thought. But glaring as are our sins of commission, they pale before our sins of omission, for while we are forcing upon the child's mind knowledge which has no roots in his experience, or calling upon him to exercise still dormant powers, we refuse any aid to his spontaneous struggle to do and learn and be that which his stage of development demands. Thus we kill the creative activity, the absence of which in later life we deplore and endeavor again to recreate. It is true that it is the exceptional mother and teacher to-day who take up this question in any but a superficial manner, but it is not too much to hope that the day will come, and that very soon, when the *practical results of the science of child-study* will have permeated *every home of intelligence, kindergarten, and school,* and when *mother, nurse, kindergartner,* and *primary-school teacher* will work hand in hand, without stepping over the line forbidden for normal physical development. From a foundation like this should arise a nation of people possessing such marked individuality and productive capability as would conclusively demonstrate the value of the work that has been done by men like Comenius, Pestalozzi, Rousseau, Froebel, Herbart, Preyer, and Horace Mann, and is now being done by Sully, Harris, Baldwin, Stanley Hall, and many others.

A great impetus has already been given by these psychologists to those young parents, kindergartners, and primary-school teachers who have been alive to the true meaning of child-study; and Froebel's love for children and his desire for their happiness is understood more clearly to-day than ever before. Much of the physical restraint formerly in vogue among kindergartners and teachers, and the too close attention to method and the *letter* of his philosophy instead of the *spirit*, have disappeared, and the freedom of spontaneous play and self-activity have taken their place, to the manifest improvement of the child.

10

When we remember that Froebel did not expect his philosophy to be thoroughly understood for two hundred years, we can easily see how, after fifty years of imperfect elucidation, there still remains a great work for the kindergartner, and a still greater one for the mother in the nursery, to produce the necessary adjustment to educational methods which is required for spontaneous development.

Sympathy and suggestion must go hand in hand with trained method—one is as necessary as the other—but the mother's work must come first, for she has the first opportunity.

She can prepare herself for this work by studying the philosophy of Froebel—not necessarily his methods—and then, by putting his principles into practice, she will find that the child's development in the nursery will be a sympathetic reflection of her own, and will unconsciously follow her own plan of study, which should lead directly into the hands of the kindergartner. It is evident to the careful observer of children in kindergartens and the primary schools that to-day parents need direct teaching more than the child, to be given in such a way as to influence children in the nursery before the most impressionable period of their lives has been passed. "This is very true," wrote Dr. Preyer, who lamented, with reason, in *Infant Mind*, that in cultivated families the children should be left alone so much with uneducated nurses, maids, *bonnes*, and that no counterpoise, as a rule, is supplied by a close personal contact with the child of the educated parents ; that the fathers have other claims upon them; the mothers, in too many cases, are hindered by so-called " duties" of society or by needless journeys. He says, forcibly, that when a child grows up from the beginning under the influence of the suggestions of cultivated people, he must of necessity take with him into the period in which the nursery is left behind forever a considerably less number of naughty ways and a great many more excellences, with the natural result of being better fitted for progress than if undesirable ways must be first forgotten, and excellences, such as obedience, be bred in him after leaving the nursery. He says the direction of attention through suggestion never fails when used systematically. It is evident, therefore, that the mother who will interest herself in child-study and its results must find, by following this course of sympathetic supervision and intelligent suggestion, that she can easily and unobtrusively prepare her child for satisfactory work in both kindergarten and primary school. The aid of a trained kindergartner of inspiring personality, or of at least a refined and educated nursery-maid, may be secured, if possible, very early in the life of a child. One, however, should be selected who has learned the value of repose in handling children, and who can *subordinate* method as a means for the development of mental and moral growth. Undoubtedly one of the greatest dangers to be found to-day in the average kindergarten lies in the absorption of method and the aggressiveness of the teacher's personality to the exclusion of spontaneity, and the self-effacement necessary upon the teacher's part for the promotion of unconscious development in the child.

We can all, no doubt, as Rousseau says, " sit reverently at the feet of infancy, watching and learning."

Sully speaks of Rousseau's belief that the infant comes

unspoiled from the hands of its Maker, and is not born morally depraved, to be made good by miraculous appliances. The accepted belief of many psychologists of to-day is that every child comes into the world loaded down with inherited tendencies to evil, from which it will eventually suffer unless they are counteracted by opposing influences. The child is certainly unformed at this period, hence may be moulded for good or evil, and in consequence man's methods in training must be carefully adjusted so as not to brush away the bloom of the "lovely grace of childhood." There is an instinctive goodness and gladness in every child that, in spite of evil heredity and depraved surroundings, will respond to sympathetic treatment. But to treat children sympathetically in order that we may obtain a clearer insight into their mental processes and know better how to guide them, we must certainly absorb the *spirit* of Froebel, who begs us to live *with* our children, not only *for* them, as so many do, and keep them happy.

I have never seen a child who was not happy and inclined to be good when well occupied. The *letter* of Froebel's philosophy was simply meant by him to be an aid in establishing a suitable environment to fit the comprehension of the children in question, and it is invaluable when properly used to keep them happily employed. But if a mother happens to be placed beyond the reach of a kindergarten, or the aid of a kindergartner, she need not despair of attempting the work unaided, for by studying Froebel's philosophy and reading his meaning with the eyes of love, she will clearly see how she may prepare for her child an environment of suggestion, and formulate for herself a method that will grasp the entire meaning of his play and occupations, with their wonderful results. Then, when she sends her child away to begin his life-work, she may feel that she has given him power with which he can easily handle the problems that will confront him daily, and that she has not only given him power, but has done it in a manner that has not hindered his *physical* development, the soundness of which will determine largely his whole future intellectual and moral life. Dr. Preyer here added : " Therefore, the controlling supervision of the *physical* development in childhood is the most important task of all young mothers." Fathers may assist in such work if they will but realize the importance of surrounding young mothers with the serene, happy conditions in their daily lives that will impel them by their great content to live with their children, as Froebel begs them to do, and watch over them with that brooding mother-love which should be the natural outcome of affection and consideration not denied them in their own relations of life.

CHAPTER I

FRAGMENTARY FIRST-YEAR NOTES

THE dated record of the spontaneous development of the child in question began when he was fourteen months old, and comparatively few notes were made during the period covering the first year. The few facts that were noted may be of greater interest, possibly, to psychologists than to the general reader. For instance, the child's first sign of early adaptation to surroundings, of which Compayré speaks, was possibly given when he was found contentedly sucking his thumb, after the fashion of many other infants, about half an hour after he was born. Both nurse and physician dwelt frequently upon the importance of the fact that when the child received his first bath he lifted his head unaided from the lap in which he was lying, thus showing to the popular mind an early inclination to know what was going on about him, again following the fashion of many other mortals, and to the psychologist great promise of brain power. He showed on the second and third days a decided disinclination to sleep in the nurse's arms, but he would invariably fall asleep easily when removed to his mother's arms. Receptiveness to sympathy may probably here be traced, for the nurse was unsympathetic.

The child noticed color when he was a little over three months old. He was lying on a bed, near a hat trimmed with stiff yellow flowers. He put out his hand and touched them. The rattling noise of the flowers must have pleased him, for when the hat was moved a little farther away from him, he stretched his body after it so he could reach and rattle them again. Dr. Preyer added an interrogation point to this incident, evidently questioning the date, for it was at that part of the manuscript that he pointed his question. When I wrote to him the last time I explained how I knew the date to be a fact, but his death intervened before I could receive a reply. The child had noticed some colored balls of red and white a few days before the hat incident. His nurse hung them near him, and he played with them while lying on a couch and kicking up his heels. He seemed happiest always when he was let alone and treated like a machine, and at even this early age he was fully able to amuse himself, as nearly all well children are when a wholesome regime has once been established.

He objected to a Raff concerto for violin and piano, but tolerated Handel's Largo, although with a quiver of his lip. This was before he was four months old. The Raff music began just as he was going to sleep; he cried bitterly on hearing it, and he was taken to the music-room to see if it would quiet him to see the performers. He cried continuously, however, as if he suffered. Then, as an experiment, the Largo was played. This seemed to soothe him somewhat, but his parents concluded that the violin was the trouble and laid it aside. (It is interesting to note that a year later he developed a great fondness for violin music, begging for it whenever opportunity offered.)

At this time a single voice singing would not quiet him, if for any of the numerous reasons of early baby-land he was not inclined to sleep; but two voices, singing in parts, would invariably have the desired soothing effect. (The record shows, later on, great susceptibility to rhythm and harmony.) The music of hand-organs always seemed to attract him, even before he was four months old. This he showed, at this early date, by pushing towards the window and jumping in his nurse's arms whenever the organs appeared. His eyes followed his aunt across the room at this same age (three and a half months), and he also looked at himself attentively in the glass several times, leaning over and putting his lips to his little reflection.

When four months old he was taken to the shore. (His first tooth had appeared before this, and soon after his arrival several others made their appearance. He had sixteen teeth when he was a year old, the result, the physician said, of careful feeding and attention to hygiene). During his shore experience he was nothing more nor less than a little automaton, for by this time he had become habituated to his nursery routine, which was kept up undeviatingly. This automatic way of living was so marked that for a week a person in a neighboring room did not know there was a baby near, nor would she believe it at first when told. This serenity was undoubtedly caused by the thoroughly regular life of the mother, the nurse, and the child. He frequently took his morning nap within hearing of the hotel musicians, one of whom was the proud possessor of a trumpet; even this could not conquer the child's regular habit of sleep. I mention this as being of probable interest to parents as well as to psychologists, although it is far from wise to put a child to sleep irrespective of noise and light.

The child's early sense of humor, which is a marked characteristic throughout the record, was shown by his manner of receiving the visits of a very jolly-looking physician who was an image of Santa Claus, and at whom he would always laugh inordinately, even when he was only five months old, whether he was ailing or not. It grew to be so noticeable that once even the physician, seeing him laughing, without knowing the cause, shook his finger at him and said to the mother: " You must make that child stop laughing," when the child laughed more than ever, and the mother pleaded her inability to control what seemed perfectly natural and spontaneous.

In the same spontaneous way he reached out his arms for the first colored servant he ever saw (a chambermaid with a fresh white cap and apron on), and promptly kissed her. (The record shows throughout a great liking for what he called " lovely white.") This won the hearts of the entire hotel staff, for it was duly retailed by the favored recipient, and after that both the child and nurse were in no need of willing service at all hours and places, and under all circumstances. At this time the telegraph ticking and the washing of the waves were his two absorbing amusements during the few hours he was awake. Sailing had no terrors for him. The yacht captains called him " our baby." His nurse held him over the side of the boat, where he would contentedly watch the water dash against it, even when out on the ocean where the waves were high. (He always showed the same content when watching the splashing of his bath, and would look intently with much pleasure at the water running swiftly from the faucets.) Once, during a passing shower of rain, he settled down contentedly in the stuffy little cabin of a sail-boat, where he apparently took in all his surroundings very quietly, just as he had done on the train when travelling to the shore, with never a murmur nor a cry, but always eager to see or do something. His wants were usually anticipated, which, with his regular life, may probably have had some influence in promoting this unlooked-for serenity.

The only time he was known to be guilty of putting anything in his mouth after the fashion of children who are continually doing so when they should not, was when sailing one day he was discovered chewing a tarry bit of rope by a family friend who declared the child was only half fed and was hungry, this innuendo being directed at the mother for her well-known insistence upon regularity in feeding the child. The rope was replaced by something that seemed equally desirable to him, which method of removal may also contain a suggestion for that parent who believes in early discipline.

When, after returning from the shore, the child was taken to the mountain, he showed a fancy for throwing pebbles and green grapes, which he picked for the purpose, while in his nurse's arms; and all this was done, presumably, from imitation of some boys who played with him in this manner.

He began to walk very early, stood up alone when nine months old, and attempted to sing when placed on a music-stool before the piano. He sang the music of two lines of "Annie Rooney" correctly, from imitation, when nine months old. His nurse-maid sang this song daily.

At this time he showed a shrinking sort of fear when he heard a noise like a hammer striking something in the next room, and also when he heard a coal fall from the

19

grate. During an unavoidable absence of a day and a
night upon the part of his mother, he cried, and apparently missed her. After her return, he would cry whenever she approached the door by which she had left
when she went away.

One evening, when he heard his father and mother
singing a duet, he joined in, in the most naïve way,
singing up and down to the very end, as if he couldn't
help it. Every one about him was careful not to laugh
at anything he did; consequently his spontaneity was
deliciously entertaining.

He would at this time recognize the voice of a favorite
servant when she passed the door on the outside, and he
would call loudly for her. He began to try to say a few
words at this period, as related in the dated record, and
succeeded in walking a few steps. He crept very little.
He seemed to give great attention to everything he did,
so no doubt he soon learned that he could do better than
creep, so far as locomotion was concerned.

Compayré says the child's consciousness flashes forth
at first in gestures, later in his babbling. Hence the
particular interest which the observation of his outward
movement offers as the sincere expression of his mental
activity. (Compare an idiotic with a normal child—the
first quiet, the latter all motion.) Besides, these motions
which we can follow and note with exactness, however
slight may be the attention we may give them, are in
themselves psychic facts, and only to have described
them would be psychology in itself. M. Anthomie
speaks of the power of penetration that the mother's
eye acquires, fixed with a sweet determination upon one
she loves. The force of the tenderness creates between
the parent and the child relations so close, a moral inti-

macy so deep, that the faintest heart-beats of the child re-echo in the ears of those that love him. Paternal and maternal love carry with them a sort of divination. Compayré says that the best psychologists of childhood are those who have followed carefully, from hour to hour, the moral development of their own children. He says if the journals kept by a mother or a father, in which a careful hand registers from day to day the smallest incidents of the child's existence, are really the most precious sources of observation, *all* information, wherever it comes from, is welcome. Mme. Necker de Saussure recommended these records fifty years ago, saying: "I strongly urge young mothers to keep an accurate record of the development of their children."

Much of the following dated record of the little life which rolled along so serenely and pleasantly may seem of slight value to the general reader, who is simply charmed with the fascination of children's ways, yet for reasons like the above none may be omitted, for we are told that the key-note of the whole psychological value of the work might prove to be found in those facts that might be omitted by one who does not know, yet hopes that herein is faithfully pictured the inner life of a child.

CHAPTER II

SECOND YEAR, COVERING DEVELOPMENT OF LANGUAGE, AND, INCIDENTALLY, THE CULTIVATION OF OBEDIENCE AND TRUST

APRIL 11, 1891.—Fourteen months old. I was reading aloud from *Punch and Judy*, which is fully illustrated. When I came to the place where Punch says, "Oh, my nose! my best Sunday nose!" Harold touched his nose, then bent over and touched mine, and, placing his head against my shoulder, he screwed up his face in a grin and laughed loud twice in succession. The book was given to him when he was a year old, and ever since receiving it he has shown great delight when he sees the picture where Punch and Judy are turning their faces to each other, and Judy says, "Punchy, wunchy, dear old Punchy!" Harold always laughs aloud when he sees this, and at any time of the day or night I need but say the words to make him laugh. Once I whispered them to him in the middle of the night, when he was restless, and he laughed loud, was diverted for the moment, turned over, and fell asleep. (The record shows to present date that he is keenly alive to fun, and advantage of the fact was often taken for diverting him from what might otherwise have proved a source of trouble.)

April 12th.—When putting away some of his blocks to-day I inadvertently put some in a basket with other

22

toys, but he reached for the little wagon in which they belonged, intimated that he wanted them all, and put them, one by one, in the basket, sometimes, however, stopping to build. I attempted to make a note of this with a pencil, which he took from me, tried to write with it, discovered that he had the wrong end of the pencil, and turned it about. The same day he saw a dog across the street. He looked intently at him and said something that sounded like "wow! wow!" He frequently says it upon seeing a little boy. He did it to-day, his manner showing distinctly that he meant it for the boy.

One day this week, while in his coach on the street, coming home, he began to throw kisses just before falling asleep. He often does this when going out or when going to bed, and, according to Dr. Preyer, some association with farewell causes him to do it.

He occasionally has an egg for breakfast, of which he is very fond. They are served to him in cups similar to those used at table. On Sunday he was in the dining-room, and as soon as he saw the egg-cups on the table he cried, apparently for an egg, and could with difficulty be diverted.

One morning last week, when watching some one dress, he brought the shoes needed, one by one, from a closet near by, and took the bath slippers back in the same way. One day recently he voluntarily went to a couch, under which stood a pair of shoes, and carried them one by one to the shoe-case, set them down before the curtain, and then turned and seated himself on the floor before us, looking up as though he wanted to be praised.

He often begs to be taken up into some one's arms to

23

watch the brushing of teeth. This suggested buying a brush for him, which he gravely puts in water now and brushes his own teeth daily. This morning, when watching his mother brush her teeth, he picked up a brush lying near him and took it to his father, saying, questioningly, "hab 'em?" He has said "hab 'em?" and "gib 'em," and "ups-a-dada" for over a month. He says the latter when lifting anything, or when jumping up and down. He often pretends to drop something from his hand, and pulls it up quickly, saying "ups-a-dada!" I think he learned this expression from his nurse. When he says "hab 'em?" he hands you something. He often picks up something from the floor—a thread or a pin — and brings it to you, saying "hab 'em?" If he wants anything he reaches for it and says "hab 'em?" or "gib 'em." He often comes with his hand closed, looking very mischievous, and says "hab 'em?" and on opening it you find nothing.

About this time he learned what "no, no" meant. A cover that was used for a water-pail in the room next to his seemed to attract him very much on account of a hole in its centre, through which we would occasionally find him poking his fists. One day he was found there pretending to wash his hands. We then began to take him away from it and say "no, no," doing it quietly but persistently. One day nurse and I followed him at intervals no less than twenty times to do this, as a matter of experiment, to find out whether he could learn what "inevitable" meant. Frequently he seemed to understand what we were trying to do, for he would often run away from us and go directly there, as if in a spirit of mischief, look at us and laugh as he stood there, while at other times he would walk up to it gravely, stand there, shake his head, and say "No, no." We had the same experience with a linen-closet, the lower shelf of which had a little door which he could pull open very easily, and the lock of which we often found him examining very intently. (The record shows a keen interest in mechanics.) We would find him sitting before the closet, door open, and all the clean towels scattered about him. He seemed to take a special delight in rumpling them. We took him away every time, saying: "No, no; they belong to mamma." He soon understood that this too was forbidden ground. From this date we began systematically to teach him to consider the rights of others, and to touch nothing that did not belong strictly to himself.

(The record shows that this was carried out unfailingly, but without severity, in order to keep the child fearless, and results recorded show complete success in the effort.) About this time we noticed how fretfulness would disappear upon sight of his hat and coat, apparently in the hope of being taken out.

A few days after the first experience with "no, no," he ran away from us through two rooms, going directly to the water-pail, crowing all the way as though he thought he would get there first before we could catch him. He did get there, and laughing as if he had done it for fun, stood waiting for nurse to take him away, and went without a struggle.

One morning this week he found a bunch of keys attached to a chain. He seized them instantly, took them to an iron bedstead, and pushed the bunch between the spring and the frame of the bed, holding on to the chain and letting the keys move up and down as he pulled the chain, saying "ups-a-dada!" taking great delight evidently in the clinking of the keys against the iron frame. He has been going repeatedly during the last few weeks to a chiffonnier, where he would stand looking up intently at the door of a little closet in it, which held a slender-necked claret-glass, of which he is very fond. He sometimes would say " hab 'em ?" when looking at the door. We regularly opened the closet and gave him the glass to carry for a while, which he did with the greatest care and pride. He would then return it, apparently satisfied, and we would replace the glass in the closet. One morning this week he broke it accidentally, but for two days he still went to the closet each morning in the same way that he did before he broke the glass. We opened the door each time to show him that it was not there, and at last he seemed to understand, and never went again.

He has shown for some time a desire to fit things together, or to drop things into holes. To-day he was playing in one room with part of a broken toy — a pointed stick with a hole at one end, through which he could put his finger. He did this a number of times, examining it intently where his finger came through the hole, when he seemed to be suddenly struck with some idea and started for the next room, going as fast as he could walk. As we never interfered with him unless we saw danger ahead, I followed quietly and saw him go directly to the water-pail before mentioned and poke the piece of wood up and down in the hole in the lid of the pail, saying " ups-a-dada !" He came away without a murmur when I took his hand and said, " No, no," dropped the piece of wood at once, and took up another toy.

We gave him some kitchen things to play with to-day,

as he seems to take especial delight in them, especially
the contents of the bottom part of the dresser—pots,
pans, etc. Among those given to him was a new salt-
box that looked like silver. Shortly after we gave him
the lid, and although it was gilt and the box silver, he
instantly fitted the lid where it belonged, selecting the
box from several things on the table. He was sitting
upon the table himself at the time. We then tried him
with a quart and a pint jar of glass, each having covers
to fit, which we gave to him at different times. He fitted
them correctly without a moment's hesitation.

He has begun dancing now when he hears street-
organs, but only when there is a suitable rhythm. If he
hears the music at a distance he drops his toys, runs to
the window, and cries to be lifted up to see. The organ-
grinders know him so well that he has them here daily.
(When seven years old he showed a marked sense of
rhythm, and although he had received very little musical
instruction, he then picked out very pretty harmonies.)
He is beginning to imitate the rag-and-slop man, giving
a very fair imitation, as he runs through the rooms, generally carrying under his arm, in imitation of the rag-
man's bag, a journal full of mechanical illustrations,
which is his pet book.

He comes to my bed in the morning after having been
dressed by his nurse, hands me my shoes and gown, saying "hab 'em?" and then hands me all the clothes he
can find that he knows belong to me. When at last,
after much of this sort of persuasion, I get up, he can
hardly wait to call his father, which he does by going to
his bedside and saying "ba"; sometimes "baba." He
has had a great fashion lately of kissing me at odd moments, often on each eye successively, especially when

27

I am lying down face upward. This evening he kissed his father in the middle of a song, while he was holding him in his arms and singing. If we say "Sing, Harold," he will hum a few notes. He did it this afternoon when out in his coach, and also this evening when his father was playing a song.

April 16th.—Harold picked up my thimble to-day and brought it to me, took up my hand, and fitted it on my finger.

April 18th.—Since the 16th inst. he has himself used the bottle of lotion that was given by the physician to ease his gums during teething. He takes the bottle in one hand, puts his finger on its mouth, turns it enough to wet his finger, and rubs his gums.

His coach parasol was used to-day for the first time since last summer, and he showed fear when placed under it. He looked up at the cover as if afraid to sit under it, and cried bitterly. I soothed and diverted him until he reached the street, when he seemed to forget it. To-day I took a dime from him to put in his bank, and when he saw it about to disappear he cried.

April 17th.—We tried to use an atomizer to-day, but he showed fear as soon as he saw it, although he had never seen one before, and he cried bitterly when I insisted upon using it in accordance with the physician's directions. He seems to show fear of some things that work in any way that he cannot understand, or where he cannot find the motive power.

April 18th.—I brought out the atomizer again, intending to use it. As soon as he saw it he left my knee, where he was standing, and walked very quickly into the other room, as fast and as far as he could go, and stood there and cried. I gave up all attempt to use it from that time for fear of making him nervous, and because force was never used if it could be avoided. When his teeth seemed to hurt him I gave him the bottle of the lotion we used and told him to apply it himself, which he did in what seemed to me to be a very grateful way. (The record shows that when he was five years old his mother felt that something should be done to habituate him to the use of the spray, if only as a precautionary measure for probable need during illness. It took her longer than a year, making the effort at intervals of probably a month, to teach him gently and without bribing or straining his nerves by using force, to use both atomizer and vaporizer. At seven it is still very evident that he dislikes them, yet he uses them bravely, showing how a victory of mind over matter may be brought about by patience and gentle treatment, and also how moral courage may incidentally be cultivated in a very young child.)

About a week ago he walked to the wash-stand, and pointed to the pitcher and cried. I gave him some water to drink, and he took a great deal, apparently being very thirsty. When offering him his bottle of milk this morning, he shook his head, said "No, no," and walked away. He seems to be strong-willed and self-reliant, but not capricious, perhaps because he trusts us.

Last night he had two bottles in his crib. One contained sterilized water for use during the night; the other was a small, empty bottle, with an unpunctured nipple tied on securely. We gave him the latter to bite on during teething. He was very fond of it, was rarely without it, and took it to bed with him every night for a long time, where he would hold it tight in his hand until he fell asleep. About midnight he was restless, and I gave him the water-bottle. He took a long drink, and when he had enough, compared the bottles in the dim light, shook the water-bottle, held it up, and looked first at it, then at the little one. At last, after doing this several times, he lifted up the little one, shook it, looked at it very closely, laid away the water-bottle, turned over, and fell asleep with the little bottle in his hand.

Quite recently, when visiting his grandparents, they had an amusing experience with the little bottle. It was mislaid during the excitement of his arrival, and when bedtime came it could not be found. He refused to sleep. The entire household took part in the search, and at last it was found under the bed, given to him, and he soon fell asleep. It may not seem wise to be so dependent upon accidental circumstances, but his mother cannot quite make up her mind to deprive him of the comfort he takes in his " bot," as he calls it. (The record shows how he gradually dropped the habit himself as other interests developed.)

Since January, when he was eleven months old, he has shown fear whenever he sees a wire dress-form that is in the sewing-room, and all our efforts to familiarize him with it seem to be useless.

April 16th.—He began to build with blocks to-day, placing five or six on top of each other with great care and precision.

The words he has learned since November, when he was nine months old, are as follows, given in the order of acquirement: "Oh, mammam," "hab 'em," "gib 'em," "ups-a-dada," "wow wow," "bow wow," "ba" and "baba" for papa (he generally says "ba"), "by-bye."

April 27.—"Ssss" (which he says to dogs, cats, etc., pointing his finger). The first week in April he said "button" and "dollar."

April 30th he said "cock" for clock, on seeing a very large clock at his grandfather's. He said, the same week, "ga" for cat, "rub-a-dub-dub," "eene, eene, mine mo," and "oo-oory-oooo" to a rooster in the immediate vicinity, which answered every time he did it. He was behind a fence, where he could not see the rooster. He had never seen or heard one, but on hearing this one crow he imitated him so accurately that the two kept it up for some time, and it was his favorite amusement during his week's visit. Said "dere" for there.

May 8th.—Said "tick-tick-tick" and "cock" for clock for the second time, upon seeing a large picture of a clock similar to the one he saw April 30th at his grandfather's. After he was dressed this morning he ran just as fast as he could toddle to his father, who was still asleep. He stood by him for a few minutes and said "up, up" several times, and looked very much disappointed because this did not waken him. He stood quietly for a moment looking at him, and no doubt puzzling what to do, when he went to the other side of the room to the shoe-closet and very deliberately took out a bath-slipper, which he carried to his father, saying, as he put it on the bed, "up, up." Then he returned to the closet for the other one, and repeated "up, up" as he was bringing it. He had to make two trips, for it took both hands to carry each slipper. By this time his father was awake, and Harold seemed very eager to begin his morning romp without more delay.

On May 10th (fifteen months old) he said "hark"; also, "boo" for book, and the word "up."

31

On May 15th he said "goo" for good. He frequently repeats the following words to himself, as if trying them: "hark," "dere," "rub-a-dub-dub," "bow wow," "by-bye," "ups-a-dada," "up," "hab 'em," "ssss." He said "now" for the first time.

On June 14th (sixteen months old) he called a boy by name (Paul), and on June 15th said "Bidyet" for Bridget. At this date he gabbles a great deal, making all sorts of sounds, and seems to understand when he is told to shut the door, kiss the cheek, bring mamma's shoes, bring Harold's shoes. He points to his eyes and his nose, or to mine, when asked where they are.

On July 16th he said "Judy," and kissed the wire form of which he was afraid in January. Since July 1st he has seemed to grow accustomed to, and even become fond of it, saying "Lovely Judy." When we speak to him of it we say "Lovely Judy," etc., and pat it kindly, and in various ways we have tried to get him over his fear of it, with the above result.

July 18th.—To-day he said "bavy" for baby, and repeated it upon looking at a picture of one. He also pronounces "l" in clock now.

July 19th.—He walked up to the baby picture which hung on the wall, and repeated "baby" in a loving tone. He also said "out" distinctly to-day. He has said "outs" for a long time, but we could not discover what he meant until this month, when we heard him say it when he pricked himself with a pin. We then traced the connection between his expression and a word used by one of the servants—"ouch"—and had a practical demonstration of the influence of an uneducated servant upon a child learning to talk, for it took a long time and much patient effort to teach him to drop this word.

He opens his mouth and shows his tongue now when asked where it is, but he makes no attempt to say the word.

He calls pussy "psss," drawing out the sound of s. Later in this month he called pussy "putty," and said "braw" for "broth."

The words acquired from July 1st to 12th are "light," "bye," "how do," "coat," "cap," "stove," "door," and "shoes." He said "fire" one day recently, when he saw a lot of stoves at a hardware store.

July 23d.—To-day he tried to say, "Peep, Bidyet," peeping around the wire form. He now says, distinctly, "rock-a-bye" as he rocks himself to and fro.

July 24th.—To-day he tried to say "potato," and he said "go away" when some one was teasing him. He frequently says "no, no," shaking his head as he says it. He understands when we tell him to "sit on the floor," or to shut or open the door. He sings himself to sleep very often. He has one favorite that I play (one of Heller's Studies on Rhythm), which he tries to sing whenever he hears it.

New words on July 26th and 27th are "bread," "blow," and "door," which he says very distinctly.

Since July 1st he has said something that sounds like "a-a-a-h," drawing it out between ah and oh, and making it slightly nasal. He says it very lovingly to his pussy, or anything in the way of pets that are alive. He will take his pussy in his arms, smooth her fur affectionately, and say it in the most loving manner possible. He has always shown great love for kittens or any live pet.

c 33

To-day, during the visit of a friend, he tried to occupy my entire attention. Hardly thinking he would do so, I told him very suggestively to go to the piano and play and sing. He went at once, put his fingers on the keys, and tried to sing for about a minute, which served to divert him for the moment and gave me the freedom I wanted.

A servant said to him to-day, " Peep, Harold !" when playing " peek-a-boo " with him. He instantly replied, " Peep, Bidyet !" although he had never said " peep " before. He always says " y " for " g " in her name. He imitates words very quickly and correctly for a child of seventeen months, and seems to understand the meaning of many more words than he says.

July 20th.—When building with blocks, pennies, or anything that he can place one above the other, he lifts both hands and exclaims, " o-o-o-o-o-o-o-e !" drawing out the long " o " indefinitely, as if very much pleased with his building. We let him amuse himself in this way for a long time, changing his materials as he seems to need them. We never change until he begins to show a little restlessness, for so long as a child is content it is folly to disturb it. In time this policy secures serenity for the child and peace for those about him.

He now helps undress himself for his bath every evening, lifts each arm or foot when told to help remove each garment, and he evidently takes great delight in the whole process and is always eager for it.

For a long time he has given an expression of distaste (sounds like " ugh !") when obliged to take medicine that he does not like, and he follows the sound with a shake of his head.

When finished taking his bottle of milk, no matter

where he is, whether just about going to sleep or if ready for play, he first hands the empty bottle to some convenient person, saying, "hab 'em." He does this every time, and we encourage the habit in the hope of inducing method in his actions. (The record shows that at seven he gives evidence of the results of this plan of action, for he invariably shuts doors when passing through them, replaces articles he may have used to where they belong, and in many ways shows a methodical manner of action, even in his play.)

He often leaves an ounce or more in the bottle. Nothing can induce him to take this when he reaches the point which to him seems final.

July 28th.—He said "baba" for papa to-day, for the first time for a long while. He has said "ba" only, with one or two exceptions, before this time.

He now says "door" frequently, and says "bruh" for brush.

Since August 2d he has said "birdie" distinctly, "bre" for bread, "bat" for bath, and "wa" for water on seeing a tub filled with it. A week ago he saw it rain very fast, and said "wat." When he sees a glass he says "wat," and will take a drink if we will offer water in the glass. He also says "wat" when thirsty, without seeing a glass to suggest it.

On August 13th he pointed to the gas-fixture and said "li" for light.

The next day he went to two gates in the yard, one after the other, and said "ga" at each one. The same day he saw a bird from a window in the nursery, and he went from one window to the other to see it as long as he could, saying "birdie," showing clearly how he reasoned about seeing farther from one window than the other.

I took up a clothes-brush of his father's to-day as I stood at the dressing-case with him in my arms. He took it from me and said, "baba, bruh." I smiled, and he said it again and kissed it. He is very affectionate, and we all try to be as responsive as it is possible for older persons to be. Children are really made very unhappy at times by the chilling manner with which their affectionate outbursts are sometimes met. Snubbing and unkind criticism should have no place in a child's education when spontaneity is desired.

On the 7th of this month (August) his father brought him a fox-terrier, called Jack, that had just arrived from England. Harold was delighted with him, and the dog seemed to be equally delighted with the child. He cried the first time the dog licked his face. We could not punish nor train the dog to do anything in the child's presence by showing severity, for every time any one spoke sharply to the dog, Harold would cry. (The record shows this trait throughout. When only four months old he would cry if he saw another baby cry. When seven years old he confided to his mother, one night before going to bed, what a little girl had told him in the day about her intention of drowning a family of young kittens. With tears in his voice and eyes, he said: "Oh, mamma, I cannot bear to talk about it! Will she do it?" His mother said no, and further assured him she would not allow it. He then said: "If she does, I'll drown the mother kitty myself; if she wants to drown the babies, she ought to drown the mother, too." Then he said: "Mamma, it nearly makes me cry to even tell you." So she diverted him with a funny remark, which he is always quick to appreciate.)

He follows his dog all over the house, plays with him happily, and loves him very much, but he tries to prevent him from touching him with his tongue. He often says to him in the most loving tone, "o-o-o-h," drawing it out at great length.

He now goes to sleep regularly in his crib. Before this he was frequently held in arms while being sung to sleep, after which he would be quietly placed in his bed, and no trouble was experienced in making the change. He seems to trust us so entirely that he will do whatever we can make him understand is for his good. This trust is cultivated by never asking him to do anything simply for the amusement of others, or to show their authority, and he always gets a reason that he can understand when he is directed to do anything, unless instant obedience is required, as in case of danger, when the reason for the command is carefully explained after he has obeyed. (This may account to some extent for the reasonableness of his disposition as it develops later on.)

August 14th.—To-day, when giving him his nap, I forgot to pull down the mosquito-netting that was hanging over his crib. He pulled at it, saying "h'm," whether in imitation of the hum of a mosquito or not I cannot say. He seems to understand all we say to him, but we are careful to use words that we think he will understand. If I say : "Take this to papa, please," or, "Take this to Sarah, please," he distinguishes, and does it cheerfully. He is always willing to do things for us, to run little errands, and if he sees anything drop from my lap when I am reading or sewing, he invariably stops his play and comes to pick it up for me. In this way he shows all the time what seems like a loving wish to

help, which we are encouraging, for it is the key-note of
self-activity, and promotes unselfishness.

Sometimes I say : " Do you want your bottle ?" He
understands, and says " Yes." When either the nurse
or I must leave the room for a moment we say : " Harold,
will you please sit still on the chair until I come back ?"
He always says " Yes," and sits there, many a time
singing to himself until we return. This plan was followed so as to be sure he would not get into mischief
from undue temptation, for he is too young yet to resist.
We always found it more effective and more pleasant
to say " do this," or " do that, please," instead of saying " don't."

August 17th.—When he awoke this morning he said
" door," pointing to it. Then he pointed to the bell and
said : " Bridget, door-bell ringing." This was his first
attempt at connecting a sentence of any length. He is
now eighteen months old.

He now calls his dog by name, adding a " y " to it,
however, saying " Jacky." He also tries to make a
sound with his lips to call the dog, in imitation of his
father's method of calling the dog to him.

August 21st.—When I was showing him his "Piggy
Book " to-day, he put his finger on each picture and then
put it in his mouth and looked very knowing. Upon
looking into the matter we found that yesterday his
nurse wet her finger to turn a leaf and he imitated her
to-day, but his action looked as if he thought he was
eating from the book. He tasted his medicine to-day
by putting his finger in it before he would take it. He
had two bottles of medicine that looked alike. He liked
one, and objected decidedly to taking the other. After
finding out, by putting his finger in it, that I was offer-

ing him the one he liked, he took it without a word.
When using vaseline for a head cold, he always helps
put it on. He will put his finger in the bottle very
daintily and rub the bridge of his nose and forehead
thoroughly, but he often puts little dabs all over his
face too, as if he enjoys it.

He tried to help me push a piece of sewing through
the machine this morning when I was stitching. He
placed his hands on the work as he saw the seamstress
do yesterday. He was on my lap at the time, where I
often allow him to sit as I sew. He enjoys watching
the machine go so very much that he will sit motionless
so long as any one will hold him, maybe five minutes at
a time gazing at the same thing. For three months he
has pulled the strap of the machine voluntarily, looking up at the same time to see the needle move. (This
interest in mechanics was allowed to grow spontaneously by providing the right environment for it, and at
seven he shows remarkable ingenuity and mechanical
skill.)

August 22d.—Some little girls who live next door came
home yesterday, and nurse asked Harold to call to one
of them, saying, "Call Mamie," which he did distinctly,
and, although he had never said Mamie before, to our
knowledge, he repeated it several times afterwards. He
always does this with new words, as if trying them.
(The record shows that he did this without any acquirement of language up to seven years, and does it still, his
favorite time for practice being after he wakes in the
morning.) She also told him to call Alice, the sister.
He tried to do so, but succeeded only in saying "Ell."

His father has been away for a few days, and to-day
he called "papa" after a man going by, and cried bit-

terly because the man did not stop. I did not notice
whether the man resembled his father or not. The
father of the little girls next door resembles him, and
this afternoon when Harold saw him he wanted to go to
him. The gentleman took him for a while, and Harold
cried when he was taken away. He evidently misses
his father very much. About a week after this he was
taken to the house of a friend where he saw a cuckoo-
clock for the first time, and learned to say " cuckoo."
Afterwards when asked what birdie said, he replied,
" cuckoo."

He has said " bi " for bite for some time. He heard
it in connection with some conversation about mosqui-
toes about the middle of August. He says " bavy " to
me in the most loving tones. He will lay his head
against me in the morning and say it when he wants to
wake me. His head just reaches my pillow as he stands
by the bed. He says it too, in the same loving way,
when he thinks he has received a special favor. Whenever I do anything that pleases him very much—smile to
him, give him a kiss, or give him a trifle to play with
that shows him that I thought of him when he wasn't
there—I notice what seems to me to be an attempt to
show his appreciation. (The record shows that later on,
when he could talk, he invariably said on similar occa-
sions to his mother, either " Lovely mamma," or " Good
mamma," or " Why are you so good ?" or he would kiss
her and fondle her and say nothing, and at seven he
still has the same habit.)

September 8th.—This morning I killed a mosquito on
the wall by slapping it with my hand. He promptly
imitated me, and also looked about the room and up at
the ceiling to see if there were more of them. He

walked about with his head back, imitating every movement of mine.

September 8th.—He tried to say " girl" to-day on seeing a picture of one in the nursery song-book. I read " Mistress Mary, quite contrary," to him this morning. When I said " Mary " he said " Mamie," evidently recognizing the similarity in Mary to the name " Mamie " that he had learned a few days before. When he wants to go anywhere or to get something, he now comes to one of us and says " hand," and tries to lead us to what he wants. A few minutes ago he said to his nurse, " hand —stair," leading her to the stairs that go down.

He heard a person on the street say " wait " yesterday, and he called " wait " after him.

To-day he called " papa " after a man on the street who resembled his father. There were other men in the vicinity, and he singled out this one.

On September 5th his father took the dog away and remained over Sunday. Harold missed the dog at once when he woke from his nap; he called and looked all over for both his father and the dog. A few days after, when I said to him : " Call the dog," he looked under the bed and called " Jacky " distinctly.

He has said " pease " for please since the middle of August ; also " ang you " for thank you. From the beginning of August he has said " hot " when near anything warm—as, for instance, a stove, a fire of any kind, a dish of hot food, etc. He also says " flies " distinctly, and " band," meaning the knit band he wears.

On September 11th he said " hugar " for sugar. He has said it several times lately, but we did not understand until to-day what he meant by it. He also said " gas " and " bites " distinctly to-day instead of saying

41

"ga" and "bi," as he used to do, pointing to the gas-fixture when he said "gas," and to some marks of mosquito-bites when he said "bites."

While driving with Mrs. N—— this afternoon he put his face to his mother's, patted her cheek with his hand, and said, in a loving tone, "mamma." Later in the day some one said "manĩ-ma." He immediately said "ma-má," which is the way he always accents the word. He leaned over to Mrs. N—— in the carriage to-day and put his hand up towards her cheek, saying, very affectionately, "o-o-o-h!" This is a very usual expression for him when he wants to show liking for any one. He always says it when he pets a dog or cat. He shows no fear of any one, and a liking for nearly everybody. To-day I showed him a picture of a dog. He said "o-o-o-h!" kissed the picture, and put it to my lips to be kissed. When I said "Call bow-wow," he called "Jacky." When he heard an engine go by to-day he said "choo-choo" for the first time.

This evening we were looking at some pictures when I said, pointing to one that only resembled a rooster: "Is that an oo-oory-ooo?" (his name for one). He shook his head and said "No."

Yesterday Mrs. N—— offered him a piece of sweet chocolate. Her little boy is fond of it. Harold tasted it and returned it, showing by his manner that he didn't like it. I gave him a taste of something I had at the time and asked him if he liked it. He made a face, shook his head, and said "No-o-o." He always shows likes and dislikes very plainly, especially in connection with food.

He saw a roulette-wheel to-day for the first time. He and N—— (a boy of the same age) were playing with it.

N—— pushed it by the spokes; Harold took hold of it in the middle and twirled it with thumb and forefinger in the regular way.

One evening this week he was allowed to remain up a little longer than usual. After his bath he was placed in his crib, the gas was lighted, and he was given his "Mother-Goose" book and a copy of a weekly journal of mechanical illustrations, of which he is so fond that whenever he sees one he recognizes it and tries to get it. The next night, when being put to bed at the same hour, he asked for the book, pointed to the gas, said "gas," and kept repeating "book" as he went to his crib. He was again allowed to wait and to have the books. The third evening he showed that he expected the same thing, so he was put to bed as usual, just as if he was expected not to protest, tucked in, kissed "good-night" as usual, after having had his bottle of milk, the netting was pulled down, the room was darkened, and "good-night" was said. He evidently accepted the intended suggestion of "no books or gas-light to-night," for he fell asleep without a protest. He is trustful and very docile, and although naturally self-willed, he generally does just as we direct. It never seems to dawn upon him that he should oppose any one. For this reason care is taken not to provoke opposition, in order to preserve this spirit for future need—when absolute and instant obedience might be required. (The above portion of the record shows very clearly how easily a bad habit might be formed by unwise indulgence. Bad in the sense of being unwise from a hygienic stand-point, for the necessity of freedom from mental excitement during the last hours of a child's day, and also of a regular hour for its bedtime, must be fully realized. It is through little

things like this that one gains the control that, later on,
will bring *loving* obedience.)

While we were out driving to-day Harold saw a lady
riding by; he opened his eyes wide and looked after her
until she disappeared, for he had never seen a woman in
the saddle before.

I gave him some sugar on the tip of my finger at
luncheon. He enjoyed pecking at it for some time, and
then he tried to bite my finger, laughing heartily each
time I snatched it away to escape being bitten.

Last night I found that the key of my bedroom door
was missing, and I felt certain that he had taken it, for
every morning he is in the habit of carrying it to another
room to open a door of which we have lost the key.
To-day we found it in the corner of a drawer in the
room to which he went daily with the key. I have
often wondered whether he intended to save himself the
daily trip, for he is a sagacious little chap.

To-day, when making up his crib, I said, " Harold,
bring me the sheet." He looked all about for something
to bring but didn't know what I meant. I touched the
sheet without saying anything, and he instantly pulled
it from the chair and brought it to me. (A quick comprehension can easily be cultivated in children by self-
restraint upon the part of the mother.)

September 14th.—To-day he is nineteen months old.
I said "moon "to him, pointing to it, and he repeated the
word distinctly several times. Afterwards I returned to
the window and looked out. He followed me and said
the word again, remembering it clearly after the short
interval. Just before going to bed he saw some of his
books. He said " book, book," and " gas " as I lighted
it. We then looked at the pictures. Every clock he

called by name, and put down his ear to listen. He
kissed all the pictures of cats and dogs, and said " puddy" to the pussy pictures and " wow-wow " to the dogs,
also saying " o-o-o-h " affectionately to each one, as he
always does to pet animals.

When it was time, this morning, he was told to call
his father. He went to his room, as he always does, and
wakened him in a very gentle, loving way by going to
his side and saying "hm-m." This morning he made
a great romp of it, alternately kissing and petting him,
and then running away. He would then return again
to the bed, put his head on his father's pillow, then say
" bye," and run away again.

He sleeps soundly, and does not want to wake, it appears, until his hour for rising, for whenever he is disturbed he seems annoyed, and falls asleep again as
quickly as he is let alone. At eleven last night I gave
him his milk, for which he wakes voluntarily at the
exact time. I placed him on my bed after turning up
the light, shook up his pillows, and rearranged his crib.
I then placed him in the crib, kissed him, said "good-
night," and drew down the netting. He looked at me
sleepily, laughed, turned over, and was asleep before I
had time to open the window and turn down the light.
When I go to my room late at night he does not stir.
I have noticed that when he is well, and eats a light,
early supper (at five o'clock), he sleeps soundly. The
least indiscretion at his supper-time, or too much excitement after five o'clock, invariably causes restlessness. (The record shows the same result throughout.)

Every morning now he wakes about six, pulls away
the netting that is over him, and calls me. I ask him
if he wants some milk. He says "yes," invariably.

45

When I give it to him, he takes it himself in his usual fashion, holding up the bottle with both hands, so that the neck is full all the time. When he has had all he wants, he hands it back to me, generally saying "hab 'em." He sometimes goes to sleep again without a word, but generally he wants to get up; if so, he calls his nurse, who takes him to the nursery and dresses him. He seems to understand that for another hour I am not to be disturbed, for he remains with her contentedly until it is time to call me, when he is all eagerness, first to get me up and dressed, and then to go to his father, who usually has a romp with him while he dresses. (It is very interesting to note how he accepted the habits of the household and adapted himself to them, as, for instance, he was quiet for an hour after he was up, and then he evidently thought it was time for others to rise, for he was heard everywhere. Habit had a great deal to do with this, and every one was careful not to disturb it by irregularity in his life. The mother claimed that he was at any rate much happier by being taught to consider others than he would have been had he been allowed, perhaps unwittingly, to be a disturber of the peace of every one around in the early morning hours.) This morning he discovered that he could slide his feet on the carpet and sit down suddenly by holding to me as he leaned against me. He did it repeatedly with great glee. Yesterday he climbed all alone up and down the steps on the porch, and he is becoming quite venturesome. This week he said "wagon" quite distinctly when he saw one of his toy wagons. He also says "ice" now whenever he wants us to give him some, and broadens the same sound for "eyes." He still says "wat" for water.

He says "mamma" and "papa" correctly, but he still says "bavy" for baby, "hugar" for sugar, "bock" for block, "bot" for bottle.

For a few days past he has shown temper, kicking and screaming when not pleased. I paid no attention to him each time that he did it beyond saying "good-bye," and going towards the door as he lay on the floor kicking. He got up at once and came after me every time, evidently forgetting all about the disturbance in his fear that I would leave him alone.

He still says "puddy" for pussy. He often says "peep, oh!" and plays it on the slightest provocation. He claps his hands and tries to clap on mine. He puts his finger in his mouth and then offers it to me. He did the same thing once when eating sugar with his finger. He grows more affectionate every day—runs up and touches us, lays his head or hands against us, saying "bavy"—meaning himself—in a long-drawn-out, loving tone that is indescribable. He frequently kisses little Mamie next door. He has selected her as his favorite out of a family of six children.

September 22d.—To-day he said "po-book" for pocket-book, "toes," "pins," and also "water" instead of "wat," and "Tottie" for Topsy, his new dog's name. Two weeks later he said "han," then "fan," for fan.

October 18th.—He wanted to sit on a chair that had a towel on it. He evidently did not want to sit on the towel, so he brought it to me, saying "towel" distinctly for the first time. It is curious to hear him use words as occasion suggests that we never supposed he knew.

From October 1st to the 21st he has said "goose," "cushy" for cushion, and "neeze" for sneeze (imitating a sneeze he heard); "baa-baa" when looking at a picture of sheep; "choo-choo walk carry papa" all in one sentence, when his father went to town one morning and he seemed very anxious to go with him; "scissors," "fork," "poon" for spoon; "Gacky" for Jacky, "Tossy" instead of "Tottie," as at first, for Topsy, and "Bahdee," the name of a friend's cat, which we were taking care of at the time.

He also said "hat" and "cuckoo" in one sentence on seeing a picture of the child N——, who lived in the house containing the cuckoo-clock. N—— had his hat on in the picture, which he noticed instantly. He also said "hanger" for hammer, and "wet" for the first time.

October 20th.—He said "winnow" for window, "coach," and "horsey moo"; said "moo" to a cow also. Whenever he hears the door-bell ring now he says "bell." One day recently the electrician was here to repair the bell. He was very much interested, and watched him closely. Later in the day he said to Bridget, "Bishy, stairs bell wats" (meaning he wanted to go down-stairs and watch). This morning he reached for his tooth-brush, and said "toot-broush." He now says "broush" instead of "bruh," as he did at first. Said "baksy" for basket, "pitty" for pretty.

When he gets cross and cries, we say "No, no, pretty," and he repeats "pitty," and clears his face at once, many a time looking up smiling with tears still in his eyes.

He pointed to the moon and said "gas." He also says, now, "buttony" for button, and "knife" and "fork." He seems to enjoy saying knife lately, when he sees a picture of a fork. He waits for us to correct him, and then does it again with the next picture of a fork in his pet book, his eyes full of fun.

He says "banket" for blanket, and "hummer" when he wants to open things. We cannot find out what word he wants to use. We thought it might be "under," as he says it when he tries to lift the lid of a jewel-case or of a box on the table.

Recently he said "hair," brushing it at the same time; also "table," lifting the lid of a side-table when saying it; and "Bishy," when he saw a picture of a coal-scuttle, associating her with the fires she tends. When he saw a picture of a stove-lifter he said "hot."

One night lately, before going to sleep, when alone in the dark, he said "Poppee, poppee—I see you, poppee. Bishy, Bahdee, poppee, poppee." We were away from home at the time for a few days' visit, and he seemed to miss them all. He pronounced "1" to-day in clock for the first time, and then said it only once. Said "tree" for the first time when out walking. He always says "thank you" when we give him anything. A short time ago I took something from a servant without thanking her, and he did it for me. He often does this when he notices the omission.

He says "mell" for smell when he sees my smelling-salts.

Says "pins" and "pail"; "wing" for ring; "dum" for drum, and "schlissel" and "key" whenever he sees one either in the door or in his beloved journal of mechanical illustrations. The latter has a page full of pictures of various sizes of keys. We told him a key was a "schlüssel" in German, and he has called the book his "schlissel book" ever since.

He said "wide, Mamie," the other day, for "ride, Mamie," when he saw a girl on a tricycle. He is accustomed to seeing Mamie P—— on one when he is at home.

D

This month some one gave him a pack of cards with a picture of a dog on the back of each one. He will say "good-night" and kiss each dog as he puts the cards aside when he is done playing with them, sometimes kissing every dog in the pack.

He says "pool" for spool, and repeats many words after us very distinctly. One morning he heard a clock strike, and said "cuckoo," recalling the cuckoo-clock we saw last summer. We are still at his grandma's, and he says "ganma" for grandma.

November 1st.—We are home again. To-day I told him to come to the nursery window to see the sunshine. He came, saying "tuntine," and all day he said it at intervals, lifting the curtain and looking out at the same time. He also said it when he saw some tin-foil with which he was playing. (For many months he called tin-foil sunshine.)

November 2d. — He counted three, four, five, six, nine to-day voluntarily. Some time ago his nurse counted a few cards for him, saying, one, two, three, four; he at once picked up three and four, saying "fee" for three, and ever since he has called his cards "fee-fours." When we count them for him he says six as soon as we say five; also ten after we say nine.

November 3d.—Instead of repeating or counting with us, he said the above numbers himself. (The record shows exceptional interest in numbers later on.)

When hearing a baby cry, he says "poor bavy."

Hearing the question, "Have you used Pears' soap?" suggested to him to say "Sares' soap," and during the day he often comes to me, saying "good-morning" and "Sares' soap" without waiting for my answer or question.

He now says "tsain" for chain, "wain" for rain, "cacker" for cracker. One day he tore his dress, and pointing his finger at it, said "o o-o-h."

To - day — November 4th — he said, "seepy" when yawning; also "seepy boy," and "here it is."

He said "there it goes" when eating something, and when holding up an envelope he said "paper."

November 6th.—Said "house" to-day, while building blocks. He also called "Carrie" (a visitor) when he woke up, and looked in the next room for her. It is very amusing to watch him running to her with open arms, saying "comes," meaning "here he comes." This morning he said "here he comes" when pushing his foot through his clothes when dressing, and he also said "here it goes" when eating some stewed celery at dinner.

November 7th.—He said "foot clock" to-day, pointing to the feet of a clock; "apple-butter"; and he said "seepy" again when yawning.

On Monday, when looking at the picture of the "pig who had roast-beef," he said "dinner—funny."

This week he has acquired the following words, in the order given : "say so"; "rats"; "cheek"; "cake"; "cook," for crook, in "Little Bo Peep"; "bucket"; "whistle"; blowed. When he saw a gentleman's comb to-day he said "papa." He said "papa's room," on entering it when returning home after a week's absence; said "crib" when going into his own room; and called "Bishy" when he saw her. Said to Bridget, "Bell bwoke, fix it." When I told his nurse he had gained half a pound, he repeated "half a pound."

November 12th.—To-day he said "stick through," putting a stick through a hole, and he said "shovel" voluntarily. When bathing him this morning in the large bath-tub, I took his head and nurse took his feet and we floated him. He showed no fear, but let himself rise to the top of the water. Next time he took his bath I took his head, meaning to do it again, but before nurse could help me he said "hand—foot" to her, intimating that he was ready for it again.

November 13th.—He said "finger" to-day, for the first time, taking mine in his hand and examining it while in bed this morning. He put his head on my pillow also and said "pittow." Later in the day he said "wats (watch) sand goes." As he said it he picked up some sand in a glass and poured it in a basket. I had just come in from a walk, and after showing me the sand he turned to the table and said "table."

November 14th.—New words to-day were: "Knock, Bishy"; "Sit down, Bishy." He begged for "crook" when going to sleep, thinking of "Bo-Peep"; also begged for my "hand," and said "find," "get," and "skate," "show it," "corn," "beans," and "take."

November 15th.—He said "sweetheart" to-day, pronouncing it "sootheart." He says it to his mother when going to sleep; for instance, he will say, "mamma's sootheart," in a loving tone. To-day he said "play—sing" to his father, pulling him to the piano, and he laughed as if pleased when he sang for him. He is always eager to hear him sing.

November 16th.—He said "pittow" again to-day for pillow when reaching for one. After breakfast he said "Dear papa, good luck," when his father left for town. Afterwards he said "Dear papa, good papa" once, and the next time when he came to "good" he hesitated a moment, and then said "luck," and he has said it voluntarily in this way ever since when his father leaves in the morning. He always shakes his head up and down when he says "luck." He also said "knock" to-day and "oh, my !"

On November 17th he said "tummer - glass" for tumbler.

On November 19th he said "ladyle" for lady, when speaking to Claudia, a visitor. He has also said "well, well" ever since her arrival, which is a frequent expression of hers. He said "come" to me after taking his bottle of milk, indicating at the same time that he wanted to go to bed. He awakened in the evening and said, on hearing his father play, "play—papa," instead of saying "papa is playing."

November 20th.—His new words to-day were "music," "yard," "nice boy," "ah," "ma-am," "say what," "what's that." For some time he has said "nice—good —ah!" when eating something he likes. He shakes his head when he does this.

This morning, when in the dining-room, I handed him a little cloisonné plate that belonged in a certain place on the table in the next room. As I handed it to him I said, "Take it and put it where it belongs," which he did very carefully, and then returned to his toys. He seems to understand many more words than he says, and uses them only as occasion requires. I often try him in this way, to keep him in the habit of obeying cheerfully, not because I want the thing done.

November 21st.—This morning he took his doll and hugged it, saying all at once, "seep" (sleep), "eye" (pointing to the eye), "hand" (taking it up in his), "foot" (taking it up), "ear" (touching it), "mouf" (touching it), "head" (laying his hand on its head). Then I put a feather in its hair, but he put it away and said "no." Later on he put it in himself. Yesterday he found this same feather among his toys, and, recognizing it as belonging to his stuffed owl, he lifted it up and said, in a very lugubrious tone, "oh—owl."

November 22d.—He said "fwend" twice to Claudia to-day. She often says to him, "We are great friends, aren't we, Harold?" He evidently appreciates her courtesy, which she always shows delightfully to little children.

When he awakes in the morning he often lies still and amuses himself by looking around the room and repeating the names of all the things he knows, as "hutter" (shutter), "gas," "door," "picture," "bed," "crib," pointing to each one as he says the word. His capacity for self-amusement when he has the right materials is increasing every day, and his physical development is quite normal—a little beyond the average in height and weight.

One day he saw a picture of a chair tumbling, and children falling from it. He pointed to the chair, which stood on one leg, and said, "rock, rock." He took hold of one of the leaves of a screen soon after, moved it, and said, "Swing—go."

November 23d.—He said "papa" to-day for the first time, having always said "baba" before. He also said "fix-pence" when he saw the song "Sing a Song a Sixpence"; he said "tar" to "Twinkle, twinkle, little star"; "seesaw," when we reached "Margery Daw"; "Horner, plum-pie" for "Little Jack Horner"; and he often says "son" only for "Tom, Tom, the Piper's Son." When in looking over the book he comes to "Ride a cockhorse to Banbury Cross," he says, "Wo, get up; rings, fingers, toes, cross." He always says "girl—naughty" for "Dolly, you're a naughty girl," as if that fact impressed him most.

For "Little Bo-Peep has lost her sheep" he says "Peep, crook," and he sings out "Dolly—wow-wow" for "I had a little doggy."

He said "lose" for the first time recently, when some money was dropped, as if he wanted to say it would be lost. Something with which he was playing rolled under his toys, and when he hunted for it he said "find." He also said "mouthful" for the first time. When he heard a cornet and chorus singing one morning from a mission Sunday-school near by, he looked up to me and said, for the first time, very distinctly, "moosic."

He found a shoe-button among a lot of buttons with which he was playing, and he tried to put it on his shoe where the buttons are, saying "shoe" as he did it.

When later in the day he heard a child singing, he looked up and said "moosic" for the second time. An unusual noise outside of his room caused him to stop his play and say, "What's that?" as if startled. One day recently he repeated after me "body busy," when I said "You keep a body busy."

This morning he said, "Bangy boy, Bishy dear, poppee kill kito." No doubt trying to show Bridget how his father had killed a mosquito, with what he called a "bang." At another time during the day he said "Well, well!" then, "Porch, head, hat," pointing to my head; as if he wanted me to take him on the porch. This evening when he saw the button-box he asked for it twice, saying "buttony." I said "No," and gave him a box of bottle-tips. He put these aside and said "No, buttony." He cried and stamped a little, but I took no notice of it, and presently he took his little wagon and showed it to his nurse as placidly as if nothing unusual had occurred. A few days ago he took up a small clock and looked at me questioningly as he did it, because he had been told not to touch it. I said "No, no; put it down." He did so, and as he came away he said "Nice *boy*," emphasizing boy. I frequently tell him he is a good boy, when he obeys pleasantly. He is evidently able to draw his own conclusions.

For the last few days he says "Thank you, mommy" —to his mother—instead of "Thank you," as he used to. He looked at a picture of some children tumbling from a chair to-day and said "fall." He has learned to drink from a glass without assistance, and he does it very well, but with great care. He is accustomed to seeing me pour drinking-water from a carafe into his glass. This morning I found him at the table with a glass before him and the carafe in his hands. He had removed a temporary cover, and had poured some water into his glass, and seemed very proud of the achievement, just as in the instance above, and he rarely comes to grief.

November 24th.—He said "chappie shobel" when asking his father for the grate shovel this evening to play with his beloved buttons. He delights in shovelling them up as if they were coals. When I took him up to-day from his nap and rocked him a while, he said to me "Rock-a-bye baby on top." He also said "Well, well!" again.

When I came in this morning to see if he had finished his nap, he said "wake," as if to tell me that he was awake. He had been lying there quietly waiting for me. He shows this serenity always when well. When he was going to sleep to-night he said, in his usual retrospective manner, "I see you, poppee; I see you, ladyle (meaning Claudia); I see you, gamme (grandma); I see you, Carrie; I see you, mommy," etc. Then he asked for his milk, took it, and said "nice boy." Before coming up-stairs to go to bed he was at table with some one who amused himself by saying "Ach, himmel!" to the boy and hearing him repeat it. After a time he repeated it three times to himself, just as he always does with new words, and it was amusing to hear his efforts with "ach," which word he said correctly.

To-day he said "N——" when he saw some poker-chips for the first time since the summer, at which time he saw them at the house of N——'s father. He heard me tell his father this evening that he had said "top" to-day. He instantly said "tree-top." He says to himself sometimes "naughty boy," as if he thought he was doing, or being tempted to do, something forbidden.

November 25th.—To-day he said "all gone" when he reached the end of something he was eating. His new words were "piece of corn," "come, Harry," "did he?" "hoop!" And to-night when going to sleep, he said, "I see you, poppee; I see you, toys; I see you, fee-fours (cards); I see you, Bahdee; I see you, Bishy; I see you, goose." It is very curious to hear him go over the day's amusements just before he falls asleep.

November 26th.—Twenty-one months old to-day, when some one said, "low—high or low," he came running to my room, and called "Lou! Lou!" confusing low with Lou. He brought a screw-driver that he found in the sewing-machine drawer in the nursery, and he did not want to give it up when I asked for it, so I simply said, quietly, but *as if I expected him to do it,* "Take it back, and put it where you found it," for we always tried to avoid forcing an issue when a disposition to obstinacy showed itself. He went to the machine at once, put the screw-driver in the drawer, and took out a knitting-needle, but as he did it he looked at me as if to ask whether he might take it. I said "No, no," and he instantly pushed it back, shut the drawer quickly, and ran away just as if he didn't trust himself near temptation. I have noticed this trait frequently. (The record shows that when he could talk and tell how he felt under similar circumstances, he thought it best to go away from temptation.)

Several days ago he discovered a door to a closet in a writing-desk. He opened it and saw ink-bottles on a shelf that he could reach. He wanted to take them, but I said "No, no; shut the door," which he did. This morning he opened the door again, and his father feared he would take up the bottles and spill the ink. I said, "I think not. Just watch him." So I said, very quietly, but suggestively, "Shut the door, dearie, and go away." He did it at once, very much to his father's surprise, saying, as he went, "Nice boy."

One day he picked up from the desk a closed box of cigarettes. As he held it he accidentally let it fall, and the cigarettes fell out, thus letting him see what the box held. He then took up another closed box of them, and wanted to pull the cigarettes out one by one. I said "No, no, dear," but he tried to get my consent two or three times by touching them as he held the box, looking inquiringly at me. Each time I quietly said "No, no," as if I knew he wouldn't do it, and the last time I said "Put them on the desk," which he did. He obeys us at all times, but we must give him time to adjust himself to what he is to do, and we must speak very quietly, as if we expect obedience to be the most natural thing to happen. I had a little trouble to teach him not to touch things in the dining-room, and for a time we seriously considered placing things out of his reach, but eventually concluded it would be better to stand some loss of valued articles, if necessary, than lose an opportunity of showing him in every direction in his life that he must learn to respect the rights of others. The servants and I therefore kept following him up, saying "No, no" whenever he touched anything, and *offered some pleasant diversion each time as the next thing for him to do* when we led him away. It was really very amusing. The shining glass and silver seemed to possess a great fascination for him, and we frequently found him standing before a tea-set of highly colored china, each piece of which represented a piece of fruit. The teapot was shaped like an apple, the handle looked like the branch. This piece seemed to attract him in spite of his evident effort to keep away from it. He would stand before it and touch the lid in a very cautious manner, lift it up gently, and put it down again, and then go away. I watched him do this several times. Once I found him out after he had been there alone, for later in the day I discovered the lids interchanged. Eventually we succeeded in teaching him to keep from touching anything that didn't belong to him, but the collisions of will were sometimes diverting.

An effort was always made to refrain from speaking sharply to him, nor was any one knowingly allowed to do so, consequently he trusted all who were about him. (The record shows how, when he was eight years old, he attempted to conceal some of his actions that did not

meet his own approval, and when gently led to tell his
reasons, he said, with a burst of tears, " I am afraid of
them all !" meaning those who were about him at the
time, and who noticed and criticised his actions—with
the natural result of reaction on the child. Before this
he had usually confided even his smallest faults to his
mother, not fearing her.) His nurse is very gentle in
her manner, and she succeeds wonderfully in diverting
him quickly from what she anticipates will be likely to
give the little fellow trouble. She possesses faithfulness,
intuition, and quick comprehension, and although not
an educated person, she has many qualities that are
valuable for assistance in nursery-training. She is perfectly truthful, mild in manner, always cheerful, tidy,
and playful, and understands perfectly *how*, and is willing, *to* carry out directions just as they are given, which
quality is absolutely necessary in a person to be trusted
with the care of children. This morning she put him in
his crib for his nap, with an exact imitation of his
mother's manner of handling him, gave him some milk,
and then turned to do something else. He drank the
milk and then turned to watch her for a few minutes.
She paid no attention to him, but finished what she was
doing and left the room quietly. He turned over, and
no more was heard of him until after nap-time. Had
she spoken to him he would have tried to keep awake,
as he often does, and in all probability he would have
missed his nap. This plan was invariably followed, the
mother interchanging with the nurse, in order to keep
him equally accustomed to both. Thus the mother could
be given the freedom required in the evening at dinner-
time, without disturbing the child in the least, and he
was as well satisfied with the nurse, when sleepy, as

with the mother. (It may mean self-sacrifice, many times, to reach this end, for it is very dear to any mother to feel that her child prefers her ministrations to those of any one else, but, for the child's sake, this feeling should not be indulged in to too great an extent. When a nurse loves her charge, she should also have some of the happiness incidental to the care of the child, and be able to win its love, that, in case of illness of either child or mother, her assistance may be of value.)

He said, this morning, "Mommy, Bishy lof," meaning he loved her. He hugged her as he said it. He shows daily how much he loves her. (I have always found it safe to judge a nurse's manner during the absence of her mistress by the evidence of affection given by the child. It will invariably be a reflection of the surroundings, for a fearless child is always a mirror of others.)

To-day, when he saw the illustration of the fat spider in the "Spider and the Fly" song in his nursery-book,* he said "Sider, fatty, ha-ha." He seems to enjoy intensely anything that will provoke laughter, and he is usually a merry little soul.

Recently he took a number of things out of the drawer of the kitchen-table, saying "What's that? What's that?" to everything he didn't know, but said "spoon," "fork," "knife," etc., to those he did know. At last he found an old steel that was used some months ago to crack ice. He remembered this at once, and said, when he saw it, "Bishy, cack ice."

This evening he did not feel very well, and he begged his mother to stay by him. She remained, lying down beside him and holding his hand while singing to him.

---

* Elliott's *Mother Goose.*

He kept asking for his pet songs, one by one. When she thought he had had enough to quiet him, she said "good-night," and stopped singing, still lying quietly, however. He soon said to himself, "Mommy seep," turned over, and fell asleep.

November 27th.—His new connections of words to-day were "knock, Bishy," and "piece of buttony" (for button). This afternoon he knelt by his mother who was lying on a couch, and said, "Ah, mamma's sute-heart" in a very winning way. These voluntary tokens of love are quite usual with him.

November 28th.—At midnight last night, when rest-less, he said to his father, "Poppee stay, carry boy."

November 29th.—As he put something in a hole to-day he said, "Stick it in." He constructs sentences very often now. When his nurse came in he said, "Carry boy." He said to me to-day, "apple—fork," and showed them to me. When I asked him where he got the fork, he said, "tappie (chappie)—table"—meaning on a table in his father's room, where I remembered it had been left last night.

November 30th.—To-day the new words were "pretty well," "smart," "shadow."

December 1st.—New words were "pull up sleeve," and "wing" (of a bird).

December 11th.—"Come, Bahdee (to his pussy); Bishy bring Bahdee." He said "big ring, noder one," to some one who was making smoke rings for him when smok-ing a cigar after dinner. At one o'clock in the night he waked and said immediately, "big ring, noder one," as if there had been no interval.

He said to-day, December 12th, while playing, refer-ring to one of his nursery songs, "Taffy—tief—beef—

home." He seems to think of these things while he is doing other things.

Said " o " and " d " (from letter-blocks) to-day, and also said "lap," "lappie—bangie—boy." We can't find out what he means by " bangie."

From December 14th to end of the month he has said "pencil"; "gettie pencil"; "find more"; "ice-wagon" and "street car," when seeing pictures of the same; "Santa Caus," omitting the "l"; "bottles," for nine-pins; "pick it up"; "put it away"; "picture"; "pipes," when he sees any one smoking, or if he sees a pipe in any one's mouth; "letter," "letter-man," when he hears the door-bell ring; "pinage" for spinach; "masala" for celery; "teakettle — coffee," when he sees a picture of a teakettle; "put it down"; "Germantown"; and "my name is Harold." When I say " You live at No. ——," he instantly says the name of the street. He speaks of me as Mrs. H——, and uses my name correctly. We always teach him any change of address by direct teaching, that he may, if lost, tell where he belongs, and we have always impressed upon him the fact that all policemen are his friends and are meant to help people, especially when they get lost. I often hear him try to persuade a little friend who is afraid of policemen to like them.

To-day he said, "Tom, Tom, saw pig run, eat beat howling steet" for (street). He was evidently thinking of

> "Tom, Tom, the piper's son,
>   Stole a pig and away he run," etc.

Other words that are new are "hello," "hello, dear," " gamme boy," " screw," " Bahdee scatch " (when pussy scratches), "ach himmel," " gesundheit." He still says "neeze" for sneeze; "down-tairs, Bishy"; says "bottle—seepy," when bedtime comes; "get a coach," when he wants to go out-of-doors; "gamma—choo-choo," intimating that he wants to go to gamma's (grandma) on the choo-choo. He remembers that he went on the train some months ago on a visit to her.

January 14th, 1892.—To-day he said "Happy New-year" three times when looking at a holiday-book. He then turned to his mother, kissed and hugged her, and said "lufly mamma."

He says "Santa Claus" now, pronouncing the "l." He takes his Santa-Claus book and explains all the pictures—as, for instance, when he reaches the one where Santa is sitting reading the names of children, with pen and ink on the desk before him, he says, "Santa Claus reading, desk, gif me pencil," holding out his hand to the picture. He often asks for "pencil—write" (pencil to write), and makes an O. He calls a big O a "fatty O." He knows W, X, H, I, O, Q of his block-alphabet, and he says X, Y, Z from repetition, but does not know them when he sees them.

He saw sleighs to-day for the first time. He heard his nurse say "sleigh" in the morning, and when out in his coach later in the day he said "sleigh, noder one," as they passed him. Since the above date he has picked out pictures of sleighs in his books, saying "sleigh, noder one," whenever he finds one.

January 15th.—His new words to-day were "here 'tis," "kitchen—outside," "missee morning" (for misty morning), "how do, sir?" "shut ee eyes." When he stumbled he said "fall."

January 18th.—Last night, after he had waked and taken his last bottle of milk, he said, "Mommy's pwecious boy," rolled over, and fell asleep. He is at his grandma's. He took her hand to-day, and pulled her into the next room, saying, "hand—gamme's hand." Last evening, as he was finishing his six-o'clock meal of milk, he discovered letters on the bottle when he held it up between his eyes and the gaslight. One of the words had two o's in it. He pointed to one and said "o," then pointed to the next and said "noder one," then cried out in delight, "dubble u," meaning "w." He said it as if he was very much surprised. He then found D, S, K, and I, and repeated them over and over, as if glad to see them, first of all, however, pointing out each one to me with his little finger. As I am writing this he is in the kitchen, and I hear him at the knife-drawer saying "fee—fee knife," meaning three. He always says "fee—fee" when he means to say there are more than one. He often counts correctly from one to fourteen. I can hear him now as he is going around the rooms exploring, saying " window, parlor window," and no doubt he has met a rocking-chair, for I hear him say " rock-a-bye, rock."

When he reached the station he met his cousin and called him by name, although he had not seen him for four months. Later he said " gamme " when he met her, knew his cousin's father at once, calling him by his first name as he hears others do. After a little investigation he said " Carrie " to one member of the family, and after quite a while he said " Alus," for Alice, to another. He said "fraid dat," pointing to a rolling-top writing-desk. (Here following out indications given before of being afraid of some things that work with a motive power that is to him incomprehensible.)

The plumbers were at work in the kitchen this morning. He heard the puffing of the Bunsen burner when he awakened from his nap, and said, "See ee choo-choo in ee kitchen," and could hardly wait to get there. He amused himself for a time to-day by pushing his coach around the room, but first he moved two chairs very carefully out of his way in order to have the entire length of the room open for the coach.

When he was asked if he wanted a piece of bread, he said "Yes," and voluntarily went to the pantry, opened the door and bread-can, took out a loaf, and brought it to the person who asked him, who cut a piece from it, and returned the loaf to him without a word. He returned it to the can, closed both it and the door, and returned, when he was given his piece of bread.

January 19th.—To-day he heard something fall with a loud noise. He said, "Break ee house down." Two new sentences were: "Pull down ee sleeve, mommy," meaning his own; and "Please, Carrie, take out ee key." When he awoke this morning he said, "Kitchen, gamme," meaning he wanted to go there, where he was allowed perfect freedom every morning.

He uses all sorts of expedients to get his mother up mornings as soon as he wakes. Says, "Get up, mommy—dess, dess Harold, mommy"; "want ee dink"; "mommy up, kitchen"; "see gamme"; and then he calls "Carrie, come," as loud as he can, for she generally comes in at this time and romps with and dresses him. When at last his mother does get up and dress, he sits contentedly awaiting his turn. He says, trying to do it at the same time, "Put ee shoes on, Harold—put ee shoes on." Then he says "petticoats," when they are put on; "Put on dess" next; then, "Brush ee teeth," "Brush ee hair," "Wash ee mouth," and at last he turns

up his face for a kiss, saying " Clean enough ?"   He takes
the greatest interest in every little thing relating to the
care given him.

January 20th.—To-day he wanted to take the dust-
pan to bed with him when he took his nap.   I took it
away, saying " No, no."   He kicked and screamed, but
I took no notice of it.   At last he said, " Too bad ;
shame !"—repeated it several times, then took my hand
and fell asleep quietly, with only one more cry for the
dust - pan, following it immediately with " Too bad ;
shame !"

January 21st.—To-day he said, " Dance a baby diddy "
(from nursery song); also said "spider," when he saw the
inside of a big clock ; and then he said " Fatty clock, see
clock ticking."   No doubt he associated the big clock
with the big spider he called " fatty spider" in the nursery song-book, for he calls a big O a fatty O.

January 22d.—To-day he picked up a tin bread-can
that was standing on the pantry floor, carried it about,
and suddenly began to turn his hand around, as if turning a handle, and say "musilay," meaning music, and that
he was imitating a hand-organ.

January 23d.—We came to town for the winter a
few days ago.   Harold and his nurse came in on a later
train.   Ever since he has said, repeatedly, " Sarah, take
Harold lufly choo-choo"; "bell ring, choo-choo"; and
every time he sees a possible chance of going out he
says, " See a choo-choo ?"   He was given a very complete toy locomotive last month, because he has shown
such great interest in engines of all sorts.   He instantly
detected various differences between his engines and
those he saw about him in his daily walks, and he did
not hesitate to mention them.   He asked questions about

every part he observed after this, wanting to know the names of all of them. In a very short time he was heard saying to his nurse, " This is a piston-rod," or " This is a cylinder," or " This is an eccentric," etc. He was told each name once only in answer to his questions.

He was taught, in Germantown, when asked where he lived, to give his name and his street-number. Last evening we began to teach him his new address, his name, and street in Philadelphia, and he repeated it several times. This evening we asked him where he lived and what was his name. He said, "Harold—Gimmintown," and then, as if a new idea had struck him, he said in one sentence, " Fil a duffia, Locust Street — choo-choo— Filaduffia."

A few days ago he began saying "Use Pears' soap," instead of just " Pears' soap," as before. We often ask him, for fun, " Have you used Pears' soap?"

To-night he said, "Papa, play—play 'Annie Rooney.'" He speaks very distinctly for so young a child.

January 24th.—To-day, when playing with his toys, he voluntarily counted one, two, three, four, five, six, seven, eight.

Later in the day, when taking off my street shoes, I asked him to please bring my shoes, without specifying which pair he should bring. He went to my closet and selected a pair of low russet shoes that I frequently wear when at home. He certainly observes much that one ordinarily considers unnoticed by a child.

This morning when I came into his room before he was out of bed, I found him playing with a toy "choo-choo" that could be wound up to run. He had no string with which to wind it up, and he evidently wanted one, for he had untied the ribbon at the neck of his night-gown, and was trying to wind it up with that.

He has begun to say a few French words: "bon soir, bon nuit," from imitation, but he knows what they mean, and his pronunciation is very good.

January 25th.—To-day he begged me to "carry down cellar to kitchen to Annie," meaning the colored janitress in the basement. She has a bird with which he is delighted, and which he evidently wanted to see. He often asks for something that we find later on brings him something else that he wants but doesn't ask for. It seems hardly probable that he does it designedly, yet it is a curious coincidence at times.

January 26th.—To-day we were out walking. As we neared Broad Street the wind blew hard, directly in his face. I said, "Turn around, Harold, and walk backward." He did it at once, much to the amusement of some passers-by, who stood still and watched him. He seems to comprehend very quickly that I have a good reason for asking him to do certain things, and even if they may appear a little unusual at the time to another, to him they seem to appear to be natural.

January 29th.—To-day he said to his nurse (who is not the one to whom he has been accustomed, but an old colored mammy), "Good-bye, honey." Other sentences were, "Mannie sit down, show ee schlissel book;" "See ee mannie;" "Mommy, good boy;" "Harold —— good boy" (saying his whole name); "Carry, Bishy, (to) lovely choo-choo." He said "Geen choo-choo" to-day, saying "geen" for green—the first time for this word. He was hunting a little green engine at the time and couldn't find it. Other sentences were, "Where's ee drum?" "See ee musee-man, winnow."

January 30th.—To-day, when in the bath-room, he said, "Baf pitty soon," no doubt anticipating his evening bath. As we passed the bath-room door he said, "Baf-yoom; wash ee hands." He also said, "Fraid ee doctor," when he saw Dr. ——, who lives next door. He said it at intervals all day. (The record shows that he never learned to like the physician mentioned, cried when he approached, and could not be induced to even talk to him. He was a very stern man, and cruel to children, as later developments proved. A curious thing about the child shows clearly all through the record that he knew instantly when meeting persons whether they liked him or not. Servants could not be kept with comfort to the little fellow when he had shown that he thought they didn't like him, and it was always found advisable when engaging a servant in any capacity to first have him see the person, and watch his manner before engaging them. In this way some exceptionally faithful servants were secured. His usual expression in this connection, as he grew older, was either "I don't like her face," or "Has she a smiling face?" One day in a store he begged me to ask a certain cash-girl, with "such a lovely face," to come home to him. (His own words.) He couldn't understand at first why I couldn't do it, for it was his mother's habit at the time to regularly engage a child to play with him daily, to keep him from becoming selfish—a fault easily acquired by an only child.

To-day some one spoke very suddenly to him when he was playing, to check him instantly in something he was just beginning to do. He looked up with a start and said, "scairt."

January 31st.—He still says his name instead of saying I, when speaking of his own actions. He said to himself to-day, as if trying to recall something, "What name?—Harold—in Gimmintown."

When out walking the other day we passed some billboards on Broad Street that were covered with pictures of engines. He was delighted with them, went up to them, touched them, and admired them to his heart's content. He didn't want to leave them, but I induced him to come on to something else that appeared to attract him. He kept on talking about them, however, after we had left them, and to-day, when I took him out on the balcony for an airing, he objected at first and said, "Out choo-choo fence." This is the first time I have heard him say "fence."

His new words to-day were "cellar," "kitchen," "Bavinia" (for Lavinia—a servant down-stairs), "clothespins"; and this afternoon, when his mother attempted to feed him some ice-cream, he said, "Mommy way, George feed." (George was a servant.)

February 1st.—He used I for the first time to-day. He is almost two years old. He said, "I use Pears' soap"; "I see choo-choo out." Then he said, "Hug mamma, oh," squeezing her hard as he said it. He also said "I want you, baby," in his play to-day.

February 3d.—He began making funny faces a few weeks ago when he said, "Hoop a loop, who's in the soup?" Now he makes the faces at me and laughs. He often looks laughingly at me and winks one eye. He is always very jolly. This morning he begged me to "go out and see man carry leg." I couldn't think what he meant, but discovered later that he had seen a man on a crutch yesterday, and was very much interested.

He now uses a great many words very intelligently—

as, for instance, when he says the words, "coming," "won't come," "here it goes," "here it is." There is always an intelligent application. To-day he found a doll that he calls "Tommy" lying in a box of toys and covered with a cushion. He said at once, in what seemed to be a tone of reproof, "Tommy seep all day in box."

This morning he said, "Poppee, get up—eight o'clock;" and at breakfast he turned to his father and said, "Papa, shame!" We couldn't find out what he meant, but he very often says, "Too bad, shame!" when anything goes wrong. I recognize the words as used occasionally by his nurse, from whom he has no doubt learned them.

Late this evening, when he woke for his milk, he said, "Too early," evidently meaning it was not time to get up, for I sometimes say the same words to him, if by chance he wakes in the morning before daylight. It is probable that his first thought on waking was that it was time to get up—and seeing it was yet dark, he concluded it was "too early."

February 4th.—He said to-day, "I love ee choo-choo," while he was hunting in *Puck* for a picture of one— which he found eventually, having seen it there before.

He was given recently a book containing pictures of various kinds of locomotives. At first his comments were not noticed, but gradually we became impressed with the fact that he was saying, as he turned from one page to the other, "This one hasn't any bell"; "This one has a bell"; "This one hasn't any cow-catcher" (it was an English engine); "This one hasn't any bell"—noticing the differences right through the book between the American and the English engines pictured there. At last he closed the book, turned to his mother, and said,

" Mamma, I want an engine *without* any book." He wanted the object instead of the picture.

February 5th.—He put a ribbon round his neck and said " necktie " to-day. He is constantly acquiring new words, with no teaching whatever. For about two weeks he has said, " Show me book," show me this, or that, as the case may be, instead of saying, as before, " book," etc. This morning he called to his father, " Poppee put on clothes—poppee, please put on clothes." (The record shows that he was always eager to be up himself and get every one else up, and later on he wished a number of times that there wouldn't be any night, because the days were not nearly long enough for what he wanted to do.)

To-day I brought his coat and cap, and prepared to take him out. He ran away from me. I asked him if he wanted to go. He said " No," went to the sewing-machine, and said, " Want to see machine go." He had not seen it open for several weeks. He shows indications now of preferring in-door play, which we are trying to counteract by finding inducements to keep him in the open air a certain portion of the day.

February 6th.—This evening he was playing with his father when his bedtime came. He said, pleadingly, to his mother, who came to take him to bed, " Mommy, go away," but he said it as if he did not expect it, and went with very good grace, as he always does when accepting the inevitable. We always give him a little time to get over the disappointment of a refusal before exacting obedience.

Last night he wanted his bottle of milk, to which he has been accustomed, but which for the last few nights we have withheld. He cried a little, saying " What's the matter ?" rolled over, and fell asleep.

He said " I think so " to-day, when answering a question.

February 7th. — To-day he said, " Mommy, get the
bottle ready "; " won't come " (meaning the milk won't
come. There was good reason for this, for the bottle
was empty, he had taken it all). He then said, " Never
mind," and went about his play. He always seems to
accept the inevitable in a cheerful manner. When his
father came in to-day, Harold said to him, in an effort
to induce him to play with him, " Poppee, make chains
(of paper rings, with which he and the nurse often
amuse themselves); poppee, sit down floor, cushion,
make big dubble-u (W); poppee make big X."

February 8th. — I heard him say to himself to-day,
" Cry it out. Behave yourself." He has often heard
me tell him to " cry it out on my lap," when he is
grieved, and he must have heard some one tell him
to behave himself, and he put the two together to-day
when he thought he needed the admonition.

He also said to one of us this morning, " Poppee use
Pears' soap? hear dat." These little sentences pop out
at us at all sorts of unexpected times, and they amuse
us very much.

When going to New York this week he said on the
train, " Choo-choo, lovely choo-choo. I love choo-choo."

February 9th. — Yesterday for the first time he said
" you" instead of saying " mommy," as usual when
speaking to her. He said " Mannie talk to you," instead of saying, as he did formerly, " Mannie talk to
mamma." Sometimes he calls himself " mannie," sometimes " man."

February 10th. — As his mother was taking off her
street dress to-day he pulled her to the closet and said,

" Put ee dess on." When she puts an apron on he always objects, and begs her to " take off apron." About
a month ago he cried because she put a jacket on over
her house dress on a cold morning. He said, "Take ee
sacque off, mamma," and persisted in it. He must have
some idea for this, but I have not found out yet what
it is.

We are still in New York ; arrived yesterday, and the
long trip must have tired the little fellow, for he said on
his arrival, " I'm so glad to go to bed." When half-way
over he said on the train, " Express-man *take* away trunk
to-day," and when, on our return, he saw it brought
back, he said, " Express-man *bring* ee trunk."

To-day when sitting on a bed he intimated that he
had disturbed it. I said "Oh no." He said "Yes, nice
boy ?" (interrogatively). I said " No." He said " Nice
boy, *I* sink (think) so." (The record shows how he often said, when a question of opinion would arise, "I
think so," as if that settled it in *his* mind. Such a characteristic, if properly guided, should develop into a sturdy
self-respect and strength of individual opinion, without
in the least encroaching upon or antagonizing the opin-
ions of others.)

CHAPTER III

THIRD YEAR. LANGUAGE AND OTHER INCIDENTAL DEVELOPMENT CONTINUED

FEBRUARY 15th (at home).—Harold is two years old. He just said "See ee Lollie (meaning Mollie) sew dess, nice dess." She made a dress for him some time ago that pleased him very much and which he seems to prize very highly. He begged me to-day to "take down-tairs see big clock tick-tick." He saw one in New York, and is confused about it, for there is no "big clock" here. He called "Delia" several times to-day (a house-maid he saw in New York), and he also called for his aunt, as if he could not quite reconcile himself to the fact that he was no longer there. On the way home he saw a lady on the train who resembled his aunt's mother and he called her "grandma" several times. For many days he has asked questions about how there could be another grandma, for hitherto he has only known of his maternal grandmother, and he could not understand for a long time that his aunt's mother was his cousin's grandma and not his. He is always very friendly with strangers when travelling, and appears to fear no one when their faces please him. He invariably smiles or speaks to some stranger when out-of-doors or when travelling. He said this morning, "See ee Lollie take ee coffee next yoom." He had seen his aunt have coffee in the room next to his when he was in New York, and he evidently thinks he is still within reach of her.

February 16th.—When he saw a picture of a coffee-mill to-day in his "schlüssel book," he said "ganma." He had seen one for the first time at his Grandma S——'s. He sometimes says "ganme," and at other times "gamma." When he said "ganme" to the coffee-mill, I asked "Is it Ganme H——?" alluding to his cousin's grandma.

He repeated her name and looked doubtful, then said again, "Ganme, ganme put ee coffee in." I then said "Ganme S——?" questioningly. He looked relieved and repeated it. He is evidently still puzzled over hearing of two grandmas. His maternal grandmother only is living, and until he heard his cousins speak of their grandmother he had heard of one grandmother only. (He was very curious, when a little older, about the degrees of relationship in one family, and I had many questions to answer.)

Yesterday he said, "See a Mary go—winnow—dada," shaking his hand to her from the window as she went away.

After having had a crying-spell to-day he said "Shamed himself."

February 17th.—To-day, when he saw a man from the window, he said "Uncle Hed" (meaning *Ed*). I looked out and saw a man resembling his uncle very greatly.

Yesterday I took him to see Dr. A——. He had not been there for two months. When we reached the street door of the physician's house his face changed, and he said, crying, "Harold fraid, hurts me." He kept repeating "fraid, hurts" all the time he was there, and cried until he reached the street again, when he instantly became serene. About thirteen months before this date this physician lanced his gums, and ten months ago he vaccinated him. He remembers one or the other occasion, probably both.

February 18th.—To-day I showed him an illustration with the song "Twinkle, twinkle, little star." He instantly said "Dr. Tar," meaning Dr. Starr.

This morning he said to his father, "Good-morning, glad to see you." He said to me yesterday, immediately after his nap, "Feel tired, rock a bit," and snuggled up in my arms and let me rock him. He is not very well to-day. This may have had something to do with his desire to be rocked yesterday, for he rarely asks for it.

He has always shown a great willingness to put away my shoes. I never thought of it before, but I remember now that he is always ready to put away my street shoes and to get my house shoes. I have concluded this is because he knows I will stay at home when I wear the latter, for to-day he refused to put away my house shoes when he saw me put on my street shoes. When I came home he called me at once to the closet and pointed to my house shoes. I took them out and placed them by the couch, then turned to do something else, forgetting to put them on. He took me by the hand, led me to the couch, and said, "Sit ee down bed, put ee on shoes," as if afraid I would go out again. I did so, and before I had said a word he took away my street shoes and put them in the closet. He has evidently reasoned out for himself that when I wear street shoes I am likely to go away from him.

February 19th.—This morning when he awoke he

said immediately to me, "Wait for poppee last night." So he had. It seems to be his greatest pleasure. To-night, when ready for bed, and after having taken near-ly all of his milk, he handed me the bottle and said, *very insinuatingly*, "Put away ee bottle, see ee poppee." I paid no attention to this, so he went to sleep. Last evening when he began taking the milk, he said, "Put in hot water." I thought the milk wasn't warm enough, probably, and was about to do as he asked when he sat up and said, "See ee poppee." I knew then that he was trying to get me to let him wait for his father, so I gave him the bottle, told him quietly to take it and go to sleep, *as if I expected obedience*, and he did it con-tentedly.

February 20th.—He said this morning when his father left for town "Fraid ee papa take ee choo-choo go to see Aunt M——." This evening, when his mother was lying by him as he went to sleep, he said, "Get up, mom-my, too busy." I suppose he remembers hearing her say at some time that she was too busy to lie down by him while he took his nap, for he often asks her to do so.

February 21st.—To-day he wanted to go out and, as he said, to "see a mannie frow a bricks away."

Two weeks ago he said, "Go ee out see ee choo-choos on ee fence." This morning he said, as he put a picture of an engine on a chair before him, "Sit on ee chair, talk to choo-choo." He also said, to-day, "Tell me what's it." He says, at times, "Mommy like ee boy squeal," when he makes the noise he calls "squeal."

He loves to hear his father play the violin. He said to him this evening, "Poppee play ee violin—please pop-pee play ee violin." When his father took the instru-ment out of the case and began, he said, "Shut ee box,

poppee," reached out and shut it with a bang, saying,
" Harold shut ee box," as if glad it was shut. It looked
very much as if he were afraid his father would put the
violin away too soon.

February 22d.—He said to-day, " This is a knuckle,"
closing his hand and pointing to the knuckle. Two
days ago he pointed to a knuckle on his father's hand
and said, " What's dat?" He was told it was a knuckle,
when he promptly made a fist and pointed to his own.

He asked me to go down-stairs, saying, " Carry Harold down to Bavinia, see ee bird cellar." Another
new effort for to-day was when he tried to hang a
thermometer up above the mantel and said, " Hang ee
up mantel-piece."

February 23d.—When he heard a neighboring fac-
tory-whistle this evening he said, " Hear it whistle six
o'clock."

When talking of a clock he said, " I go see it six
o'clock " (his usual bedtime). When he was screaming
to-day he said, " Mannie make a noise."

He was trying to find a big ring carved in the mantel
this morning. The mantel was draped recently, so the
ring was covered. When hunting for it he said, " Find
big O. Harold find it. Big O go to sleep," and then
when he had discovered it he said "I find it." Then
he dropped the curtain and said, " O gone to sleep."

He is very fond of his new nurse, Annie — an old
colored mammy. To-day he said to her, " Open closet,
build a house." His blocks are in the closet. A few
days ago, when asking for a drink, he said, " Drink *fresh*
water."

He is very fond of Mrs. A——, who is a neighbor at
present. This morning when she came in he climbed

on the chair before her, dangled his legs, and said, "Harold sit on chair, talk ee lady." She began to talk to him and asked him what he wanted to say. He looked at her very shyly and said, "Lof lady." He calls her "ee lady up-tairs," and often begs to go to see her.

February 24th.—To-day he said at various times, "Did she take 'em out?" (alluding to some action of his nurse in regard to some toys) "lufly wheel," and "lof Dr. T——," meaning a physician who called recently to see him.

He wanted a book of photographs this morning, which he called "Uncle Henery's book," because it contained a picture of his uncle. He said "Mamma, give Harold pictures," then said to himself, "*Ask* mamma gib Harold pictures," as if approving of his method for getting them.

He said to Annie to-day about a broken toy, "I *thought you fixed* it." He also said, "Hang it up on a nail," pronouncing the "g" hard when saying hang.

Another sentence was "Bring ee chair see ee mommy sew."

This afternoon he was very much interested in watching a fox-terrier over the way while its owner was teaching it to jump over the fence. He said, "See mannie jumpit dog." When I directed his attention to the dog, I said, "What is his name?" He said "Germantown dog," remembering his own fox-terrier which he had at Germantown six months ago.

February 25th.—He saw the reflection of the gaslight to-night on a dark-colored bottle, and he called out instantly, "Gas on bottle."

His mother wanted to use something to-day to which

he objected, and he said, "Mommy no use dat, put away on mantel-piece, mommy go away."

His new words and sentences to-day were: "No, I like piggy slippers"; "See him put a bread out"; "Mommy write"; "I got it"; "Harold hold it—glass-water," when holding a glass of water, of which he seemed very proud.

February 28th.—This morning on waking he said, "What time is it, mommy?" "shave," "poppee shave," "*is* gone to shave." Later he said, "I must fix it; too bad break teakella (kettle) again" (alluding to a toy teakettle).

When we say "Do you like Dr. E——?" he says "No." "Do you like Dr. A——?" "No." He has unpleasant recollections of both of them that could not have been avoided. "Do you like Dr. F——?" "Yes." He (Dr. F——) has been very pleasant with him during a recent slight illness. "Do you want to see him?" "No." (Because he fears he may have to do something unpleasant when he comes. If convinced that nothing of this kind is to be asked of him, he is always ready for a chat and a romp with him.) He sometimes says, as if to reassure himself, "Mommy won't hurt you, poppee won't hurt you, doctor won't hurt you."

To-day he said, while playing and puzzling over something he did not understand, "On odder side. What's dat? I can't find it—on odder side"; "I think so"; "Did you fix it?" "Did you stick him?" "Whack, piggy," when hitting his wooden pig. He also said, "Shoot Tommy" to-day to his doll. Said to me, when going to bed, "Take it off—the shoes"; "Take it off—the slippers"; "Poppee put on shirt, put on trousers, an' take a baf"; "Annie, take it off."

Before going asleep he said to me, "Glad to see you," "Sweet enough to kiss," which I often say to him after washing his face. He also said "Good-afternoon," and this evening he said "Just one light burning" when he saw the other lights lowered that he might sleep. We asked him how many gaslights were burning in the room. He said, correctly, "One, two, three gases." When carried through the next room he said, again correctly, "Just one gas burning." Afterwards he noticed the light of the Bunsen burner and said, "One—two gases." We asked him if there were any more. He replied, "I don't see it." There were none. He is evidently going to be cautious in reaching conclusions. (The record shows this is true.)

When his father was ready to leave for the day, with coat, hat, etc., he said, "Good-bye, papa, go out steet." He always says "steet" for street. To-day he said, "Bring out *the* cars." He said "the" twice to-day, instead of "ee" as usual. He also said to himself, "Is dat funny? Dat *is* funny."

He said to Annie, before she put him in his crib, "Annie, lie down on mommy's bed and hold Harold's hand." His mother often does this when he is falling asleep, and as she was not there at the time, he tried to induce Annie to do it. He said, to-day, "See clock on wall tick-tock-ticking." Also, "Listen to the gas," as it flared, and to his father, "Poppee, smoke pipe, make rings." When on his father's lap watching him making rings, he discovered cigars in his waistcoat-pocket. He grew alarmed, said, "*I* not near them," and insisted on sitting on his mother's lap to see the smoke rings, glancing from time to time, as if afraid, at the pocket holding the cigars.

To-day, pointing as if with a gun, he said, "Bing, shoot bird." When Lavinia's canary was brought up to amuse him he said, "Poppee, buy new bird." Then he asked me to sing "Moller Goose—fol—la—three—birds," meaning the song of

> "Three crows there were once
> Who sat on a tree,
> Fal-la-la-la-la-la," etc.

I think I sang it over at least two dozen times. He kept repeating, "More—*birdie listens*," pointing to Lavinia's bird, and kept time with his finger, sometimes singing with me. It had not occurred to me that he wanted me to sing for the bird. He was ill at the time, and I sang because I thought I was pleasing *him*.

To-day he said "Oh, mercy!" twice, at intervals. He heard his colored nurse say it. He also said to me when I was at the piano, facing him, however, "Turn around and play good moosic." He says "Mommy's precious boy," "mommy's pettie boy," "poppee's darlin'," when asked whose boy he is.

When he wants me to sing he specifies now, saying, "Sing 'Jack and Jill,'" or "Sing 'Little Bo Peep.'" When we go over "Mother Goose" together, he says some of the words and I say the rest, and wait for him to say his. In this way we go over the entire book. He seems to know them all very well, although he is just two years old. The following are his words for "Jack and Jill":

> "Jack—Jill—hill—water,
> Down—crown—after
> Got—trot.

> "Caper—bed—head—paper
> In—grin—plaster
> Vexed—next—disaster."

He waits for me to say some words, just as if he wanted me to have a turn—not as if he didn't know them all.

This evening he said, " Dink water, baf—sim (swim) baf-yoom."

When he hears the door-bell at breakfast-time he says, "letter-man," and "gib ee letter." He says to me, questioningly, "Want ee coffee?" He also says "bread-and-butter." Once he asked for "*nice* bread-and-butter." When he has junket for dessert for dinner he says, "Junket, lufly junket." When he gets rice-pudding he says, "Rice-pudding day."

He says "tomach" for stomach, "kib" for crib; and says, distinctly, "medicine," "piano," "violin," "working," "stocking" (although he often drops the s), "Santa Claus," "tongs," "sugar-tongs," and "spoons." He says "pockee-book" now, instead of "po-book," as he used to.

March 1st.—To-day, while he was trying to go to sleep, he said to me, as I came into the room to get something, "Shut the door; Harold go asleep." I left quickly, and he was soon asleep. Later in the day his mother sat down to darn some stockings, when he said, "Mamma, don't sew papa's stockings; hang it up."

To-day I let him look at a photograph of himself that was taken in July last with his dog in his arms. He looked at it intently, suddenly turned, and said, "Where's the bell?" I remembered then that six months ago, in October, we had tried to get a good picture of him, but failed, and one only was finished, in which he held a bell. Harold saw this bell in the one finished picture, which we sent away at the time it was taken. He hasn't seen it since, yet asked for the bell to-day, when looking at a different picture.

To-day he called to his nurse, "My nice Annie."

This afternoon he was busy playing with a little play-mate. I thought I could steal a nap, and threw myself down on the couch. He said, instantly, "Open ee eyes; no shut eyes." I was so sleepy that I closed them unconsciously, but every time he would call out, pleadingly, "No shut eyes."

This evening he said to his father, "Papa, play violin"; "Papa sit down eat ee supper." To Annie he has said for over a month, "Annie, build a house wi matches." (This is a favorite occupation of his with safety-matches. He will amuse himself a half-hour at a time with them).

This evening we asked him if he loved Dr. A——. He said "Luf Dr. A——." We asked him again, and he said "No." Then we asked him if he loved Dr. T——. He said "Yes, love Dr. T——." We are trying to get him to forget his unpleasant recollections of Dr. A——, but he seems to remember too vividly to forget easily. To-day his mother wanted to dress a cut with antiseptic lint, and he said, "Mamma, put ee cotton way." When she picked it up again he said, "Put it on *Annie* finger," as if his finger was to be spared. Then he said, as she took the salve, "Mamma won't hurt Harold wi grease; papa won't hurt Harold; doctor won't hurt Harold; doctor put satchel way. Doctor come in, see soldier picture," which he thinks is a great pleasure (one of Detaille's).

At dinner this evening he said "Papa, gib some pease"; "Papa, gib Harold crust"; "piece of crust"; "good crust"; "nice crust." To-night he said, "Put ee stockings on, go see papa in next yoom," when I took them off to get him ready for bed. He is full of little ways of pleading to stay up at night with "papa."

When going to bed to-night he said, in his usual pleading way, "See papa eat oysters next yoom." This afternoon he said "I *must* find it," emphasizing must.

March 2d.—He said, to-day, "Harold sneeze"; also "Too bad; Harold broke it."

I gave him a small music-box that had a handle similar to a winding tape-measure, and at first he called it a "tape-measure."

March 3d.—His new sentences to-day were, "Put this on the top," and "Stand up and look at Bridget," to a picture he saw in a fashion paper that he called Bridget.

He made H, X, and A with matches, and told me what letters they were. We sometimes give him a box of safety-matches to build letters with, and it pleases him very much. At times he asks for them, but does not get them. This evening when he received the box he took out all the matches, shut the box-slide, hit it to make sure it was shut, and set it aside in a very decided way, as if to say, "Now I *have* the matches, I shall do as I please with them." He then built houses, letters, and engines, and amused himself for a long time.

A short time ago he saw a picture of a screw-top glue-pot in a journal, and said at once, in an excited way, pointing to it, "What's dat?" I said "A glue-pot." He looked at it doubtingly for a while, then said, very decidedly, "That's the doctor's; doctor won't hurt you; don't like bottle doctor." I then noticed that the bottle resembled an ether-bottle used once when etherizing him. When I asked him where he had seen a doctor's bottle, he looked at the end of the mantel where the one used had been standing. He then said, although it was his beloved "schlüssel book," "Put the book away;

don't like the doctor's bottle." He asked for it again, however, after a while, as though it had a fascination for him, yet he showed apprehension when he saw the picture.

When he heard some one moving in the hall later on in the day he started and said to me, "Doctor won't hurt you." Had his mother thought he would notice and remember so much she would have cautioned the physicians and have saved him much nerve-strain. It is a mistake no doubt often made, for knowledge so often comes too late, and children suffer. (The record shows that it took more than a year for the child to recover from the nerve-strain, which could all be traced to the fact that he was allowed to be in the room while preparations were being made to etherize him. These facts may serve to illustrate where physicians and surgeons may make a few practical deductions from child-study.)

He said, to-day, to his mother, "See birdie sleep, mamma; hang it up, gas"; "Tommy kiss O's, kiss choo-choo," putting the letters and engine to Tommy's mouth. (Tommy is a stuffed rag doll). He then said, in a reflective tone, "Tommy's face very dirty." Dr. A—— had said the same a few days before, and Harold said it as if, now that he came to think of it, Dr. A—— was right. He then said, "Tommy sit up," trying to make him sit. He accomplished it, and eagerly said to me, "Harold made Tommy sit up." This evening when he saw a picture of a tape-measure he thought of the music-box he had received recently, for he asked at once, "Mamma, gib Harold musila-box." She gave it to him, turning over another page of the book as she did so. He turned the handle of the music-box and said, "Find tape-measure."

She turned back one page again to the tape-measure picture, and he looked for and saw that it had no handle, so he looked about the room and said, "Mamma, find other tape-measure," signifying he wanted the one we used that had a handle. He saw the points of resemblance, yet knew each thing for what it was.

He has said " sterilized " distinctly for several weeks.

He said to-day, " Soldier picture; sing to soldier picture," the one of Detaille's alluded to before, of which he is very fond.

He spoke of snow the other day when he saw it falling.

This evening he asked, "How many gases burning?" When we reached a picture in the *Iron Age* of a large stationary engine, he said " What's dat?" I said, " Machine." He repeated the word, looked at me, then said " machinery " twice. How he learned it I do not know. He must have heard some one say it in this connection.

For several days he has said a number of times, " Mamma, take him arms." He does this when he does not feel very well, and it always makes her watch him closely that she may try to correct any disturbance before it goes too far.

He wanted his "schlüssel book" this evening, and when his mother gave it to him she said, " Tell mamma you are her darling boy." He hugged her, and said in a tone of great affection, " Mamma's darlin', *precious* boy."

March 4th.—He said to-day, " This is a knife to cut some bread," pointing to bread - knife. He also said, " Papa dress *too*," the first time he has said too. Said " bing " for bring.

He said to Kate, a visitor, " Love Kate, sit down on Kate's lap, tired of sitting on Annie's lap."

Other sentences at this date were: "Mommy's good boy"; "Stella (a playmate) not here to-day"; "Bring it up the spoons, Stella;" "I love it, the boy," alluding to little Walter, with whom he played occasionally ; "Shut this window."

He put one of his father's bamboo canes in a hole in a chair this evening, and amused himself for a long time making it go up and down and bend.

He said to Annie to-day, " Annie write to Susan, gib ee dis one pencil, write to Susan." She told him a few days ago that she must write a letter to some one called Susan. He said to me to-day, "Thank you, put away nice little gas-light," returning to me a gas-burner I had given him to play with. Then he said, " Mamma, try to reach it, mantel-piece."

As soon as he hears a piano, even if it is next door, he asks for his toy piano, and begins to play.

March 6th.—A new sentence to-day was "Stand up and wind the tick-tock up."

One day recently, when not well, he said, "Just a while lean on here" (meaning my shoulder), "Annie's arms break." She must have complained in his hearing of her arms being tired or being ready to break.

To-day he had spinach for dinner, the first time for a month. He recognized it, and called it "pinage."

His new sentences to-day were: "Write Baby Mc-Kee"; "Where's it?" and "No, got enough," when asked if he would have more of something.

He also said again to-day, " Doctor won't hurt you, table."

An old servant called Bridget brought him a balloon to-day. He seemed afraid of it, and said, " Don't ee like ee Bridget ball. Needn't go near it. Hang it up." He has not seen her for six weeks. At first he looked shy and turned away, but turned back again, and looked at her as if glad and surprised, saying " Bridget."

He said to his father to-night, when he went to bed, " Good-bye, papa, until to-morrow, see you again."

This evening as I sang about " Good-night to birds," he sang " Good-night, Bavinia's bird."

March 7th.—To-day he said, " Got a pain in tummach, mamma." At night he begged to lie in "mamma's bed," and was ill all night. He cried constantly, "Take him, carry him in mamma's arms, walk floor."

March 9th.—This evening at dinner he picked up a piece of crust lying by his father's plate, tasted it, said, " Don't ee like ee papa's crust, want a drink," and said, also, " Get a spoon and feed him"; "Harold feed himself"; "Want some meat"; "Want some juice" (roast-beef dish gravy); "Want some tato," and so on, as each dish appeared. As he grew sleepy he said, as if afraid she wouldn't do it on account of dinner, " Mamma, take me ; lie on mamma's bed, hold hand."

He began lately to say, in a conscious way after making a remark, "Hear dat, papa?" Every one began at once to be more careful, and the servants were cautioned, for fear he would lose his unconsciousness, and results justified this care. He has now no thought as to how his words appear to others.

He said to-day, " Fraid ee mamma sew, put ee down ee needle." Also, " Fraid ee mamma go away ; fraid ee papa take a choo - choo go to see Aunt M——, New York."

He goes over a pet journal of mechanical illustrations in a curious way. He has some association with each picture. When he saw a poker, the name of which he did not know, he said "Bishy," meaning a servant he had seen using a poker ; when he saw a stove - lifter, he said "hot" (he may have found that out by experience, for he sometimes gets into the kitchen). His favorite illustrations are a page of screws, one of keys (after which he calls the book his "schlüssel book," for we told him the German word for key), and a very complete illustration of a locomotive, but he will sit contentedly, turning over page after page, and talk to himself about all the pictures. He does this also with *Mother Goose*, and seems to know nearly all of it, sometimes humming snatches of the melody, but he prefers the "schlüssel book," and finds something new in it every time he looks it over, and is always eager to show me his discoveries. It is astonishing to see how he amuses himself from morning to night when we do not confuse him with too many things. One time we give him blocks, another time take him to the kitchen and let him reign until naptime, when cook gets a chance to tidy up again. When there, he will go from one utensil to another, point to them, and say "What's dat?"

Every evening now he says to his father as soon as he is in the house, "Papa, play ee violin," and while he plays he will rest quietly in his nurse's arms. When his father stops playing, to go to dinner, he says, "Put ee violin seep." He found somewhere a fan shaped like a violin, and an egg-beater that he uses as a bow. He calls these "my violin," and goes about the house playing and singing at the top of his voice.

Yesterday I held him up at the window to see a chute coal-wagon. He looked at the men taking out the coal for a while, and then said, "Make ee wheel go round." I didn't know at first what he meant, but afterwards I saw them lower the cart, and understood. I had not noticed the wheel before.

This evening I gave him a bottle of milk that was a little bit warmer than he is accustomed to. He instantly handed back the bottle after touching it, and said, "Put his bottle in the cold." He often says "his" now for "ee."

To-night, when giving him a mustard foot-bath, he protested, and lifting his feet out of the water said, "Don't like ee mustard." He heard me tell nurse to put the mustard in. Probably if he had not heard this he would not have noticed the difference, especially if I had diverted his attention when doing it.

March 11th.—This evening he said, in about one hour after receiving a toy violin, "Daden's bow; poor bow fell!" (to his own when it fell). "Mommy sing 'A Maggie pet.' Poppee don't want to play violin." Then to his own, "Sweet violin, nice violin, lovely violin; mamma kiss violin, Harold kiss violin" (doing it). "Don't want Dr. A—— to play violin." (This doctor lanced his gums when he was teething.) When told he was to go to bed, he said, "No; Harold must play violin. Go clock" (meaning go *see* clock). "Harold go to bed? I t'ought so. Pretty violin. Oh-h-h, is it broket again? Where is the oder piece?" (when a peg fell out). His mother said, "Can't you find it?" He said "No. Come find it, mommy; come find it, mommy; find tick to Harold's violin." Then he said, meditatively, "Poppee don't play piano. Mommy don't play violin" (noting difference, as usual). "Poppee's violin in big box." Then, after seeing something about the violin that made him point and exclaim "W" very eagerly, he went to bed as if he had to go but did not want to.

This evening he said, " Feed children supper. Poor children cry; I get it. I get *Moller Goose*," running to the next room to get the book to bring it to me. I never looked to see to which song he alluded. He broke his toy violin after dinner and said, " Poppee fix it." When his father returned it to him he said, voluntarily, " Thank you, papa. Harold *play* violin."

March 12th.—This morning he said to his father when he left, " Good-bye, poppee; see you soon again"; then, " Mommy, get violin " (meaning his own); " daden's bow next yoom; fraid ee poppee put it seep next yoom" (again meaning his own, fearing his father had put his away with his own).

To-day, when looking over a puzzle-block game that had a large picture of an engine on the box-cover, he found a small piece of the engine inside, which he promptly called " little choo-choo," pointing to the bell on the piece at the same time, and saying " ting-a-ling-a-ling." He then said, eight times in succession, "*big* choo-choo, *little* choo-choo," again noting difference.

When dressed in the morning now he goes to the door and calls, " Annie come and talk a you." She asked him who gave him the engine. He said, " Mamma bing it this muding," (morning). Sometimes he says words correctly, and at other times he does as above—*i.e.*, saying " muding " for morning. He is not corrected, for we want him to find out for himself from observation the correct way to pronounce words. When he asks the names of things he is told carefully, and we see that he says the word correctly, but what he learns himself we let alone. We want to find out how much he can absorb from surroundings without direction. So far he has learned a great deal through his own activity. He

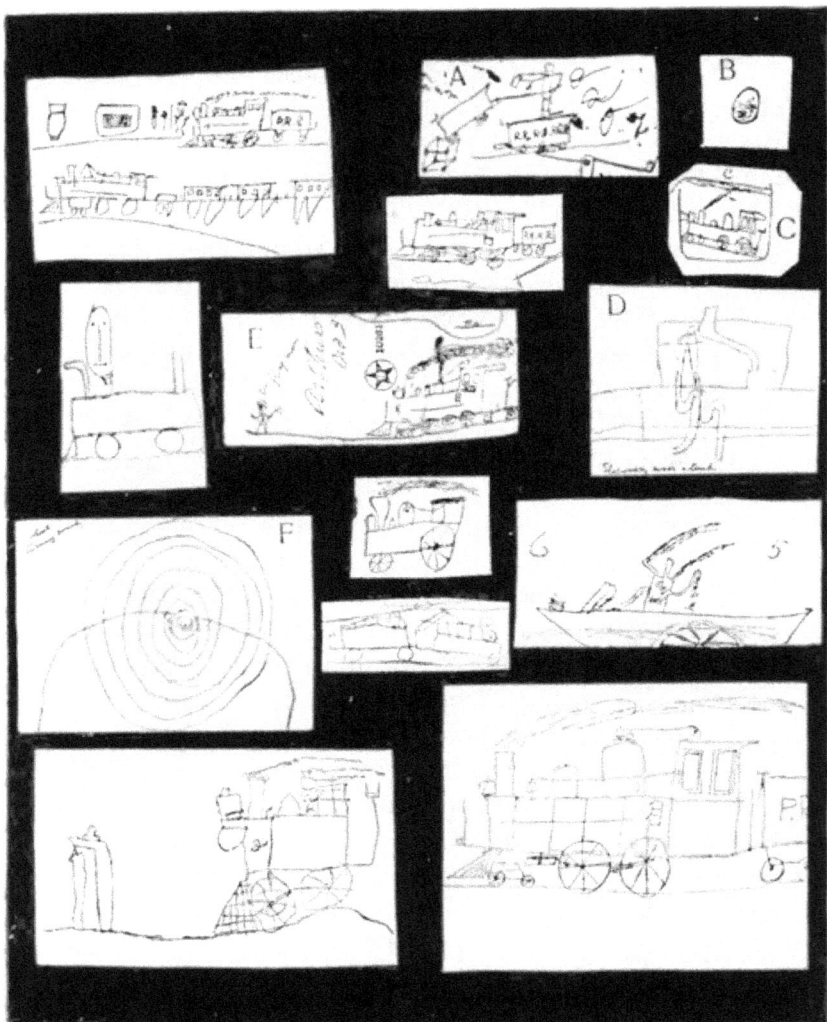

NO DATE DRAWINGS

A, stand-pipe B, folded paper frame for drawing of boat ; C, machine-stitching for frame , D, stationary wash stand ; E, flag-man ; F, wheel turning round.

is never at rest, brain or body, and it keeps us busy to
see that he has sufficient diversion without confusion to
occupy him from morning to night. So far as is possible, routine is depended on for all that must necessarily
be done—*i.e.*, feeding, naps, going out, bathing, and bedtime—and we find that he takes all of them as incidental
to what appears to him to be his great occupation—*i.e.*,
play. (The records show that he was never happy unless
occupied—always asking, "What may I do?" when he
could find nothing himself, and but a few words of suggestion were necessary, as a rule, to send him at once to
a new occupation.)

When he awoke to-day from his nap he was fretful
until he thought of his violin. Then he was happy, and
wanted to stay home with it instead of going out in his
coach. His mother let him take it down to the door
with him, and diverted him sufficiently to take it away
when he left. It might have been wiser to have openly
taken it away, offering something in its place, for he
cried as soon as he missed it. As soon as he came home
he asked for it, and said, "Fraid a mommy take it way,
violin." He then asked me to "play it and sing fiddle,"
meaning "Hey diddle-diddle, the cat and the fiddle."

To-day he said he had a pain in his "tummack," and
asked for his medicine (soda-mint). When he had finished taking it he took the spoon and said "More;
Harold feed himself." He evidently likes the sugar in
it, and I fear the pain is imaginary. He has shown an
inclination several times to use sophistry in getting me
to do something he wants very much, so hereafter I
shall try to let him know that he can have things for
the asking only, and trust that he will ask for what
may reasonably be granted. (The record shows that

this method corrected his sophistical efforts to a great extent. Some one may have said something in his hearing to impress him with the fact that an inducement must be offered to get certain things, but I think he has reasoned it out for himself that he gets certain things under certain conditions—as, for instance, the soda-mint sweetened when he says he has a pain. The only other times we have noticed this inclination have been in the morning, when he tries to induce us to get him up very early, or at bedtime, when he wants to stay up longer than his usual hour. We are generally deaf to his entreaties at each time, but we are quite accustomed to hear him say in the morning that he wants all sorts of things, each one calculated to make one rise—as, for instance, "Want a drink," which he knows he will get, or "Harold hungry," etc. He is not allowed to get up before seven, for we want him to have the habit of waking and rising regularly, and his hour of waking has gradually been regulated from five to half-past six in this way, and we will soon reach seven, by simply chatting and playing with him and giving him a drink of milk and his toys, but insisting on his remaining in bed until seven. Such training is of value, especially when travelling, for he will sit contentedly and amuse himself without disturbing his neighbors.

To-day he had two pitchers to play with, and poured a little water from one to the other. He said to me in a tone of great delight, "Harold pour." We risked his getting wet to give him the pleasure—and, as in everything he does, he showed care.

This morning we went out for a walk. Before we started he asked to go to see the "choo-choos on ee fence." I promised to take him there, but allowed myself to be diverted from doing so at once. When we were several blocks beyond the "*choo-choo*" street, he evidently realized that we had gone too far, for he turned about and said, "See choo-choos!" When we returned and reached the place, we found that the posters had been covered with others, much to his disappointment, which I tempered by directing his attention to something attractive beyond; and as we passed a provision-store he was delighted to see some dressed turkeys hanging there, and called them "roosters."

This afternoon he crept down half a flight of stairs, unaided, when following his nurse to the bath-room. As he did it he no doubt remembered that he had been told not to do so, for he called, in a very insinuating way, "Good-bye, mamma," as if he wanted very much to go, yet felt it was not quite right. His mother honored this feeling in him and let him alone.

This evening he asked for a piece of candy. I suppose he calls "flake manna" candy because it tastes sweet; yet I do not know how he can have any conception of candy except from hearsay, for he has never eaten any. I gave him a piece of the manna and he ate it, then asked for more. I said "No." He then took up a quinine-chocolate that he had refused to take before, and asked to lie on mamma's bed to eat it, and ate it all. Then he came to me and asked again for "more piece of candy," as if he thought I would be so pleased to see him eat the chocolate that he would get the manna as a reward. Hard as I found it to deny him, he did not get it, for he must do what is right without being bribed, and he must learn that he must not attempt to bribe. (This is a great evil in training children, both at home and in school. Using bribes, marks, honors, or

G   97

anything of the kind, should not be allowed until a child has reached years that bring with them some judgment as to the real value of things. A child should learn to do a thing because it is right in itself to do it, not because some one else wants him to do it, and he should see by example that those about him follow the same rule, then doing right will become a life-long habit.)

March 13th. — This morning when dressed he said, "Mamma draw the curtain las night six o'clock; Harold go asleep. Hear dat, papa?" as if proud of going to bed so early. To-day it snowed, and he said, "See— the snow falling down!" He put his finger on the reflector of a speaking-tube to-day, moved it, and called Lavinia so that she heard it.

When his father was dressing this morning he said, "Papa, put clothes on; what coat, trousers?" opening the door of the closet and looking in as he spoke, as if he wished to know which to get for him—showing, as usual, his desire to help others.

March 14th.—Said "Fool ee Annie dat time" to his nurse. She often says to him, "Fool Harold!" when she plays with him.

One morning when he was trying to get his mother to rise, she showed a strong disposition to lie down again after having risen. He called out to his father, in a tone of great apprehension, "Fraid ee mamma lie down, papa." Poor little chap, he seems to feel the responsibility of getting us up in the morning, and, as every one but himself is up late at night, it is pretty hard work.

March 15th.—This evening at dinner his father said, jokingly, "Will you have some of the edibles?" He replied, "Don't like edibles."

March 16th.—To-day he said, "Mamma, lift ee in ee

arms see horsy, see bird-cage." Also, when his father left with a travelling-bag, "Papa, steet, New York, Aunt M——y." He evidently thinks that every time his father goes out of the house with a bag he goes to New York to see Aunt M——y.

March 18th.—When his father came in this evening he ran to him and said, "Iss, papa," kissed him, brought his little violin and bow immediately, walked up to where the big one was, stood there, and said, repeatedly, "Papa play big violin." When at last his father did play, he walked around the room as usual, playing his. It is a very quaint sight, for he holds both violin and bow correctly, for his father found it was just as easy to show him the right way as the wrong. It is on this principle that he is shown correctly how to do anything that he is likely to use in later life. One evening recently, when amusing each other with their violins, Harold's father used his bow on Harold's violin, naturally with increased sound. Harold instantly cried for " big bow" to use it himself on his violin, and it took a long time to restore his content with his own bow. (This shows how readily a child may be made unhappy by comparisons.)

This evening at early dinner he was allowed to sit at table. He had bread-and-milk, and asked for a spoon to "feed himself." I spoke incidentally of Mary (a former servant). He said at once, "Did you see Mary? Did you see George?" (Mary's husband, of whom he was very fond). He had not seen nor heard of them for some time.

This morning he found a picture of a clock in his pet journal which looked not unlike one in a friend's room. He called it "lady's clock," and handed me another copy of the journal, begging me to "Find nodder lady's clock." I did so, and he was delighted, repeating many times "Find nodder lady's clock." Then he looked closely at them, said "Won't go," then looked up at the clock on the wall and said, "Ganma's clock; don't touch."

One morning before I had risen he was very quiet, and we discovered him on my desk pulling at the pendulum of a clock which he calls "ganme's clock" because she gave it to me.

March 19th.—When his father kissed him good-bye this morning he said, "See papa out er winnow on steet." I held him so he could see him for a moment as he passed out of sight. He said, "There he is—*gone*," and turned away as if ready for something else. He is a very philosophical little fellow.

This evening he said to us, "See Mrs. Pancer." We asked him where. He said, "On ee steet at ee corner." We found out afterwards that he and his nurse had passed a Mrs. Spencer at the corner of a street in the afternoon.

The other evening when in his own room he lost a peg of his violin, one that came out very easily. We all went out to find it for him. Since then he begs us every evening to come out and find it, leading each one of us to the same place, because he still misses it. We really found it the first evening, but put it away, unknown to him, for we thought he would soon be satisfied without it, and it was so loose that he was constantly losing it. I suppose it would have been kinder to the little fellow to have fixed the peg in so that it would stay.

To-night he said at dinner, "Want some oysters.

Papa want some water? Harold pour it out." He always wants to help wherever he is, and he is still encouraged in it, although at times it is trying to wait until he has done what he is aiming at.

He saw a bird go down a chimney to-day, and said, "See little bird go down hole." He never saw a chimney from the top, so he must have reasoned that there was a hole because the bird disappeared. When he saw flowing water and sleet on snow to-day, he said, apropos of each subject, "See water run," and "See water on snow."

He was very sleepy when he was put down for his nap, and as soon as his head touched the pillow he said, very decidedly, "Draw curtain, mamma." It sounded as if he could hardly wait to go to sleep. When he saw her lying on a couch later in the day he said to himself, "Mamma resting."

When he went to see Mrs. A—— to-day he asked for "birdie." She has a stuffed bird that she gives to him occasionally to amuse himself with while we chat. To-day, after receiving the bird, he said, "Put birdie on ee trunk." We did so. Then he looked at it and said, "See birdie on ee trunk," then took it up and caressed it, asking me to kiss its eyes and its tail. As he said tail he pointed to the branch upon which the bird's feet were resting. I then showed him where the tail was.

When looking out of the window to-day he said, "See ee bird in cage," indicating that he wanted to move so he could get something in his line of vision. I did as he wanted, and found that from a certain part of the window-ledge he could see a bird in a cage in a house across the street. He had evidently discovered this before, but had said nothing about it, for we were not aware of its being the case. He is constantly surprising us in this way.

A violinist and harpist played before the house one day recently, and he insisted on having his violin and being put on the window-ledge, where he stood and played for a long time, much to the amusement of the musicians outside.

When he was being dressed to-day to go out with his nurse he said, "Take the chair away." It appears she has to remove a chair in the down-stair's hall in order to get the coach out of the door, and he meant that she should get it ready while I was dressing him.

He began running up and down before his father this evening, saying, "Boom, boom, bumpety boom; shoot papa, bing!" pointing his finger as he did it.

March 20th.—To-day he said, "Call papa"; "Ring bell"; "Mamma resting"; "Papa, play big violin"; "Call papa; papa, come home, play big violin." When he came in from his airing he said, "Had good time on steet."

This morning to amuse him I suggested that he go to the door, call Mrs. A——, and say "Good-morning" to her. He called "Mrs. A——" four times, waiting until she answered; then he said "Good-morning." This occupied him for quite a little while, and I had a few minutes' freedom until he was ready for something else. Yesterday when I heard Mrs. A—— going downstairs I said to him, to divert him for a moment, "Call good-bye to Mrs. A——." He did so, and added, "Frow a kiss to Mrs. A——." He loves her very much, and it pleases him to do these things, at the same time it cultivates a kindly feeling to others. He appears now to love nearly every person he meets.

To-day he said, "Mamma tore her dress. Too bad!"

He heard us say alcohol, and said, instantly, "Don't like alcohol bottle on ee mantel." He is rubbed with it, and doesn't like the smell. He says the word very distinctly.

For several months now he has said, when eating, "Put away, got enough," and he will take no more.

To-day he said, "Make a tick-tock. Harold make a tick-tock." He has stopped saying I, except occasionally, and uses his name (Harold) instead. He told me to-night to "Make lamp light again; make gas-pipe light." He also asked to go out this afternoon by saying, "Mamma, get ee coat and cap and take Harold bye," following it up with "Annie no Harold bye" (meaning he preferred that his mother should take him out instead of his nurse).

When his mother tried to cover his bare feet this evening with his night-coat, while holding him on her lap before placing him in bed, he said, "Mamma, coat no on feet." He always shows a desire to have them bare at this time, and it is curious to hear him say "no" for not.

March 21st.—"Hello, Alfred!" he said, to-day, looking in the next room to see if it was an errand-boy he knew, for he heard some one moving about. He saw it was his nurse, however, and then said, "Oh, that's Annie!"

This evening he said to his father when he came in, "Take off gloves, poppee; take off fingers."

His mother had a headache and he said, "Annie's forehead, mamma's forehead—poor mamma's forehead!" He said "Big pin, little pin" repeatedly to-day, to two safety-pins of different size.

103

On March 22d he said, "Now, Tommy, sit up; now, Tommy, eat some breakfast"; "Tommy like boy squeak." Tommy is his pet rag doll, and he talks to him a great deal. He also said that "Tommy go in a hole." We couldn't find out what he meant.

March 23d.—As I poured all the water from a carafe into a large basin this morning he said, "Big water, little water; little water gone out."

March 24th.—New sentences to-day were "Lots of good times"; "Lots of good fun."

March 25th.—He asked me to "Sit on ee knees." This is the first time for the word knees.

March 26th.—He said to-day to himself, "Papa says no, no. Harold; papa says turn those pins around" (meaning pegs in violin). He said later to me, "Harold want to write." He has never asked for this before. He has a great notion of comparing—*i.e.*, "big violin, little violin"; "big cup, little cup"; "big pin, little pin," etc.

March 27th.—He was delighted to sit up to early dinner this evening, and said, "Harold see papa eat supper. Harold see mamma eat supper too. Harold eat too. Lots of fun. Lots of good times."

March 28th.—I washed "Tommy" to-day, and when he saw him he noticed it at once and said, "New Tommy, nice new Tommy. Tommy clean." But first he rubbed him with his hand and said, "Tommy wet." The doll was not yet dry.

March 29th.—He said to-day, "Fraid mommy lay down herself." This is the first time he has said "herself." When he came in from his walk, Annie asked him what the gentleman said to him. He replied at once, "Shake hands."

He is very much interested in clocks, and insists on stopping to see every clock he can find in the windows as we go along. He rarely misses one, and keeps on the lookout for them during the entire time we are out walking. In consequence, we take quite a long time to walk a very short way, for nearly every window has a clock. I fear it will soon be a question as to which one of us is the more clever in selecting a route—whether it be one minus clocks, or almost so, at any rate, to suit me, or full of them, to suit him.

Every evening when his father comes in it is still the same old story, " Poppee, play big violin ; Harold play little violin "; and, " Poppee, put rosin on bow, mamma dance, Harold play—lift dress and dance, mamma." She has danced for him several times, to show him the motion of her feet when waltzing.

His mother was ready to take him out this afternoon, but had not yet taken up her gloves. He said, " Mamma, get gloves." He seems to observe every little thing. We need make no effort to influence him to notice things. He misses very little, and seems to remember everything he once sees or hears.

(The record shows that when he was old enough to ask questions about things that puzzled him, he remembered every answer he received with but one telling. His usual form of questioning at this age—two years— was " What's dat ?")

When he had his bath this evening he soaped his hands, washed them, and dried them with a towel I gave him. Then he held them out to me and said, as if asking me if it were so, " Harold's hands dry ?" touching each one as he said it.

Yesterday he saw a baby in the window across the

street. He said, " Baby has white dress on." I asked
him if he wanted to have a white one on. He said, " No;
Harold has Aunt Mollie's dress on." This is the colored
gingham he prefers to all his other dresses. He is a
sturdy little fellow. It never makes him unhappy to
see others have what he has not. (The record shows
this to be the case right through, and he was always
content when told he would receive things he asked for
" some day," because he was given reason to trust those
who promised him anything. The record shows also
that it was always found to be the best plan to buy his
presents when he was not along, for he soon reasoned
out for himself that his part was only to select what he
wanted to have " some day," and care was taken to see
that he frequently received the things he selected. For
this reason he never gave any one trouble about buying
when taken about to see things.)

He has never mentioned color in this way before.
He notices when his mother has a black dress on, saying, " Mamma has black dress on." He also asks for
his " red cap." or " white cap," as the case may be.

March 31st.—This morning, when Mrs. A—— and I
were engaged, he walked up to his father's violin with
his own in his hand, and began to laugh aloud, paying
no attention to us. As he laughed he said, in a low
voice, " Papa come home, play big violin. Papa *will*
come home this evening, play big violin," followed by a
long-drawn-out "Oh," and laughing to himself quietly.
At last he turned to us and repeated the whole perform-
ance in a very comical manner. His laughing was all
pretence, quite noiseless, and not at all like his spontaneous laughter, but as if he were trying to prolong his
enjoyment.

April 3d.—He wanted to go to sleep at once this evening when put to bed, and called out, " Papa, better shut the door." There was a slight delay, and he said, "Mamma, *shut* the door!" emphasizing *shut* in a marked manner.

He saw Annie throw a kiss to him with her hand, and said, "Annie put a hand on a kiss."

April 4th.—To-day he stroked my face, kissed me, hugged me, and said, very lovingly, "My darlin' boy!" He also said to his nurse, "Annie, Harold's darlin'."

April 7th.—When we took a walk to-day, he saw a pussy in a yard across the way. He stopped, bowed his head, and said, "How do, pussy? Glad to see you, pussy. Pussy come and take a walk."

To-day he said to himself the whole of the nursery song "Ding dong dell," without any assistance. I asked him this morning where his father was. He answered at once, "Gone to Filaduffia."

April 10th.—When out walking this morning with his mother it grew very windy, so they hurried home. As they went along he pulled at her hand and said, "Hurry up fast, mamma"; then, "Walk hard, mamma, windy," running as he said it.

To-day he said, "Sit hard, Aunt C——." I couldn't find out what he meant. He sat down on the floor then to try to button his shoes, and as he did it he leaned over them very closely and said, "This is the way Aunt C—— does." I recognized the position at once. He is very imitative.

April 12th.—He amused himself to-day by watching a sprinkling-wagon go up and down the street. I heard him say to himself several times "Here it comes again."

107

He also said to a sleeping dog, " Get up, dog," and to one he met, " How do, dog?"

April 15th.—When at dinner to-day he looked around and said, " I see no apple-sauce." He likes it very much, and has it nearly every day for dinner, but this day it had been overlooked.

This morning, when he went to the window to see his beloved choo-choos pass by, we heard him say, " Good-morning, Mrs. Y——," saying the name of a neighbor whom we thought he would not remember from his previous visit (he was away from home). We then saw that Mrs. Y—— was at her window. He knew her at once, although he had not seen her for four months.

Last night his mother put him to bed after having dressed to go in the rain to a concert. He said to her, " 'Fraid mamma go away. Mamma got rubbers on. Mamma got shoes on. Take hat off, mamma; tay with Harold." All this was said in a very pleading tone. She removed her hat and rubbers, and he fell asleep contentedly. As he invariably sleeps until eleven, after once getting asleep, he can be left without trouble if no sign of going is given while he is awake.

(The record shows that when he was old enough to understand, he was told every time that his parents expected to be away when he was asleep. This was done to keep him free from any knowledge of deception. Minot Savage tells a story of a boy in Boston who said of his father and mother, who promised him a ride daily but never took him, " There go two of the biggest liars in Boston." I have also heard of a child who evidently met deception somewhere, who said that since liars wouldn't go to heaven there wouldn't be many people

NO DATE DRAWINGS

A. "a disappearing cannon"; B. "a man having his hair cut—the boy is pulling the long hair of the woman who is cutting the man's hair"; C, "ostrich looking back as he runs"; D, reversible picture.

there; maybe grandma, but she was sure there wouldn't be any men there.)

To-day he saw one of his white dresses lying *on the grass* to bleach. He became very cross and said it would get dirty, not understanding the process. He saw his beloved colored gingham *on the line* and said, "*Aunt Mollie's dress* get clean."

He has been watching his cousin prepare a bed for planting tomatoes. He was allowed to dig in the ashes that were used. Next day he said, "Mamma, get shobel, dig powder," meaning the ashes, which to him seemed like powder, yet we do not know how he learned anything about powder.

April 16th.—This morning John S—— came in. Harold knew him at once and went to him very soon. They were very friendly about four weeks ago, at which time Harold was very much pleased with my explanation of a metronome to John S—— and J——'s cousin who called on us at the time. John S—— asked him where the clock was (Harold called the metronome a clock). He replied, "Clock asleep." We had put it out of sight after John S—— left, because we could not easily control Harold's desire to have it while he could see it, hence his own conclusion of "clock asleep."

The engines pass and repass all day on the railroad back of his aunt's house, and he stands at the window at intervals all day long. He shows that he reasons, for as an engine passes out of sight at one window he crosses the room quickly and looks for it from another window, from which the engine may be seen as it turns a curve in the track.

To-day I asked him if he wanted to go to see his father

on Friday. He said, "Don't like Friday." Then I said Saturday. He said, "Yes, go to see papa, Saturday." I then said, "Papa will play the big violin." He smiled and said, "Harold play *little* violin."

April 17th.—This morning, as he was lying in bed for a moment with his mother, he said, "Mamma, put head on Harold's dry pillow." Some milk had just been spilled on the end of the pillow towards her. He shows quite a great deal of consideration for her in many ways. To encourage him in this he is always given some kind word or a kiss in return, and care is taken to let him see that it is appreciated. He said, afterwards, "I don't want to go to sleep, mamma. Get up and dress Harold." His sentences now are rapidly becoming fuller, and he often uses every word necessary to form a complete phrase. Since his mind is not so much occupied with the big words—having acquired a considerable vocabulary—he is beginning to notice the connections more, and also the little niceties of accent and pronunciation, yet his attention is not directed to this. He takes it all very naturally and easily, without the least sign of physical or mental strain. By nurturing the physical, he runs along mentally so rapidly that no doubt he will soon have to be repressed a little in suggestion in order to keep things even, for uneven development is always a cause for alarm.

When he looked out of the window this morning and saw the snow, he said, "Snowing, mamma," pronouncing the "g" distinctly. He put his violin between his knees to-day in quite a professional manner, and said, "I want to wind it up," then turned a peg and touched a string. Then he took his bow and drew the rosin over it to the very end, saying, "This is the way that papa does."

Then he drew the bow across the violin, and because it made no sound he said, "Rosin no good."

He asked me to-day to sing "Baby, baby, oh, my darling baby" (Emmet's song, which he heard for the first time about a week ago, when his father sang it for him).

When out walking with me this afternoon he saw a clock on a steeple fully a quarter of a mile away, and said, pointing to it, "There's another clock." (He gives frequent evidence of being far-sighted.)

We called on some one to-day who gave to him for amusement a board of marbles used for solitaire. The centre hole, as usual, had no marble in it. The *instant* Harold saw the board he said, "Want anoder one," went to the closet from which the board was taken and said it again, looking for the marble he thought was missing. He observes very quickly. When we returned from there we stopped in to see his metronome friend, John S——, who showed him a guitar. Harold said at once, "John's violin got no bridge on."

April 18th.—This morning when he waked he hugged and kissed his mother, saying "Mamma"—very lovingly —"have lots of good times wif mamma." She asked him if he wanted Annie (his nurse). He said "No— mamma," dwelling on mamma, and by his tone intimating that he preferred to have her. (He always seems so glad to have her instead of the servants that she gives him much more time than was originally planned for. It is evident that it is better for him. With even the most faithful service there is constant need for intelligent and sympathetic supervision at very short intervals, to watch the gradual unfolding of a child's mind, and to nurture to the best of one's ability its physical development.)

April 20th.—We have returned home again, and to-day when Annie left the room for her coat and hat, while Harold was waiting, ready for her to take him out, he said, "Fraid Annie go out herself," for she was rather slow in returning. Then he said, "See an ah-ah-ah-ah-ah," meaning a derrick, imitating the noise of one. For a long time afterwards he called a derrick by this sound. I think his nurse said it to him the first time, but I do not know. Probably he tried to imitate the sound of the creaking. His father protested at last, thinking the child should always be told the correct name of anything he noticed, and he was then taught the word *directly*.

April 21st.—This morning he said, "Want to see Aunt M——e taking coffee in next yoom," remembering his visit to New York two months ago.

To-day I cut some paper engines for him. The moment he saw them he said, "Harold's choo-choo." Last Christmas his cousin Harold sent him one cut out of paper, and the last week of our recent visit there he also cut some for him.

April 22d.—To-day I had the little fellow with me all day long. He was very docile and loving, and appeared to be perfectly happy. He came to me constantly in between his play, to hug and kiss me. I gave him a scissors and paper for the first time. He is twenty-six months old now. He took up the scissors to try to cut. He knew it had to be parted at the blades, but he did not know how to do it, so I showed him the place for his thumb and fingers. He didn't need a second showing. For some time he tried and tried to cut, without success.

I let him alone, watching, however, to see that he did not stick or cut himself, for the scissors was a small, sharp-pointed one. The blunt scissors made are too heavy and too clumsy for the delicate work of a child. I therefore gave him a small embroidery scissors, wishing, however, I had a blunt yet equally delicate scissors. (It would no doubt be possible to have the regular embroidery scissors blunted.)

After he had struggled for a long time with the scissors and piece of paper, he announced in a tone of triumph, "Cut a piece!" and showed me a piece like this, that he had succeeded in cutting off. He was very much elated, and at last he started in to cut off all the projections on one of the paper engines I had cut for him. He cut one after the other, saying as he went along, "Harold cut off whistle; Harold cut off bell; Harold cut off wheel," etc. When he reached the pilot he looked up at me interrogatively, and I said, "Cowcatcher." He did not repeat the word after me. He went right on with his sentence, "Harold cut off cowcatcher." His memory seems to be very good. He often repeats a word of three syllables correctly after hearing it only once. After he had cut away all the parts, he held up the body of the engine and said to me in a tone of pity, "Harold cut off whistle; engine all torn." I asked him if he wanted another. He said "Yes," so I gave him one similar to the one he had cut. I often folded paper fourfold before beginning to cut them out for him, because it pleased him very much to see me hand four engines to him instead of what appeared to be only one. He took up the paper engine I gave him, took his scissors in his other hand, looked at them both, looked at me, held the scissors to the whistle, and to each part, and said, "I don't want to cut off whistle; I don't want to cut off bell; I don't want to cut off wheel; I don't want to cut off cow-catcher," and he didn't do it either. All this occurred without my saying a word. He evidently did not want to see the engine destroyed, and although he wanted to have the pleasure of cutting, he desisted that he might not destroy it. (For a child two years and two months old, this appears to be an exhibition of the self-control one should endeavor to cultivate in children.)

I then gave him as a reward (without saying it was such) long strips of paper to snip, in order that he might enjoy the cutting without feeling that he was destroying something. He also had to-day some large-eyed buttons and a long string threaded in a bodkin. He found one button that stuck on the extreme end of the bodkin. He held it towards me and said, "I make a chimney."

Later in the day we called on Mrs. A——, his "lufly lady." He saw a chimney from one of her windows, and said, instantly, "Harold make a chimney," referring to the button.

He also had some large screws during the day. (His mother keeps on hand a supply of the things likely to amuse him, for he appreciates each one very much, and is often diverted from crying by the production of a new set of toys.) He played with the screws for a long time, comparing them to the pictures of the screws in his "schlüssel book." Then he put one in and out of his mouth as if it were a cigar, saying, "This is the way papa mokes."

He had beans next. These he put one by one in his mouth. I said, "No, no." He blew them out of his mouth in a very funny way, and said, "I don't want to eat beans." His mother kissed him and said, "Mamma's good boy," for he always expects this when he obeys. Several times to-day he fretted for what was denied him. Each time his mother said to him, as she often does, "Put your head on mamma's lap and cry it out," which he did every time, crying quietly for a moment, when he would say, "I don't see Harold." Then she says, "Here he is," when he looks up smiling, many a time with tears still lying on his cheeks. The storm is then over, and he will go on with his play. He is very persistent and strong-willed, but if care is taken not to oppose him openly, guiding him only by suggestion, he shows a willingness to do right at all times. It appears as if he might become obstinate if he were treated harshly or with less regard for his feeling of individual right, of which he shows a strong sense. (The record shows all through that he has a keen sense of injustice and a strong belief in his own rights, but it shows also that he believes in the rights of others as much as his own, for he tries very hard for a little fellow to show that he respects them. If any question ever does come to an issue, which his parents try hard to prevent, they keep on patiently until he obeys. This is usually very soon, but before compelling obedience they satisfy themselves that he is perfectly well, in order to avoid nerve strain. If ill or restless from causes for which he is not responsible, they lay aside all rules until he is himself again, and effort is made to hold only sufficient control to exact instant obedience in case of illness or immediate danger. It would seem that this is all that any parent or person in charge of a child has the right to exact in *absolute* obedience, and all so-called discipline, breaking of the will, etc., is to be deprecated, as breeding obstinacy, deception, nervous conditions, and many undesirable qualities. I have frequently found that even bad children — many times mistakenly called so — will respond delightfully to treatment that is kind and sympathetic, yet *perfectly just*. The record also shows that Harold had several playmates at times who were considered almost unmanageable at home, yet in *his* nursery they were perfectly well-behaved, probably in part owing to the opportunities open for diversion by the surroundings offered, but equally, no doubt, to the invariable rule of sending home *all* the children when *one* quarrelled, no matter whether it was Harold or one of his visitors. Decisions were absolutely impartial, and the children all felt as if there was an appeal made to their honor, for they saw that all suffered when one disobeyed. In this way they learned to play together for hours without dissension. A curious fact, noted in connection with the entire record, is that the children who were fed properly and received proper hygienic care were the most docile. Those who gave evidence of careless handling or of nagging by servants were invariably the most difficult to impress with consideration for others. Social reformers may find this of interest.)

One day recently I cut some large paper engines and cars for him, making them about a yard long, by using long pieces of newspaper. I did not fold the paper double, as I did before, but cut each train separately. He took up two in the most critical style without saying a word, and looked first at the smoke-stack of one, then the other, and so on with each part of each train. He seemed satisfied, and put them down without a word. Fortunately I had cut them very nearly alike. He is very quick to note differences.

When it was raining one day he looked out of the window, and said, "I don't see the sunshine." Then he said to a servant in the room, "Maggie, look out and see the rain." Just before that he had said, "It's raining *again*." Yesterday he used "again" in the same way. First he said, "Here it comes"; then a little later, "Here it comes again." He came to his mother to-day and said, "Sit on mamma's lap." She lifted him up. He then said, "Sing, mamma." She sang a song from Elliott's *Mother Goose*, which was always used, because the harmonies are sufficiently beautiful to cultivate a taste for good music. He then said, "Harold sing," and he joined in her song, piping up his little voice as high as he could get it, singing all the words of the song she was singing. He appears to know the words now of all these songs. She then sang a dance song, and he stood up on his bed, held his skirts with both hands, and swayed back and forth, saying, "See Harold dance." He did not move his feet, but kept perfect time with his body movement. He heard Mrs. A—— play a waltz later in the day, and he beat time correctly with his hands, never missing the rhythm as she changed from one part to another.

Mrs. ——, who plays exquisitely, was here the other day, and while she was playing something with marked rhythm he begged to go near to her. He had previously refused to go to her, and no amount of persuasion would induce him even to look at her at first. He was carried, however, to the next room, and he showed interest in the music when he was placed by her side. He closed his eyes that he might not see her, but moved his body in his mother's arms in perfect accord with the music, and said, "Mamma, dance." At last he begged to go into the next room and be rocked and soothed. It appeared as though he needed to be soothed because he had been under two opposing influences—his love for the music, and his feeling against the performer. When Mrs. —— had finished playing she spoke of his keen sense of rhythm. He begged his mother to hold him for a long time, which is unusual, and then said, "Mamma, sing a song of fixpence," and seemed to be himself again.

(Compare this experience with his different action at four months in Chapter I., page 16, when Handel's Largo and Raff's concertos were played in his hearing.)

One day I gave one of my visiting-cards to him. He has had none since we gave him one two months ago with Dr. T——'s name on it, which we read to him at the time. He kept Dr. T——'s card at that time among his toys for several days, always calling it by name. The card I gave him to-day was larger than the original size he first saw, yet he noted the resemblance at once, for he said "Dr. T——'s card." When I gave him another of mine he said the same thing.

When he doesn't feel very well now he says, "Harold has a pain, poor dearie; mamma's dearie. Pain soon all over," in the most compassionate tone. He is very brave about bumps. He always sympathizes with the thing bumped into instead of thinking of himself. We have encouraged this in order to get him into the habit of looking away from himself at the world about him instead of becoming introspective and self-conscious. He even goes so far as to kiss the pavement, if he falls on the street, and say "Poor pavement!" We never check him in this even, for fear of starting the tide the wrong way. It seems that it is in just these trifling things that the great value of the "letting alone" with supervision system becomes apparent. Evidently the nearer one can get a child to a regular habit of action under certain circumstances, taking it for granted that the habit aimed at is a desirable one, the easier it is to take care of that child physically, morally, and mentally. (The record shows that the effort of trying to establish a regular habit of action for body, mind, and spirit resulted in a remarkable happy life for the little fellow. He thinks everybody loves him, and with rare exceptions he loves everybody.)

Last week, after having let forbidden things alone for a long time, he touched the little tea-set in the dining-room that had first attracted him. His mother followed him and said, "No, no," doing just as was done before. He persisted, however, in taking off the lids that pleased him so much. She then said, "Shall mamma tie Harold's hands up?" He said "Yes," not really knowing what she meant. She did this very lightly and gently with her handkerchief, but more in fun than for discipline. He was very much surprised. He had no idea what tie meant, or else he thought it wouldn't be done, for if it can be avoided he is not punished in a way to make him feel that he is punished. He is allowed to reason out cause and effect when he has done wrong, and he is, consequently, very reasonable when he understands matters. When he saw his hands tied he began to cry, and said, "No tie Harold's hands up." He nearly always says "no" at the beginning of a sentence, instead of saying, for instance, "Do not tie," etc. His mother said, "Well, go to papa, and tell him you are sorry and will not do it again, and ask him to take it off." He did so, saying "I sorry," when his father, with a kiss, removed the hand-kerchief. I suppose he didn't even know what sorry meant, but, once begun, even if in play, the affair had to be carried out to the end, although his mother really did not mean at the time to teach him instantly and in this way that he must not touch the china. It was her intention when she saw him touch it to let him handle it carefully in her presence and appeal to his love for her to let it alone when she was not there, which he would have done, for he is always amenable to treatment of this character. Unwittingly, however, this lesson was learned in another way, and probably no harm was done, but care is taken that even in play nothing is done to make him afraid. He now walks to the china set, looks at it, and says, "No, no, mamma tie Harold's hands up," and it hurts her every time he does it. She often goes to him and kisses him and says, "No, no, Harold is mamma's good boy who doesn't need to have his hands tied up."

(The record shows that about a year later she chastised him, very lightly, it is true, but still she laid her hand upon him in a moment of vexation, evidently as much to her own surprise as to his, for she realized her mistake, and promised never to do it again. The little fellow seemed to love and trust her more and more from that day on, and what appeared to be his proudest boast afterwards to his playmates was, "Mamma never whips me." He never knew what whip meant until he heard other boys use the word. Nor did he ever hear the word "naughty," to know what it meant, except in the one instance mentioned (page 54), until he began playing with outside children. To control matters like these it was a well-understood thing that if servants spoke of forbidden subjects in the hearing of the little fellow, it would be considered sufficient cause for dis-

NO DATE DRAWINGS

A, man looking through telescope ; B, naptha launch ; C, cannon — a, explosion, b ball ; D—a, Harold's copy of b ; E, hospital, doctor, nurse, patient, and visitor ; F, gun shooting a man ; G, "boys sledding by moonlight — a is hill they had to go over "; H, pussy's face ; I, figures for his toy theatre ; J, steamboat, and two negroes in a rowboat ; K—a, gun with bayonet ; b, hammer of pistol ; L, his idea of a machine for generating electricity to run trolley cars—a, engine making it ; b, trolley ; c, c, wires from engine to switches and batteries ; d, d, conductor of power to car ; e, switches and batteries ; M, sea serpents after fish and boat.

charge. As a counterpoise to the care and gentleness required of the servants, many unexpected privileges were granted them through the medium of the child, with whom they naturally associated these pleasures, thus keeping a kindly feeling for him in spite of the extra care required of them for his sake.)

Diversion is a great aid in getting Harold out of little tempers. He is keenly alive to anything that is humorous or that possesses the least element of fun. When any one succeeds in making him laugh he forgets his anger. I notice that he laughs quicker at an attempt to do something and missing it than at anything else. When putting on his overshoes, for instance, his nurse has a habit of pretending that she has pushed so hard that the rubber flies to the other end of the room. This always brings a peal of laughter. Once in a great while, when he is ailing or fretful, and we have a hard time to bathe or dress him, she will pretend to hang something on a nail that is apparently just a little too high for her to reach. She will jump at it and miss it at the most important period of my work, and will do this possibly two or three times while I am getting him ready for bed. She thus gives me the greatest possible amount of comfort by her faithfulness and quick comprehension, and has given a bridge many a time for getting over troublesome places by her quick adaptation to the little needs constantly arising. This is the true spirit of Froebel, and she lives *with* the child in his play, for she has leisure and aptitude and enjoys the fun as much as he does. He is very quick to see when the spirit is lacking, and he will not suffer any attempt at a make-believe liking of play. He wants the genuine love for it every time.

We never let him cry if we can help it. A well-trained and healthy baby does not want to cry, for he is sufficiently occupied in trying to find out the meaning of the world about him. Experience has shown what his cry means at different times. When he is angry we keep away, and then go to him as if nothing had happened when it is over. He always wants us for "lots of good times," as he calls them, so he quickly dries his angry tears. If he is hungry, we give him his food if it is near his regular time, or, if not quite near enough, we prepare it in his presence *very deliberately*, gaining all the time we can by the interest he shows in the work as we go along, and which has a tendency to stop his crying. He rarely gets hungry, however, between meals, for he is accustomed to method as to time and quantity in the way of feeding. When he is ill and cries, we can always tell it at once, and we find that this cry means that instant relief of some kind is needed. He has a peculiar little cry, almost a gasp, it might be called, when he is giving up the battle after he has been crying from anger. It often comes just when we are seriously considering whether we might not in that instance give up to him, and it always brings relief. It is certainly true that a mother has as much occasion for self-discipline as has her child. He is very quick to see a chance of gaining a victory, and he sometimes uses it mercilessly, when I leave him alone to keep myself strong, and he will then yield gracefully and very lovingly, coming after me at once. I notice that when I keep all sound of coercion out of my voice in giving him directions, he is willing to do as I say. Were I to command him, he would become antagonistic at once, and be hard to control. I found this out by an experience that need not be repeated if his rights to consideration will be respected as being equal to my own. Because any one happens to be in authority is no reason why it should be exercised unnecessarily. The strongest character is the one that does not take an unfair advantage of opportunity. It is hard to comprehend why so many parents think it necessary to scold children when they are, as they suppose, training them. It inclines too much to the methods used when training animals to act in the circus-ring to appeal to wisdom. Intelligent and loving obedience to the wishes of considerate parents is a beautiful thing to witness, and it must be productive of great good in the development of character. Abject obedience, however, in response to commands that are given without rhyme or reason, by parents or servants, just as it may happen, is something to be banished completely from nursery training, if the moral development of the child is desired. Let mothers beware of giving absolute authority into the hands of *any one*.

(The record shows that no one but the parents were allowed to use any authority over Harold, and even his father frequently sent the little chap to "ask mamma," in the mutual effort to keep authority in one direction only, for the purpose before stated—of possible future use. There seemed to be very little occasion for the exercise of this authority in his ordinary life, for a suggestion or an expressed wish was usually sufficient. When that failed, an appeal to his reason or love invariably ended the matter. He always seemed to feel that he was expected to do right.)

April 23d.—This morning at breakfast Harold said, "Papa, eat *her* egg." I said, "No, papa eat *his* egg."

He repeated it after me, and some time afterwards said it over twice, very carefully, emphasizing *his*.

He is beginning to say "I" much more frequently than before. When he waked this morning he crept over into his mother's bed as usual, hugged her, and said, "Have lots of good times wif mamma."

April 29th.—To-day, when in Mrs. A——'s room, he suddenly dropped his toys and came to me in an excited way, begging to be held and rocked. As I rocked him he kept saying, "Don't like it; go down-tairs. Don't like it; go down-tairs." We couldn't understand what the trouble was until I saw a screw-top bottle standing on the dressing-table, and then I understood it all. The poor child cannot get over the recollection of the ether-bottle. It took some time to pacify him, and it could not be done until I took him out of the room. As we left he looked excited, his face was flushed, and he said again, "Don't like the bottle."

Ever since, every time he hears the door-bell, he puts his hand to his face and says, "Doctor won't hurt you."

April 30th.—To-day he told me, without crying or showing any disturbance whatever, that he had hurt himself at the door. I discovered that he had done so some time earlier in the day. He often bears suffering without flinching, but yesterday when he rolled down a few steps, he came to me crying and said, "Harold fall down ee steps and hurt hisself." Later he told me this again. I then said, "Harold should have sat down before trying to creep down the steps." He promptly sat down on the floor and looked up at me, evidently not understanding my meaning, and I do not wonder that he did not when I analyze my sentence.

May 4th.—To-day, as we passed a toy-store, I let him go in and select a toy for himself. He took a calliope on wheels, and pushed it all the way home, a distance of about four blocks. When we reached home he sat on the floor and held the toy so that he could turn the wheels to make the music. He had evidently studied out for himself on the way home, by alternately moving and stopping the toy, that the moving wheels caused the music, for he had never seen one before. He then went to the machine-drawer for a screw-driver, returned to his toy, and tried to take out the nail that held the handle which was in his way when turning the wheel in his lap. He asked me to do it when he found he couldn't manage it. A curious thing I notice about him is that he does not care for toys simply because they are toys. He has frequently refused them, one after the other, when offered any from a selection in a toy-shop. When he finds one that to him seems to have a purpose he will gladly take it. He has often surprised shop-keepers by leaving without taking anything that he could have within his limit. He usually has the amount limited before he goes in—as, for instance, "Harold, you may have a quarter, a half-dollar, or a dime to-day," and he is content to keep within his limit. (The record shows that when he was older he would save until he had enough money to buy something of importance—as, for instance, a tool-chest, a tricycle, or an express-wagon, and it was always for something that he could make use of. He was never allowed to receive money from any one but his parents.)

He is allowed to choose for himself as often as possible in matters that relate to himself only as an individual, but care is taken to indicate to him the probable result if he should make a wrong selection. The greater part of his regular amusement comes from finding out and playing with the things he finds about the house — i.e., clothes - pins, blocks, pictures, kitchen utensils, etc. Very few toys are purchased for him that have no purpose, and he never receives many at a time.

Last evening I heard him sing " Ding Dong Bell " all the way through, using the right words and singing the melody correctly.

He heard us speaking of a cat to-day. He instantly said, " Crumpety and lame," associating cat with Mother Tabby Skins in *Mother Goose*. He often tells his mother to " Look (at) sunshine, mamma." He evidently loves it very much.

May 8th.—To-day when he saw me take up his gold-link dress buttons, he said "Hadn't for a long time," and repeated it to a little playmate. He has not seen them for a long time. He heard the door-bell ring. The servant down-stairs had forgotten to turn off the connection, and the bell outside of the nursery door rang too. This happens frequently, and annoys us very much. He said, "Did you hear dat bell ring? Maggie. turn dat bell off."

His first greeting to any playmates coming in is, "Come, build a house," taking their hands and leading them to his toys.

May 10th.—To-day he found his little photograph-book, which he has not had for some time. He seized it eagerly, and said, " Have it for a long time," meaning that he *didn't* " have it for a long time."

May 14th.—To-day he was out all the afternoon. We took a long ride on the street-car, to an extreme end of town. He gave a sigh of satisfaction and said, "Had a lovely ride on the treet-car." He now says " treet " sometimes, instead of "steet," as formerly. Evidently he cannot manage the *r* and *s* together. He then drew me in the right direction and said, " See the choochoos." We had been to this place about a week before, when he saw some large engines, and remembered it.

May 15th.—To-day he went to the sewing-machine and touched every moving part. He touched no part that was stationary.

May 16th.—We returned to the country to-day for the summer. As we crossed the bridge leading to our street he kept saying, "Want to see Bahdee, Bahdee, Bahdee." (The name of the cat he left behind when he went to town, four months before.)

May 17th.—He said to his father this morning, "I see a little baby in papa's eye," meaning his own reflection.

I gave him some water to pour from cup to cup. He then asked for a little pitcher belonging to him, evidently preferring to pour from that. When I gave it to him he said, " Dear little *white* pitcher." He still shows a great liking for white things.

He now helps me put away one set of playthings before bringing out another. If I help very little and loiter, to try him, he will do much more than his share of the work without seeming to notice that he has done nearly all himself.

In June he took up a postal-card and said, " I want to write a postal-card. Write a postal-card to Annie." (The nurse we had in town, who has gone away.)

When we were walking along the street to-day he picked up a stick shaped like this, ⟋⟍, and called it a " tick, tack, too." He found another, and said, " Here's

another tick, tack, too." Later, when we were looking
at a scrap-book, he saw some cards with crosses like this,
——+——, and he said, "Tick, tack, too, again," and said,
"Want to see more tick, tack, toos." He picked out
every picture that had a cross. He also picked up a
half-broken match that looked like this, ———┐, and he
said, "Tick, tack—" Then he stopped and said, "That's
a hammer." I then noticed his association with the
illustration of the nursery song:

> "Is John Smith within?
> Yes, that he is.
> Can he nail a shoe?
> Aye, marry two.
> Here's a nail, there's a nail,
>   Tick, tack, too.
> Here's a nail, there's a nail,
>   Tick, tack, too."

The illustration to the song represents a man holding a
hammer that is not unlike a picture of a cross, and he
noticed the resemblance to all the things he had just
called "tick, tack, too."

August 4th.—To-day, while I was reading, I heard
him say to himself as we lay on the floor:

> "He brushed his teeth with carpet tacks,
> Polly, wolly doodle all a day."

He heard it in June, when in New York, two months
ago.

Day before yesterday he said, "Dr. —— come to see
Baby —— (a little friend of his); put him on table.
Baby —— see what in Dr. ——'s satchel. What did Dr.
—— (mentioning another physician) do with satchel?
Dr. —— (mentioning the first one) has choo-choo in

satchel for Baby ——." It was said to himself in a very meditative manner, with no apparent fear or excitement, more than a year after the time he was so impressed with the ether-bottle.

(From now on all records other than cuttings and drawings were taken at longer intervals than before, yet they serve to show the growth made during the time no record was taken. It was during this period that the child was busy with scissors and pencil, giving concrete results of a method of training that evidently excited self-activity to a great degree.)

September 23d.—This morning I directed Harold's attention to half a dozen sparrows on a roof near by. They flew away one by one, and left only two, then one, then the last one went. He turned to me and said, "He got too much alone, he flew away," recalling the song of

> "Three crows there were once who sat on a stone,
>   Fal-la, la-la, la-la;
> But two flew away and then there was one,
>   Fal-la, la-la, la-la.
> The other crow felt so timid alone,
>   Fal-la, la-la, la-la,
> That he flew away and then there was none,
>   Fal-la, la-la, la-la."

This morning he told his father he had cried last night. His father asked him why. He said he wanted to see him take doggie out walking, which was the true state of affairs. He has not the slightest fear of his father, and looks upon him in the light of a delightful playmate. He has often begged his mother during the day to promise to let him have him "all alone" until his bedtime. If she promises, and forgets to allow him his father's undivided attention, he invariably reminds her of it in a very much injured tone. He seems to feel that he never has enough time with him, and he counts Sundays from the Monday previous, saying, "How many days, mamma, to Sunday?"

This morning he tripped over a newspaper, and said to his mother, "I didn't *mean* to do that, mamma." When being dressed he waved his foot with a long white stocking partly on, and said, "This is a boat with a sail." He looked out of the window and saw a grocer boy coming in. He called, "Hello, Gordon!" then said, "Must go down to see Gordon." This same boy draws pictures of some sort for him every morning. He began it voluntarily, and after that Harold insisted upon having one daily. He generally asks for an engine.

September 24th.—This morning, when he showed me his father's watch, I said, in a tone of surprise, "Is it twenty minutes of nine?" He dangled the watch a minute, and then returning to his father, he said, in a very sedate way, "This watch is slow, papa."

November 6th.—This morning when I was putting him to sleep at nap-time, I placed him on the bed and left. I returned a moment later, when he evidently did not expect me, for he was creeping back to bed and saying to himself, "I promise you I won't creep off the bed again; that's right; that's a good boy. You will forgive me." He seems to know as well as we do when he is doing wrong, and if we give him half a chance he rights matters himself.

(The record shows that as he grew older he took great pains to tell his mother several times that he wanted to do right because it was right to do so. One time he was found crying because he had transgressed. She said, "Never mind, Harold, you were a little bit careless this time; do better next time." And he replied, between his sobs, "But I don't want to be *careless.*" He could not be diverted until his sense of fun was aroused. Then he had a romp, and forgot all about it.)

Yesterday he couldn't at first take upon his spoon some cranberry-sauce that he was eating. He carefully scraped it to the middle of the dish, and taking a crust of bread pushed it on the spoon. He shows himself equal to the occasion many times, and he always prefers to help himself if he can do it. We do not offer to do *anything* for him that we see he is equal to, for he is very ready to come to us for assistance when he wants it, for we never turn him away, and thus we gain leisure and he strength by letting him do for himself.

He has shown a disposition lately to get out of his crib at nap-time, with the hope of inducing me to let him off, so I resort to pulling the crib away from every piece of furniture in the room upon which he can possibly step as he tries to get out. To do this I pull it down into the middle of the room before putting him in, when he says, "Pull crib down the middle because Harold was bad boy to get out of bed." He howls sometimes when he sees me do it, but he always goes to sleep at once when it is done. It is really very amusing. I wonder if he thinks he can't get out. He climbs all over it in every way during the day. Maybe it is "moral suasion" that influences him, or he may realize that I intend that he shall go to sleep, and accommodates himself to circumstances. But I often wonder why he doesn't get out, for he could easily do it.

Some time ago he saw two of his engines heading in opposite directions. He pointed to one and said, "This one is going to C——n Avenue Station, and this one to

131

G——e Avenue Station," mentioning the two stations between which we live. He pointed in the right direction each time. He also knows in which direction to look for " papa's train from town."

December 3d.—To-day, for the first time, he drew a " choo-choo" himself. (See illustration opposite.) As he drew it he explained each part, as noted, and handled his pencil very rapidly. He is just two years and ten months old.

February 1, 1893.—This morning he said to me, " May I walk over to call papa?" I said " Yes." He jumped out of bed, and, carrying his pencils and his beloved "schlüssel book" under his arm, he went through the hall, singing out at the top of his voice, " Old rags, old rags, any old rags to-day?" When he had called his father he ran away from him all around the room, as if in mischief, and wouldn't even allow him to lift him upon the bed, where he usually sits and watches him dress, and keeps up a running fire of comments and questions that are very amusing. As soon as he saw his mother come he let her place him on the bed and cover him. He evidently looks to her for discipline and to his father for pure fun, which is as it should be. He loves her dearly, but as he sees her so much more frequently than he sees his father, it seems a pity to spoil one minute of the time they are together by an attempt to assert authority.

(The record shows that as he grew older he often spoke of the good times he would have with mamma and papa when he got big enough to take care of them. He once told me, after having heard fairy-stories about princes and marriage, that when he got married he would live with mamma, as he would never want to

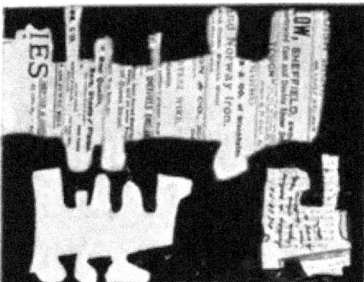

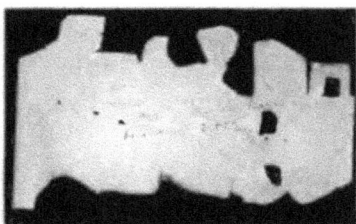

A CHOO-CHOO CUT OUT OF PAPER

A CAT

EARLY CUTTINGS

WHAT HE CALLED AN ATOMIZER

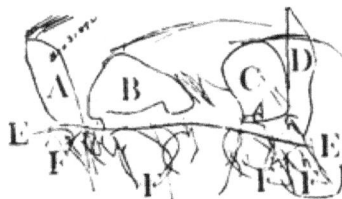

THE FIRST CHOO-CHOO

1892 AND 1893 DRAWINGS AND CUTTINGS—THE CHILD'S EARLIEST EFFORTS

His explanation of "the first choo-choo" was: A, smoke-stack; B, sand-box; C, steam-drum; D, cab; E E, one line for boiler; F F F F, wheels.

leave her. One of his greatest anticipated delights was that when he would be ten years old he could go to "papa's office" and take the letters to the post-office. This wish on his part gave rise to a story that I told him—"When H—— is ten years old, what will he do?" —and which he demanded repeatedly. It is worth noting that his greatest pleasure seemed to be that he could then help papa, just as he was now learning to help mamma. Who will dare to say that Froebel did not understand children when he urged mothers to let them make their hearts glad by allowing them to give presents and by *helping them to help others.*)

To-day I sat down for a moment in the kitchen, and as I was giving directions I took up and looked into a cook-book that was lying on the table. He passed by, looked at me, and said, "Are you looking what Mrs. R——r says?" mentioning the author's name correctly. I do not know how he found out her name. He is constantly surprising us by knowledge of this sort. We go along blindly when we think that children do not see things. I have no doubt at all of the fact that children know us far better than we know them, and were they able to express themselves in terms that we in our self-assumed strength could understand, I think we would be glad to change some of the cruel methods of training children that prevail at present. The pity of it all impresses one when one thinks of the opportunities that are wasted. Child-study is a work for all, but parents have the *first* opportunity.

Last Thursday, at the C——n Avenue Station, Harold was properly introduced to a very good friend. He was very shy, would not speak to her when I told him to say "good-morning," and apparently took no notice of her. When we reached home he said, "I was scairt of Mrs. ——," saying her name correctly enough to let any one know of whom he was speaking, although it was a peculiar name, and I hadn't the least idea that he would remember it. In the evening he told his father all about it, and mentioned the name several times. In spite of his peculiar accent his father knew whom he meant.

He has been going around lately saying, "I'm a little girl. I am six years old to-day." This is clearly imitation. A little girl said it to him a few weeks ago, and he himself is only three. He gives constant evidence of a retentive memory. He tells me constantly of little things that occurred a year and a half ago, personal matters that he recollects clearly.

February 2d. — He said to-day, "Doctor won't put medicine on my face; my cheeks are well," referring to the ether-bottle again. He asked the other day, in reference to this same event, "And did they all go away? and did Dr. —— go? and did Dr. —— go? and did Dr. —— take his satchel? and did the *one* doctor come back next day?" Then, "What did he do, mamma?" She always replies to this question, "He said, 'Good-morning,'" and tries to divert him. The other day he asked his father if he had been laid on the nursery-table, and if he had had a blanket and a pillow, etc. He evidently realizes that he can get no information from me, and he is now trying to get his father to tell him. He always says "Ask mamma," so eventually the child will have to give the matter up, as he would have done long ago had more care been taken in regard to his impressions at the time. (Ignorance is responsible for many evils, but who is responsible for this ignorance? Will women

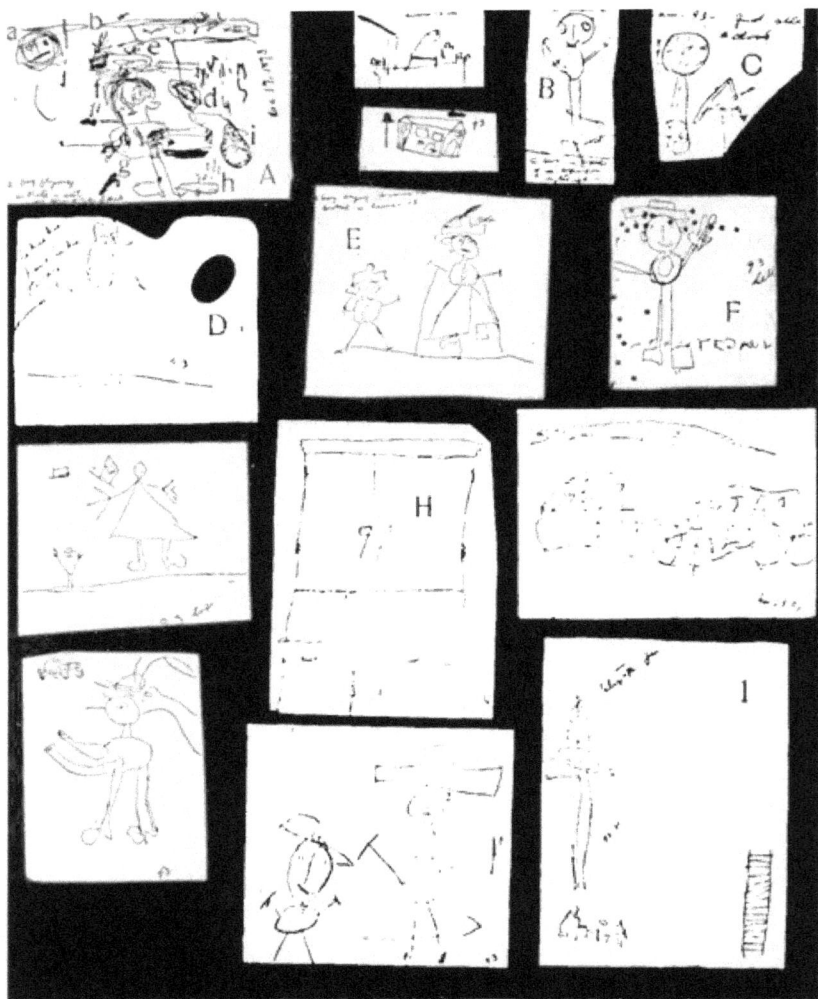

1893 DRAWINGS—THREE YEARS OLD

A, a boy flying a kite: a, man in moon; b, sky; c, kite; d, big knot in string; e, hat; f, curly hair; g, shoulder; h, foot turned over; i, watch; B, a boy in front of an engine "frightened"; C, first attempt at drawing a clock; D, "he has his hand in his pocket"; E, "a boy crying because his mother is lame"; F, inverted letters; H, kitchen dresser; I, telegraph pole.

ever be taught in the future, that looks so promising, that which they should certainly know? How few even understand the questions of hygiene or food, not to speak of their connection with the promotion of moral and mental development. Might it not be well for *all* reformers, educators, and philanthropists to follow the method adopted by *some* to-day—*i. e.*, beginning at the foundation and seeing that children are treated as they should be? and might they not better utilize hereafter the vast sums of money they now expend for the cure of much that might be prevented by helping to educate the *mothers of the future* as well as *those of the present*, taking up the work in a forceful manner in connection WITH existing schools as well as in a scattered, general way, as is now being done? This is so truly a national question that even the various governmental powers might wisely concern themselves with its practical application, in which lies the key-note of social and political reform.

February 3d.—To-day Harold saw some photographs of two cousins, who are totally unlike in appearance, each representing a distinct type. He had not seen the girls for nine months, but he knew the pictures at once. After having designated them correctly *once*, he pretended ever after—for mischief, evidently—that one was the other.

He knows all the nursery songs now, *words* and *tunes*, and if we make mistakes when repeating them he always corrects us.

He blew soap-bubbles *successfully* for the first time to-day. When he began he couldn't find his clay pipe, so he ran away, and soon returned with a beautiful one, and said, doubtingly, "Is this Harold's?" He feared it wasn't, for good reason. I went with him to see where he had found it. He led me to a drawer devoted to his father's pipes, which he had never attempted to disturb before. I did not want to disappoint the little fellow, so I said he might have it, although he has been taught not to disturb another's belongings. He then amused himself by blowing bubbles for a very long time—blowing them along the floor and stamping upon them.

The other day, when in a sleigh, the driver touched one of the horses with the whip, and Harold said, "He has no business to whip the horse." (The record later on shows how he always had great sympathy for horses—once, when six years old, going so far as to persuade a neighboring green-grocer to promise never to dock his horse's tail.)

Yesterday he said to me about a little playmate whom he loves, "Mamma, isn't Christine a lovely girl?" He saw some little girls on the street a few days ago, and he admired them very much. As he directed my attention to them he said, "I like little girls to come home to me." Mary T——, an old playmate, who used to come regularly to play with him, came to see him a few days ago. He was so delighted to see her that he hovered over her all the time she was with him. He paid no attention whatever to me. He said to her once, "I love you, Mary." He had not seen her for a year. He remembers the names of three servants and a laundress who were with us during the last year. He calls his present nurse "My Mary," as some of the other incumbents possessed the name of Mary also. He never forgets his first nurse, and often asks for her. When she comes to see him, at intervals of possibly six months, he always knows her.

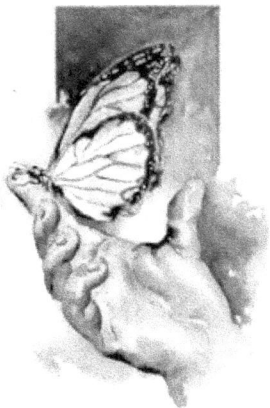

HIS PET BUTTERFLY FEEDING ON
HIS FINGER

AN EFFORT AT DRAWING A ROUND FRONT FOR AN
ENGINE

EARLY PRINTING

AN EFFORT AT THE HORIZON

A PIG

AN ENGINE AND TENDER

1893 AND 1894 DRAWINGS

1893—Printed letters; an engine and tender. 1894—An effort at the horizon; a pig; an effort at drawing a round front for an engine.

He has taken to winding string lately. To-day I was very much amused to see him place a small paper-box upon a chair, in which he dropped a spool of thread, letting the end dangle outside. He covered the box with a small drawing-slate, to keep the spool from jumping out as he wound the thread. I do not know how he discovered that the spool would jump out when winding briskly, but I suppose he must have tried it when I was not looking. He pulled his little chair up to the larger one holding the box with the thread, and began pulling out the thread hand over hand. This he did for a long time. Then he came to me and said, "I got myself stuck," meaning he had become entangled in the thread, which, although a natural sequence, was of no importance, when one considers that he had provided for himself a satisfying occupation for the time being. He plays in this way by the hour, chatting with me all the time, but going on with his play as if it were a work to be finished with the end of day only. He comes to me occasionally for a suggestion, saying, "What may I do?" But he usually finds occupation for himself for the whole day when I provide sufficient material for diversion, telling him that it is all for his amusement throughout the day. The kitchen-maid frequently lets him "clean the dresser," as he calls it. He takes out all the pots and pans, attempts to sweep the floor with a brush, and then he hangs the utensils up again where he thinks they belong. This amuses him immensely, and it occupies him long enough to give others a considerable time for rest from supervision.

February 4th.—To-day he said, "Cousin Eddie be a boy, mamma. Why doesn't papa be a boy?"

Last month he said, "I played fall up and down the

137

stairs *several* times." This was the first time he said "several."

February 5th.—To-day when he said "where," he emphasized the *wh* by blowing it out of his mouth very forcibly. He told nurse that she must not say "*me* face," but "*my* face." He told some one else not to say "*ain't*," but "*isn't*." He frequently asks me to tell him if it is correct to say certain words in a certain way, and he evidently thinks of it himself between times. He told me to-day that he would go to God when He was ready for him. He said God would give him wings to fly to Him. He has evidently drawn these conclusions from answers that he has received from some one beyond our control. I mentioned God quite unintentionally in his presence recently, and ever since he has kept up asking questions about Him—"whether He is a man, has a gown, a bath-tub, where He lives," etc. He was told at this time of God being over all the world, caring for it, as his father and mother were over him and the family. His love and power were spoken of. Harold now calls to Him in a very original way. The other evening he walked to the window in his night-dress, pulled down the slats of the shutters, and peeped through to the sky, calling loudly, "God, God, come down and bless papa, and bless mamma, and bless Harold!" He shut the shutters then and went to his crib, saying he heard God say He would come. (To the present date he shows the same belief in hearing an answer to any prayer he offers. He says his "think" tells him.)

February 7th.—He said to-night, in connection with some kindergarten songs, "Mamma, will you and I go to New York and buy a *new* book of songs, and I can *read* and READ and READ?" When we sang the kin-

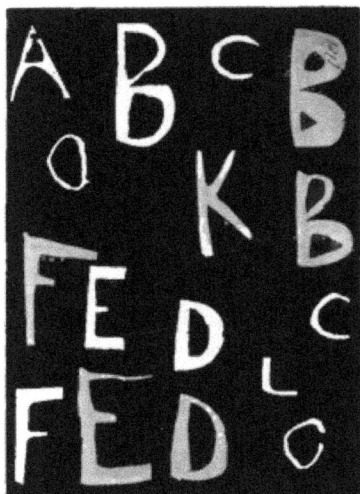

EARLY CUTTINGS

EARLY CUTTINGS

LOCOMOTIVES, A BAGGAGE-CAR, AND A STEAMBOAT

1894 CUTTINGS

Among the cuttings not designated, the one on the lower left hand of the group is intended to represent a mule, and on the lower right hand an ostrich turning his head

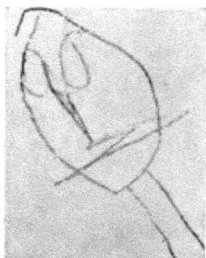

AN EARLY EFFORT IN 1893

dergarten song of exercise to-day, he tried to imitate my movements the second time. The third time he did it correctly, and he often repeats the whole song now. From time to time I give him memory exercise in this way, but I do it very gradually.

CHAPTER IV

FOURTH YEAR. RECORD OF SPONTANEOUS DEVELOP-
MENT AFTER THE CHILD WAS THREE YEARS OLD,
WITH SELECTIONS OF DRAWINGS AND CUTTINGS,
ALL MENTAL PICTURES, DONE AS A RESULT OF
SELF-ACTIVITY, AND ACCOMPANIED BY THE CHILD'S
EXPLANATIONS

FEBRUARY 14, 1893.—To-day Harold is three years old.
He awoke at seven, asked for his books and to have the
blind raised, and sat up to amuse himself, as he does
every morning, if he wakes before it is time for him to
be dressed. This is when he does most of his cutting
and drawing, after having been fed. It is a regular
habit to place his material at the foot of his bed every
night, and in the morning we have a serious time of it
picking up papers and throwing out what he allows us
to call trash.

This morning, instead of cutting, he read " A Froggie
Would A-wooing Go." He knows every word of it
from memory, turns the pages at the right time, and
takes great delight in using various tones and gestures
to illustrate each phase of the story. When he had finished reading it and I said it was time to rise, he
called to his father in another room, as he usually does,
saying to me, " Is that loud?" Receiving no reply, he
shook his head, said " He won't hear," and went on with
his play until the maid came to dress him. Shortly
after his father had left for his regular train, rather more

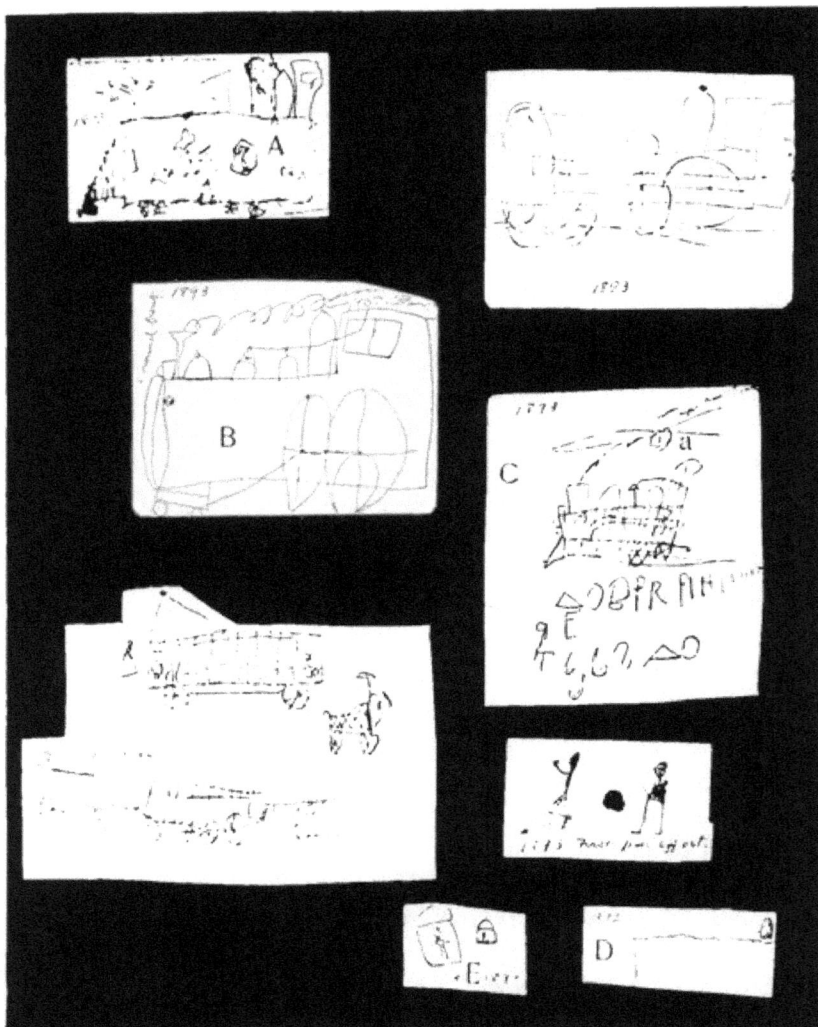

1693 DRAWINGS—ENGINES

A, "This is a man raking the fire, mamma"; B, round front to engine; C, "engine out at night time—a, is the moon"; D, "envelope and stamp"; E, "pictures on the wall."

leisurely than usual, Harold heard one go by and said, "That's papa's train; he didn't miss *that* one."

I took him out to-day to buy a birthday present. As we walked along he told me he loved to go out, asked if he was going to the barber-shop, and when I said "No," he said, "Then where are we going?" I said, "To buy a present." This delighted him. He is always so reasonable about buying things for himself that we take pleasure in giving him little surprises of this kind. When he asks for anything beyond his limit, he is always perfectly satisfied if we tell him that some day he will possibly get it. He seems to enjoy the anticipation, and many an hour have we spent looking at "possible" future gifts, while he was incidentally learning to control his desires. (Sometimes I am able to give an order, unknown to him, to have something that he has just admired sent home next day, and he thinks it a wonderful thing, next day, when he receives what he saw and admired the day before. In this easy way, by thinking ahead, we keep him happy all the time, and also very busy, for his toys all require work or motion upon his part. When he was five, and using tools, his mother at Christmas-time spent two hours in a hardware-store hunting out various little odds and ends that would please him—different sizes of nails, screws, pulleys, hinges, rings, silver wire, a gimlet, etc.—and of all the Christmas presents received this one pleased him most, and the whole lot cost forty-nine cents.)

While we were walking along I told him he was three years old, and his father thirty-three; he promptly asked me how many threes his mother was old. He saw some rabbits for sale and thought he would like to have one for his birthday present, so I allowed him to choose one and take it home himself. He picked out a black and white one, and wanted to come home at once "to build a house for it." When we reached a bridge on our way home, on which he invariably stops to see the "choo-choos," he wouldn't wait a moment, although I suggested it. He said he didn't want to, he wanted to go home and build a house in his nursery for his rabbit. Home we went and built a house out of a store-box. He was happy for the whole day, feeding and caring for his pet. He talked to it as if it could understand him, and at bedtime he bent over the door of its house and said, "Good-night; I'll call you in the morning."

He was so sleepy he could hardly keep awake long enough to ask where his paper choo-choos were. When I told him, he was content, nestled up against me, and fell asleep. He hadn't quite forgotten them, but it was evident that his engines will have rivals in live pets.

(The record shows a love of nature and animals that is fully equal to the evidence given further on of a strong bent for mechanics. He had at various times as pets—mice, kittens, dogs, butterflies, rabbits, snails, tad-poles, spiders, frogs, crabs, etc., and he seems to have learned in this way to be gentle with anything alive, having been known to lift even a worm out of harm's way when digging in his garden.)

He received his first locomotive a year ago, when he was two years old. To-day (three years old) we discovered him very busy with a string and one of his present stock of locomotives. He soon called to his mother to come and see what he had done. "See the connecting-rod, mamma; see how it works," and so it did. He had fastened the string to the centre of the driving-wheel, connected it with the cylinder, and was

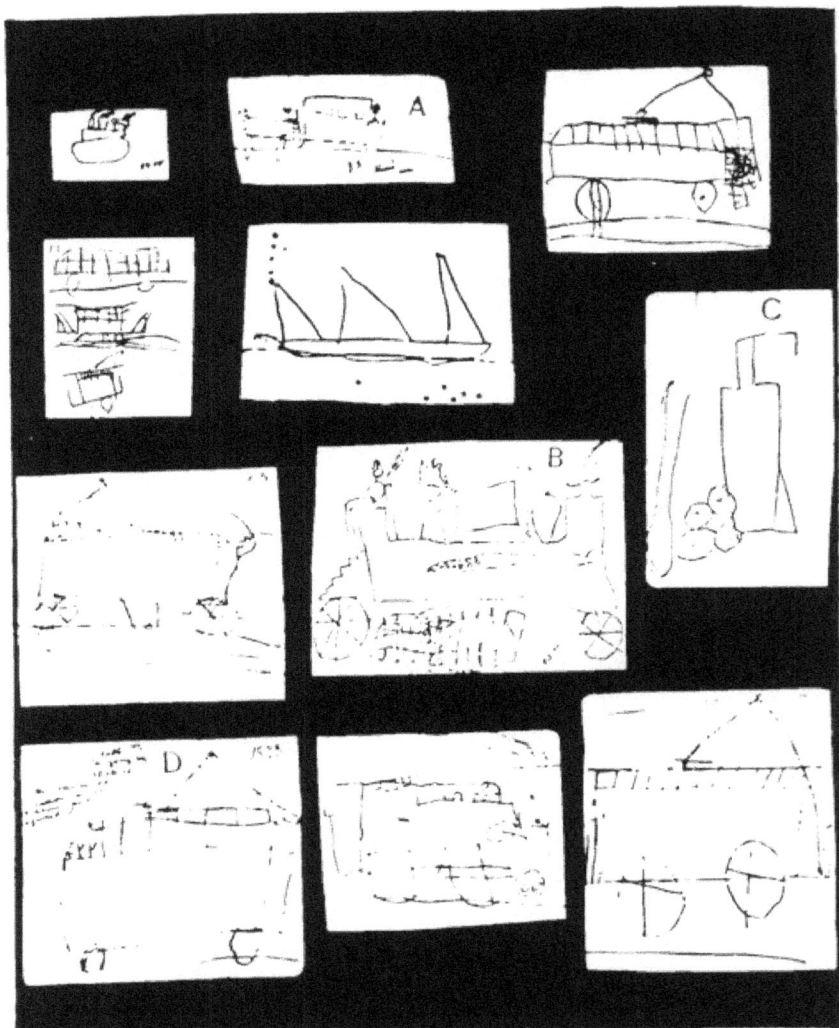

1893 DRAWINGS—BOATS, TROLLEYS, ETC.

A, street-car ; B, fire engine — engine going over a bridge ; C, stationary engine ; D, the child recognized an old Philadelphia traction car on a country electric road, and called it a cable-car going by electricity, then made the drawing.

delighted with the result, possibly because he felt that he had replaced to *his* satisfaction the connecting-rod that had been inadvertently broken off a day or two before, but just as likely because he felt he had achieved something, which characteristic seems to be distinctly noticeable in all children that are not feeble-minded.

During the afternoon he was singing " Little star that shines so bright . . . when I my homeward journey take," etc. When he reached the word journey he sang on, "When papa goes to town he takes a journey, when papa comes back he takes a journey," and went on with his play, not noticing that I had heard him. He doesn't seem to mind my presence—for when busy he apparently forgets all about me—yet if I leave he misses me at once. So I usually attend to my duties and read a great deal when sitting in the same room with him while he plays. Last night, when he woke for a drink, he saw his mother writing a letter, said " Don't write, mamma," turned over and fell asleep.

February 15th.—To-day he had some yellow-jack candy for the first time. When about taking him out-of-doors, his mother put a piece of it in her mouth, unknown to him. As she put on his coat he looked at her quizzically and said," I want a piece of yellow-jack; I smell it; mamma, open your mouth." She did so, but only partially. He said " Wide"; so she let him see that she had taken a piece. He smiled and said, "I smelled it." She then told him he could have a piece when he came in. He remembered this, and she had no trouble to get him to come in when it was time. This was not done to bribe him, but simply because it would be the most natural time for him to receive it, after going in again, instead of sending some one back to get a piece for him when he

143

spoke of it. He was never waited on to the exclusion of every one else's comfort, although all his wants were attended to, and often even anticipated; but this was done without his being conscious of it, and he was allowed to help himself and others so far as possible. When he began at this date, as he did, to demand service from the servants as if it were his right—politely, it is true, yet authoritatively, as if he recognized their position—he was taught, by examples that were pointed out to him, why a servant should be treated gently and courteously, as well as any one else with whom he had to do, and how, by not demanding, he would receive loving service. (The record shows clearly, later on, how he became uniformly gentle and kind with people who were not harsh, no matter in what condition of life he found them. And one of the greatest problems now before his mother is how to fully explain to him how he shall kindly adapt himself to the people about him without losing his own rights.)

To-night he asked me if his rabbit had teeth, and if it would bite or kiss.

February 18th.—Before going to sleep to-night he said, "Mamma, I want to talk to Katie a few *moments*." This is the first time he has said "moments." He is constantly saying words that are unusual for so young a child, and his understanding of their application is sometimes ludicrous, but generally surprisingly correct.

February 20th.—He heard the word peacocks to-day, and said, "Mamma, do peacoucks couck? Do peacoucks eat pease?"

February 21st.—He said, to-day, after the severe windstorm, bitter cold, and frosted windows of yesterday, "Mamma, it isn't cold to-day, the windows don't rattle."

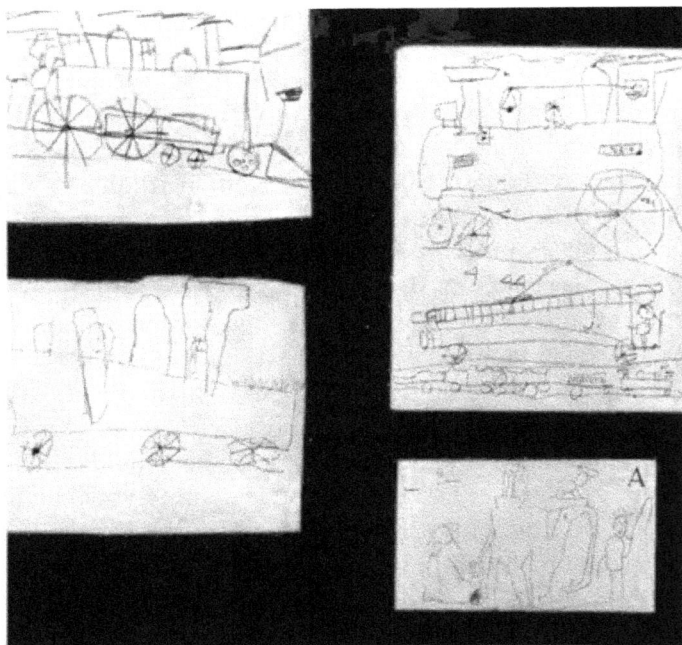

1893 DRAWINGS—ENGINES—THREE YEARS OLD

A. elephant, and children taking a ride ; engines and trolley cars

1893 DRAWINGS—THREE YEARS OLD

A, effort at writing "Thank you," after asking how to spell it ; B, b, b, early efforts at engine, pussy, and steamboat ; C, called it "writing his name," and the frame, he said, was a pipe with smoke curling around ; D, "man in the moon "; E, "man in the rain"; F, head and hat ; G, "a man without any arms—they were cut off, like the music man's legs"; H, effort at horizon ; I, engine and man in the moon ; J, his stuffed kitty ; K, house and woman

March 22d.—As we crossed the ferry going to New York to-day, he said to his mother as we came in the slip, "Oh, mamma, why does it make soap-water? See, the water is all soapy."

At the station he heard torpedoes on the track and said, "Is that thunder?" (This is the time that he first observed the differences in boats, and his constant questions during a week's visit and much ferry-crossing were, "What's that?" and "Why is that?" Every question was answered so that he could understand, by building up from what he already knew, and he carried home with him a vast increase to his fund of information that is being acquired by persistent questioning.)

November 23d.—He said, to-day, "Lorenzo *learned* me to cry." I said, "No, he *taught* you." He then said, "It is *I* that learns, isn't it?" He is three and a half years old now.

December 25th.—His prayer, as follows, on Christmas evening, was voluntary, for we let him pray just as and when he feels like it. He said, "God bless papa and mamma, and God bless Harold and Katie (his maid), God bless my Christmas-tree, God bless Santa Claus, and everybody you can find in your house in the sky."

To-day—Christmas—he said he felt so happy and pleased with Santa Claus for giving him such a nice Christmas-tree. He selected voluntarily enough toys to fill a large portmanteau—taking books, old and new toys, fruit and candy—"to take out," as he said, "to some poor little boy who hadn't any papa." He has divined or heard in some way that Santa Claus comes where there is a "papa." When he asked me in such a way that I could not escape answering, I explained to him that Santa Claus represented the spirit of love abroad for

K   145

everybody at Christmas-time, and, like the Brownies, we couldn't see him. I have not explained to him yet about Christ, so I could not go on with the idea, but he accepted the suggestion, and seems to revel in the fanciful thought of Santa. We went out to find the poor little boy, and we had a difficult search, after a long walk, during which he said to himself, "I will be the little boy's Santa Claus. I pity the poor little boy without any papa."

We found a mother with three little tots in rags. They had no tree, no toys—in fact, hardly enough to eat. Harold is very shy, and I had to persuade him to hand his toys himself. I wanted him to taste the pleasure of giving. He did it very shyly, and it was a pretty sight to see the ragged urchins crowd about him, each to take what he offered without any question as to which would get the most. When we returned he was well content and happy all day through, although he had given away many treasured toys. The chief beauty of the act was that no one would have found it out, not even his parents, if it had depended upon him for the telling, for he never spoke of it again, and seemed to have forgotten all about it, nor did any one else ever mention it in his presence.

When he was nearly four years old his uncle and Aunt C—— came to see us, and while I was engaged with his uncle he took up a new book that he had just received and brought it to me, begging me to read to him about the pigs in it. The book had a number of illustrations, and nearly every one had the picture of a pig in it. To divert him, his aunt called him to her, saying she would read to him. As it was twilight she could not see to read, so improvised the following verses

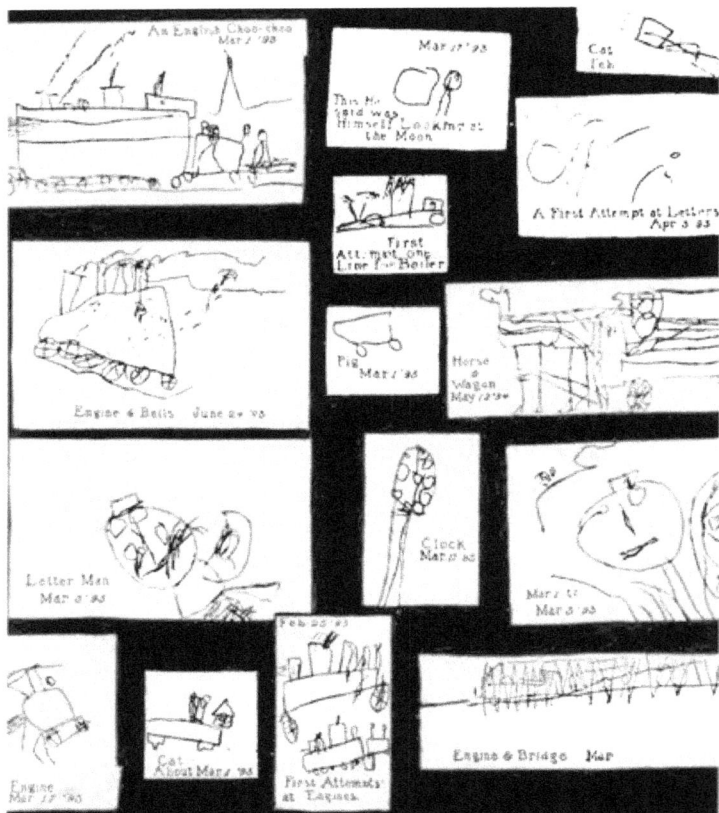

1893 DRAWINGS

With the exception of the horse and wagon, drawn in May, 1894.

to catch his interest and keep him from disturbing our conversation. It was the first time that Harold had heard any of us use "baby talk":

"A piggie, wiggie, wiggie,
Went to beddie, beddie, beddie.
On his pillow willie, willie,
He laid his headie, headie, headie.

"But piggie, wiggie, wiggie,
Couldn't sleepie, sleepie, sleepie,
So out his beddie biggie,
He creepie, creepie, creepied.

"He jumped, he hopped, he trotted
Across the floor so bold,
To reach the shining faucet,
With water, oh, so cold!

"He splashie, splashie, splashied,
He dashie, dashie, dashied,
The water, water, water,
On his facie, facie, face.

"He wet his eyesie eyes,
His cheekie, cheekie, cheeks,
His nosie, nosie, nose,
His headie, headie, head.

"Oh, the water, water, water,
Was so cold, so cold, so cold,
But he laughie, laughie, laughied,
For it felt so good, so good, so good.

"Then back to beddie, beddie,
Went piggie, wiggie, wiggie;
He slept, you may believe it,
Like any piggie wig."

He was very much amused, and begged her to tell it again. Then he went for his engine-book (one that was full of illustrations of English and American engines), and said, entreatingly, "Aunt C——, read the engine-book funny—puffy, puffy, puff."

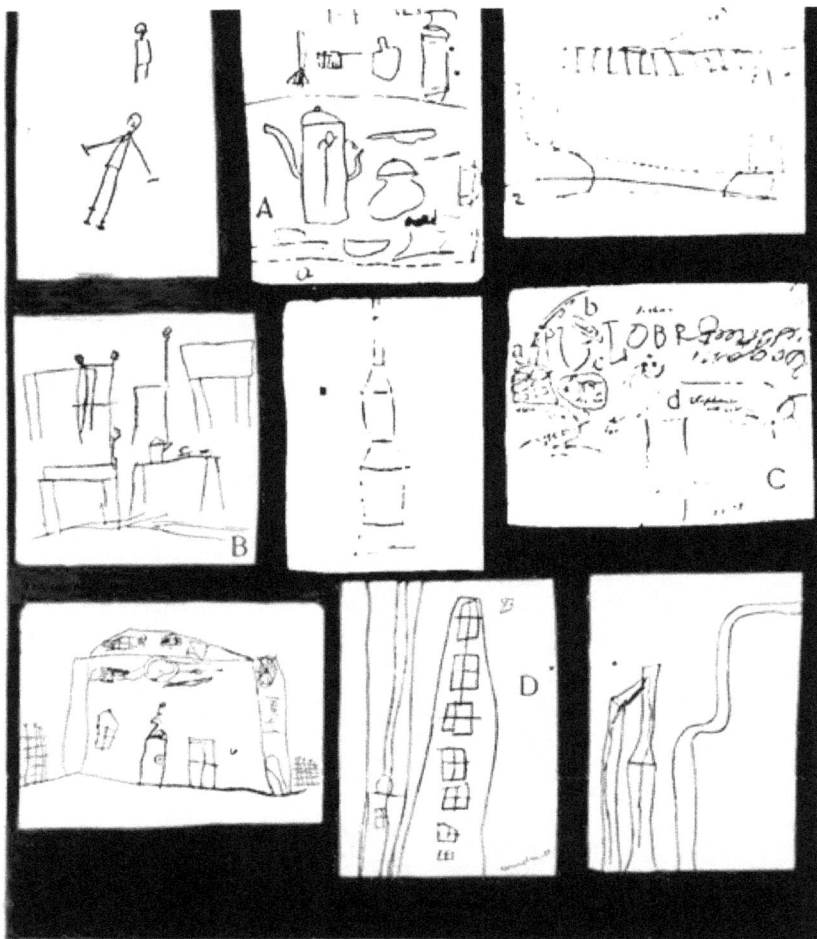

1893 DRAWINGS—THREE YEARS OLD

A, kitchen utensils; B, kitchen chairs, table, etc.; C—a, kitchen stove; b, inverted letters; c, dog with bell in his nose; d, elephant with bell in his nose; D, windmill

CHAPTER V

FEBRUARY 14, 1894.—To-day I was trying to draw a
pussy for Harold, and when I drew the whiskers I said,
"Doggies don't have whiskers." He said, "No, they
have only fleas."

February 19th.—He was looking at a large picture
of a naval review, and pointed to a three-mast vessel
and said, "I never saw one like that before." Then
pointing to two walking-beams, one at each end of
the picture, he said, "There are two ferry-boats like I
saw on the ribber when I was at Baby N——'s house.
There's a sail-boat. There is no tug-boat here. What's
that?" pointing to a cannon. I said, "Don't you remember seeing a cannon over at the square where there is a
statue?" He said "Yes." and asked what the wheel
under it meant, and the tracks. His father then explained
about its being a carriage to wheel around the cannon.
He instantly asked whether there was a hinge there to
make it go around.

February 20th.—He told his mother the following
story very seriously to-day, without a break from beginning to end.

About a month ago I told him about "The Brownies

and the Rain-drops," making it up for him as I went along. He was very fond of it, and asked for it repeatedly, so I wrote it down. The one story may have suggested the other, but he has heard of the Brownies and had their books for a long time, and he has also heard of "Jack and the Bean-stalk" independently of my story. (At seven he still begs to hear both stories from time to time.)

HAROLD'S STORY TO HIS MOTHER

"Harold saw a house, and what do you suppose he saw right by it?"

His mother said, "I don't know."

He said, "Why, a great big bean-stork" (stalk), "and Harold climbed up the steps to the top of the house; and what do you think he saw there?"

"I don't know."

"Why, a little Brownie. He said, 'Why, how do you do, Master Harold?' and Harold said, 'How do you do, Master Brownie?'" (He then said to me in an aside, "His name was *Mustard* Brownie.") "'Won't you come down with me, Mustard Brownie?'" Then Mustard Brownie climbed down on one side of the steps, and Harold on the other, and when they got down to the ground Mustard Brownie took Harold's hand, and they walked and walked and walked until they came to Harold's house.

"Harold said, 'Won't you come in this beautiful house and live with me, Mustard Brownie?' and he said he would, and went in with Harold. And what do you suppose Harold's nurse said to Mustard Brownie, hopping on the floor?"

"I don't know."

150

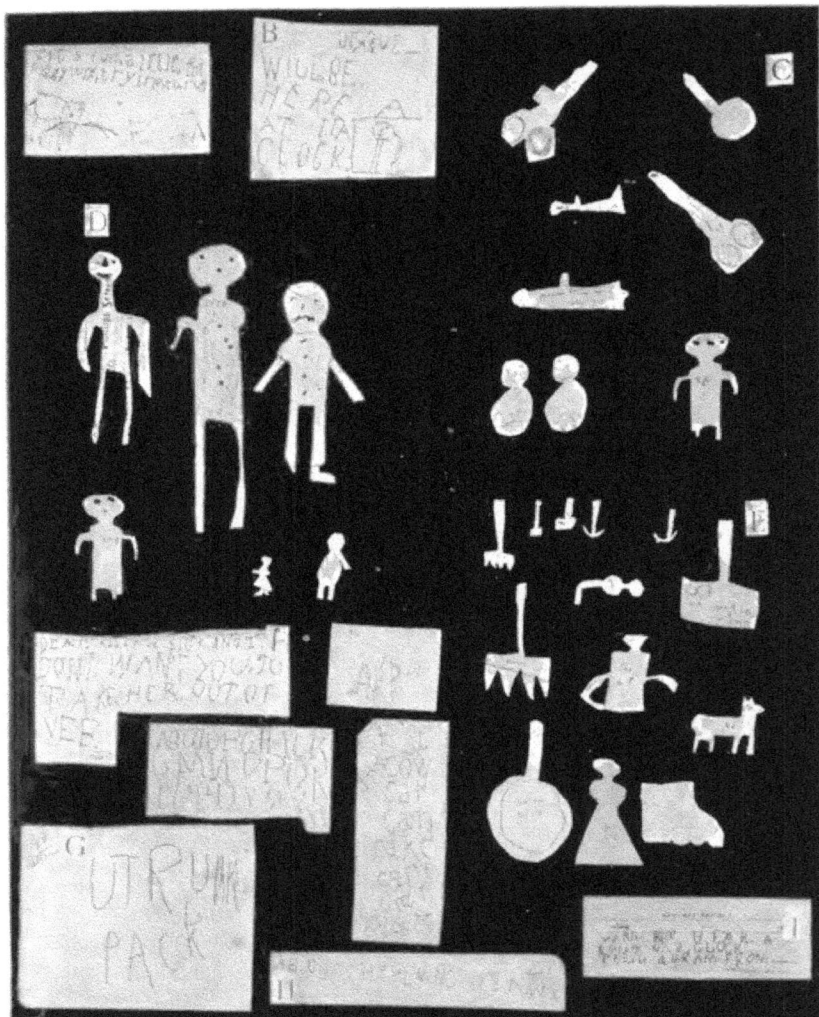

1894 CUTTINGS AND 1893 AND 1894 PRINTED LETTER WORK

1894 CUTTINGS—FOUR YEARS OLD

A shoe ; B, elephant ; C, a range with lots of fire - holes ; D, "a Venice boat," he called it, with a ventilator and window ; E, bell.

"'Why, where do *you* come from, Mustard Brownie?'
And he said:

"'Harold saw me on top of the roof of a house and
brought me here.' And what do you suppose he did
then? Hopped around on the floor and played with
Harold's toys; and that's all."

The following is the story supposed to have suggested the preceding one of the child's:

THE BROWNIES AND THE RAIN-DROPS

One moonlight night a wee little Brownie met another little Brownie, who was much older than himself,
and he asked him a question that had been bothering
him all the long, long day: "Have we mammas and
have we papas?"

"No, we are only Brownies—make-believes, the children call us. Come, let us go up to the sky and see the
rain-drops."

"But how will we get there?"

"Oh, upon a butterfly's back. I think there is a field
full of them here."

So away they went to the field, where they found
many beautiful butterflies asleep amid the flowers.
Brownies always travel at night and know just where
to find what they want, for they are very wise. To
the first butterfly they saw they said, "Please wake up
and take us to the sky to see the rain-drops."

"Certainly I will. We want them here, we are so
thirsty."

So up the Brownies jumped, but, alas! they found the
butterfly's back was *too small* to hold them. They

asked another. He said, "Oh yes; I will gladly go, I am so very warm. We want the rain-drops here." But, alas! he was *too broad*. The next was *too thin;* the next *too fat.* Another was so soft that the Brownies feared that they would go right through him. The last one they tried was, oh, so hard! His back was as sharp as the edge of a knife.

The butterflies couldn't take them, yet wanted so much to have the rain-drops, and the Brownies, too, wanted very much to learn how and where the rain-drops lived. The poor flowers in the field, also, were so very thirsty. What could they all do?

Well, the Brownies walked along, wondering and wondering, when they chanced to see what looked like large, beautiful trees, with steps running up the sides of the trees. Now these wise little Brownies knew all about the story of Jack and his Bean-stalk, and they thought that perhaps they had found a fairy bean-stalk. They picked out a tree that seemed higher to them than all the others, and then they began to climb—high, higher, and yet higher, for every time they thought they were near the top up would seem to go another lot of steps. They kept on, however, puffing and panting, until at last what do you think they saw? (Here Harold always says, "I don't know," waiting expectantly.) A beautiful white cloud, floating very near the highest step, and sitting upon the cloud was another little Brownie. How did he get there? They looked and looked, but after so hard a climb they hadn't any breath left to *ask* him how he came. Very soon, however, after they had rested a little, they turned to find out all about it, when what do you think they saw? (Harold again says, "I don't know.") They saw he was go-

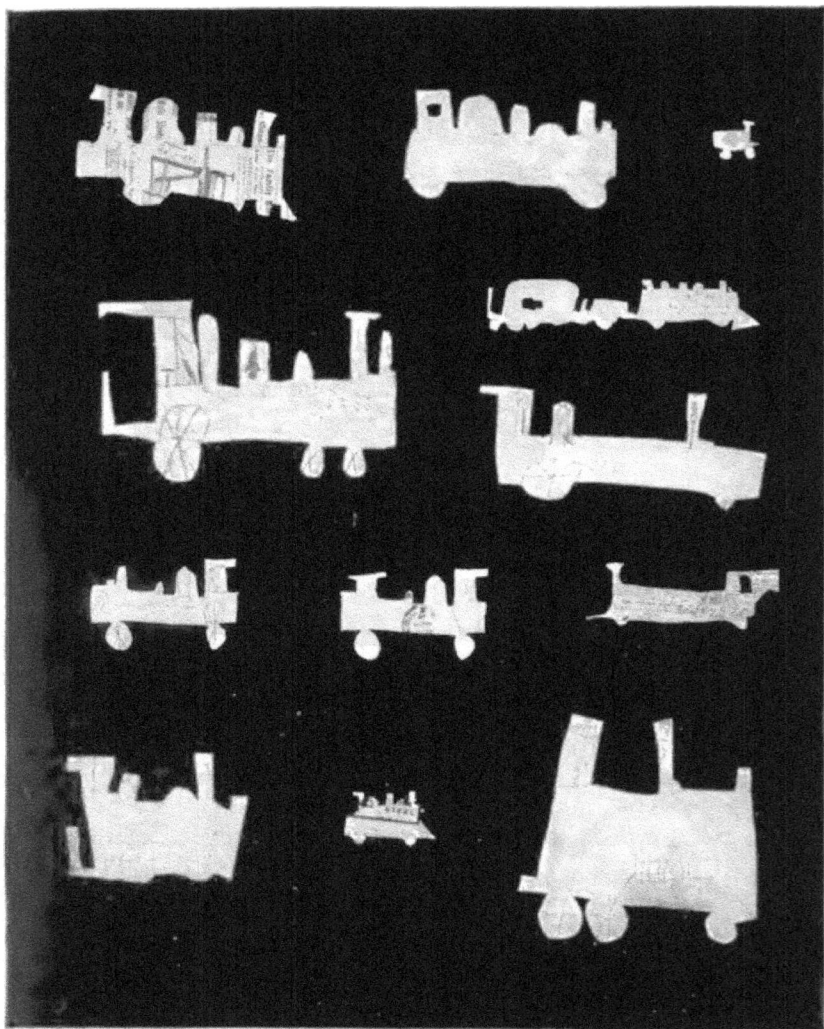

1894 CUTTINGS OF ENGINES

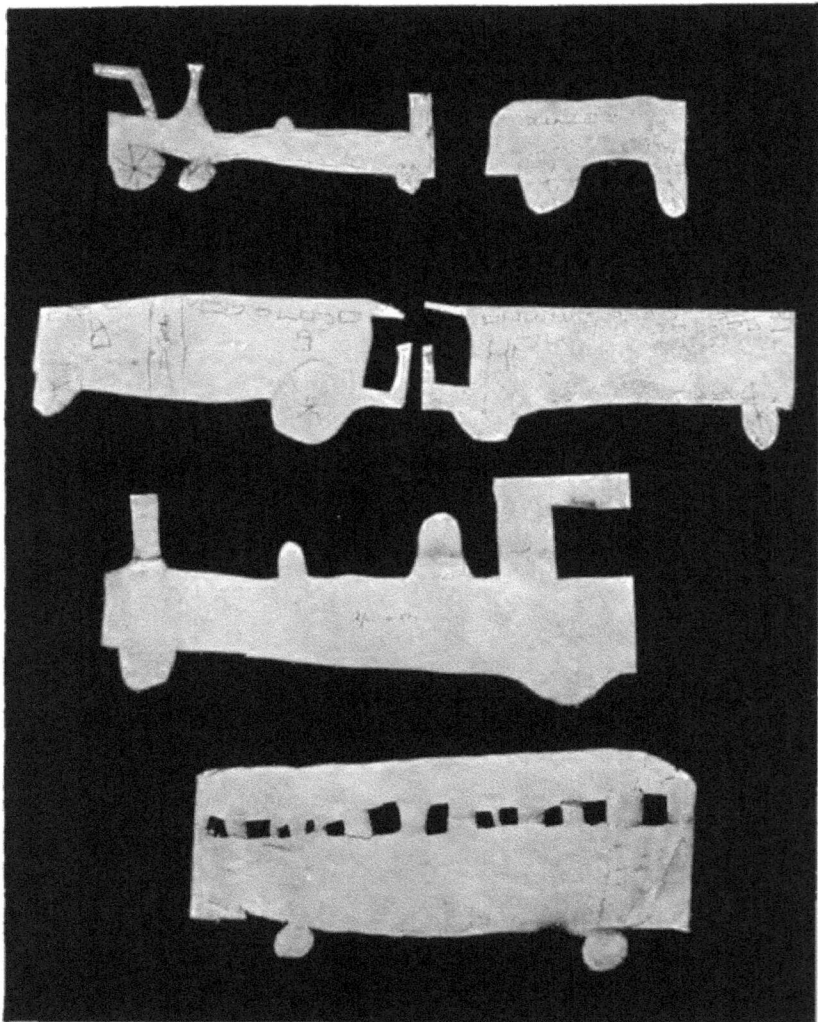

1894 ENGINE AND CAR CUTTINGS—FOUR YEARS OLD

ing down, down, down, far away from them and the cloud. What could it all mean? They soon found out. First they saw some rain-drops, like great, big, lovely drops of dew, all gathered together in this beautiful white cloud, one close against the other. They shone and glistened, and were almost too beautiful to look at.

The little Brownies were quite afraid to speak to them, but they did try to say in a whisper:

"The butterflies and flowers are *very* thirsty."

The big drops heard them, and answered, saying:

"Yes, we know, and we all are ready to give them a drink. Now sit very still and watch us." And just think of it; the big cloud opened very gently, and the drops all rolled out, one by one at first, but very soon tumbling one over the other, just as fast as they could go, flashing and splashing, and whispering gently all the way down to Mother Earth, because they were so very glad to give a drink to the poor thirsty butterflies and flowers. As they were tumbling out, two of the last big drops turned very quickly to the Brownies and said:

"Your ladder is gone. Jump upon our backs if you want to get home before daylight comes."

Now we all know very well that Brownies are good-natured little things, but they never let any one see them, so they knew very well that home they must go, and that very quickly. Their ladder was gone. They felt a little bit afraid to ride down to the earth on the rain-drops, yet what could they do? The big drops promised them they would go very gently, so each Brownie jumped up upon the back of a beautiful shining drop, and sailed away, down, down, down, in the most delightful way, and *where* do you think they found themselves when they reached the end of their journey? (Harold says, " I don't know.")

Why, one was upon the back of the fat butterfly, and the other was upon the back of the thin butterfly, and they heard both butterflies making a quiet little noise of pleasure because the rain had come. They did not see the Brownies, though, *for the sunshine too* had come.

December 25th.—He said, voluntarily to-night for his prayer, " I love you, God, but I can't always do what pleases you." The last was not suggested. He had been told that God liked to know that little boys loved Him, so he folded his hands, buried his face in his pillow, and whispered the words. Afterwards he said he had something else to tell God, and repeated, "Please, God, tell mamma to bring, next Christmas, for my kitty" (said kitty is a stuffed cotton-print one) "a pair of crutches and a bed." He told me to-day that she was lame. All imagination. He idealizes her—she is everything to him. He takes her to bed with him every night.

December 26th.—To-day when I read to him, " So Tray put his *fore*-feet in the milk," he asked, " Do two and two make four?" thinking I meant *four* feet. Knowing there were two front and two hind feet, he made his first attempt at adding. I said, " Yes, just this way," holding up my fingers; "two fingers and two fingers make four fingers." He held up his little hand, separated the fingers in twos, and said, " This way—one, two; one, two," counting each group. I said, "Yes; now how many altogether?" He counted "One, two, three, four," and was satisfied, which he is *only* when he understands the replies he receives. He never gives up questioning until he understands. I have often

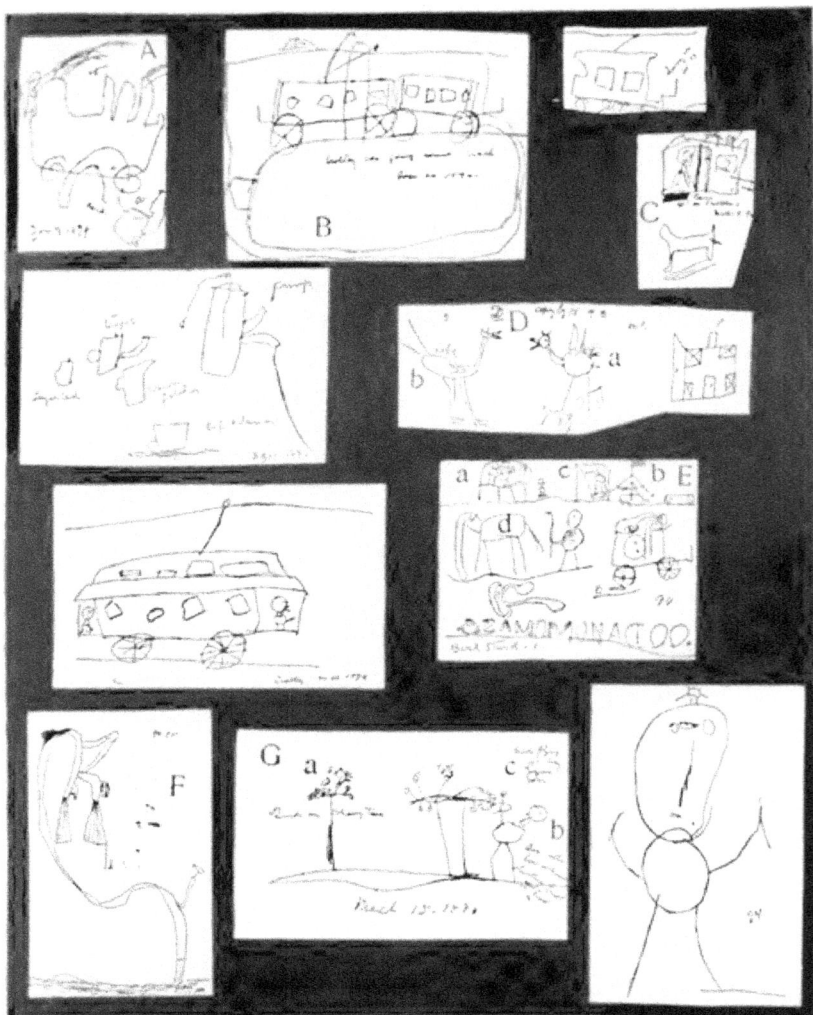

1894 DRAWINGS—FOUR YEARS OLD

A. duck ; B, trolley car going round a track ; C, "Harold lame on crutches and mamma looking out of the window"; D—a, is copy by child, reversed, of b, done by another person ; E, scenes at a country fair—a, band-stand ; b, merry-go-round ; c, swing ; d, elephant-keeper with goad ; F, faucets and pipes ; G—a, bird on cherry-tree ; b, boy with bow and arrow shooting bird on apple-tree ; c, bird flying away.

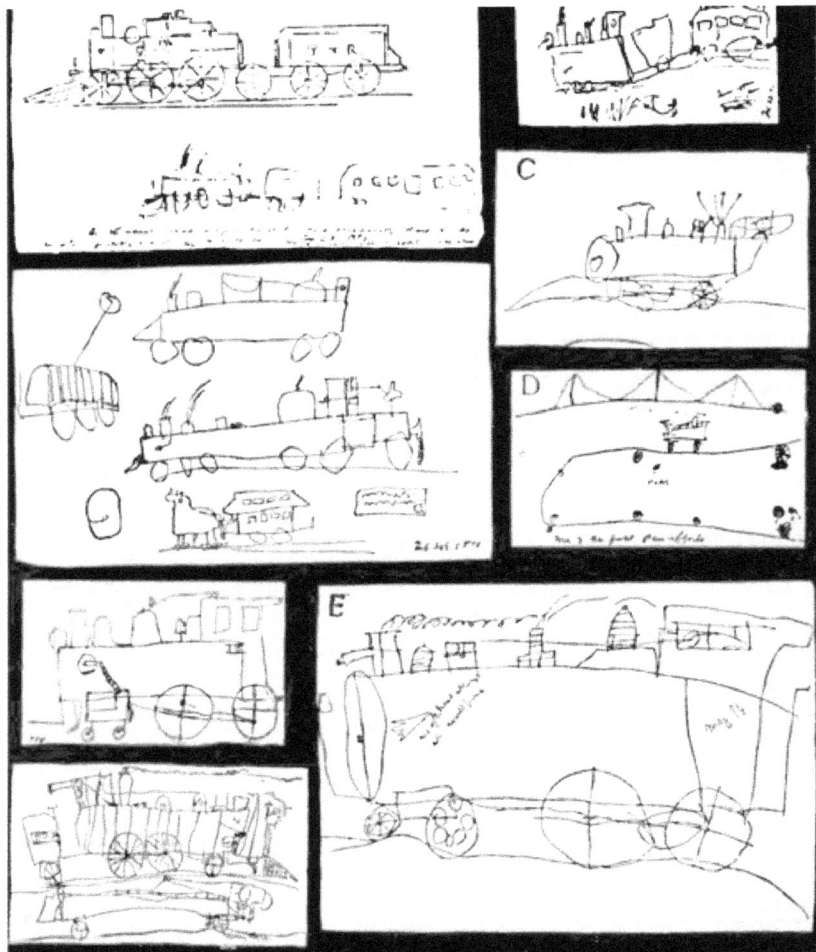

1894 DRAWINGS—FOUR YEARS OLD

A, engine from copy, February 25, 1894—as Harold's interest increased in engines his father would draw one for him, as above, probably once a fortnight—Harold always made additions to his own copy; B and D early pen efforts; E and C first attempts at a round front for engines—he seemed never to have observed this feature before.

heard him say, " What ? What did you say ?" meaning
that he did not understand—not that he did not hear ;
but until I would explain to others they would frequently answer in the same words, over and over again, to
every " what " he gave. He did not know how else to
ask, and because I always understood what he meant
by " what," he thought others did.

I did not explain to him at this time about *fore*-feet
meaning front feet, for he had enough to consider with
his " two and two make four."

We usually find out some way of making things clear
by going from what he knows to the unknown—as, for
instance, he asked once what a " calf " was, and I said,
" A little cow." He said, " Oh, is that the way ?" and
asked no more. We can always trust to his asking questions when he observes anything new, for he knows that
he will be answered. He now possesses a fund of information, acquired by questioning and from surroundings, that is equal to that of a much older child, yet
he has gained it all without the slightest effort beyond
self-directed amusement, with no sign of precociousness,
and without sacrificing in the least degree the opportunities that were needed for correct physical development.

He asked me this evening why we were not made to
eat everything. I said things were made for different
uses ; grown stomachs, if well cared for when little,
could digest almost anything. Then he said, " But no
—listen : why don't we eat vaseline instead of using
it outside ?" I said we could, but we wouldn't like it.
He is no doubt puzzling over internal and external uses
of things. He asked me to-night how to spell " gan," of
the word " Hogan." I said, " g-a-n." He then said,

"Hello, Harold, here you are again. How do you spell that?" I said, "a-g-a-i-n," and he was satisfied.

He is very fond of *Slovenly Peter*. When asked what kind of a book it was, he said, very emphatically, "*Slovenly Peter* was made for naughty boys. You could read it to good boys to make them happy, and to naughty boys to make them good; that's what it's made for." (An incipient reviewer.)

The following story, which I wrote for Harold when he was about four years old, gives our experience with some pet mice, and shows, incidentally, how he was taught to be gentle with live creatures. He asks for it again and again:

TWO WHITE MICE

"Whitey" and "Squealy." This is what Harold calls them. Whitey is the dearest little ball of fluff when sitting on her haunches cleaning her coat with fists made of the smallest pair of hands you ever saw, for her front feet looked like little hands that have only four fingers and no thumbs. They are ever so much smaller than the hind feet, that have five toes that look like a thumb and four fingers. These hind feet are very strong, and Whitey often stands up on them like a kangaroo, lifting her nose high up into the air to sniff at something which she doesn't quite understand, but knows is there. Harold says she has only four fingers for each front foot, with no thumb to get in the way, because she can roll them up into fists more easily, which mousie always does when cleaning her fur, making them go so fast that you can only see something pink that is moving but has no distinct form. Harold also says mousie has

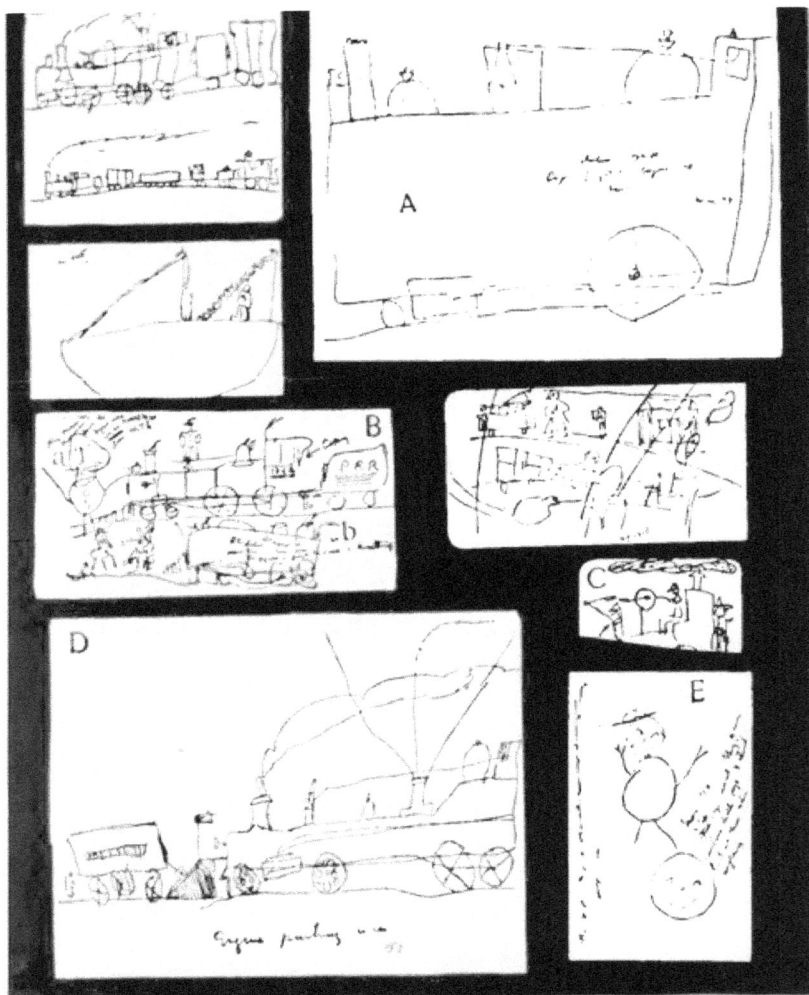

1894 DRAWINGS

A, copy of a picture of an old English engine—done from memory; B, he drew a, a man before the engine which some one else drew—he also drew b, an engine to run over the figures in front, which were also drawn by some one else; C, fire engine; D, engine pushing a car; E, he said, "Aren't they funny smiling little boys?" "I think I'd rather look at those than anything."

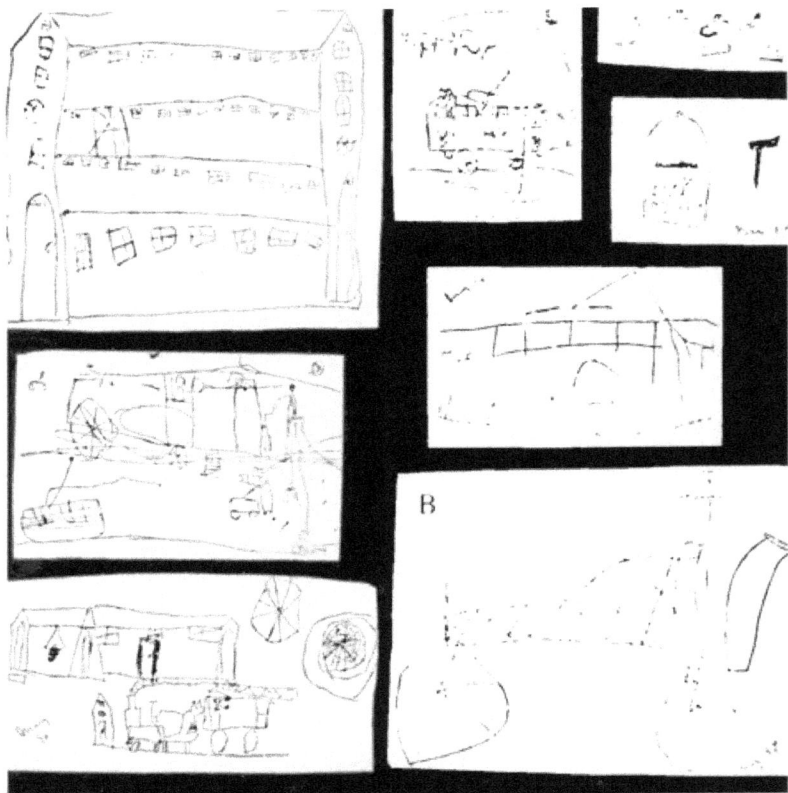

1894 DRAWINGS—FOUR YEARS OLD

A, "a man shooting an ostrich"; B, "baby coach."

five toes on her hind feet so she may spread them out to stand on. Whitey's sense of smell, as is true of all mice, is wonderful. We often place a bit of cheese within several feet of her, just to see her drop everything instantly and run straight to the tempting morsel, where the least little bit of a nibble seems to satisfy her.

She is a very dainty eater. She lives chiefly upon canary-seed, and to see her sitting beside us so fearlessly, holding a very little seed in her fore-paws, nibbling away to her heart's content, with a most knowing expression, is a sight worth working for. It takes only a little patience and kind treatment to secure this result.

Squealy was not so easy to teach as Whitey was, and he gave us a great deal of trouble. He squealed every time we touched him, which gave him his name; he would climb out of his box and run away. One night he gave us a half-hour's chase before we caught him. He would nibble holes with his sharp little teeth through the bottom of the box or in the cover on the dressing-table, where we tried to keep him for a while, thinking he wouldn't try to jump off. He would chew at the edges of any books or papers he could reach; in fact, he never seemed satisfied except when in mischief. Whitey, on the contrary, showed a genuinely sweet disposition, never squealing when we took her up, and never giving trouble of any kind.

We took them with us to the country one day when making a visit, and had a most exciting hunt for Squealy the first night, just about bedtime, when we discovered that Whitey was alone in the box, which had been set very carefully in the middle of the floor, far enough away, so we supposed, from anything that could be reached. As we knew the roving disposition

of Squealy, we took this precaution, but we were not
sufficiently foresighted, as events showed. We hunted
under beds, bureaus, and chairs, up-stairs and down,
with candles and without, and at last gave up in despair when we happened to spy him upon the curtain-
pole near the ceiling, his little white head with his pink
eyes almost invisible, peering over the top of the equally
white curtain. His eyes were shining as if he enjoyed
our worry. He sat still, watching us, and it took but a
moment to get him and place the box in a safer position,
farther away from the curtain, to which he had evidently jumped; but we did not feel secure so long as we had
him visiting, for we never knew where we would find
him. We did not mind this very much when at home,
as we were careful to keep doors closed, and all articles
of value away from him.

When he began to fight, however, we thought it best
to do without him. The scampering and squealing that
we heard at night was, to say the least, disturbing, especially to those who wanted to sleep and were not accustomed to noise of this sort. We had grown so used
to little things of this kind in our nature-studies, that
we were entirely unmindful of the fact that our little
family did not live very happily when together; but one
night, after a particularly noisy time, we surprised a
little dark mouse on a visit to the white ones. He
disappeared very quickly, but evidently returned again,
for the racket was astounding. Finally there was a
terrific squeal and a big thump. Upon springing up
and striking a light we discovered poor Whitey on the
floor with blood on her back, where either Squealy or
the brown mouse had evidently bitten her. She had
fallen or been pushed from the top of a large trunk,

1894 DRAWINGS—FOUR YEARS OLD

A, "a man out walking in the wind, which blew his hat-string from his coat button"; B, "two men on a boat"; C, "cannon and man shooting"; D, "boy and his mamma telling him not to do something"; E, "frightened girl"; F, "man walking in the rain"; G, Chinaman; H, windmill to work machinery below; I, "girl out walking"; J, New York fire-boat; K, "baggage man at depot"; L and M, engines running over men; N, effort at horizon; a, sun; b, steamboat; c, captain on sail; d, ship with four sails; e, ship with two sails; f, cannon on war ship; g, big sail boat.

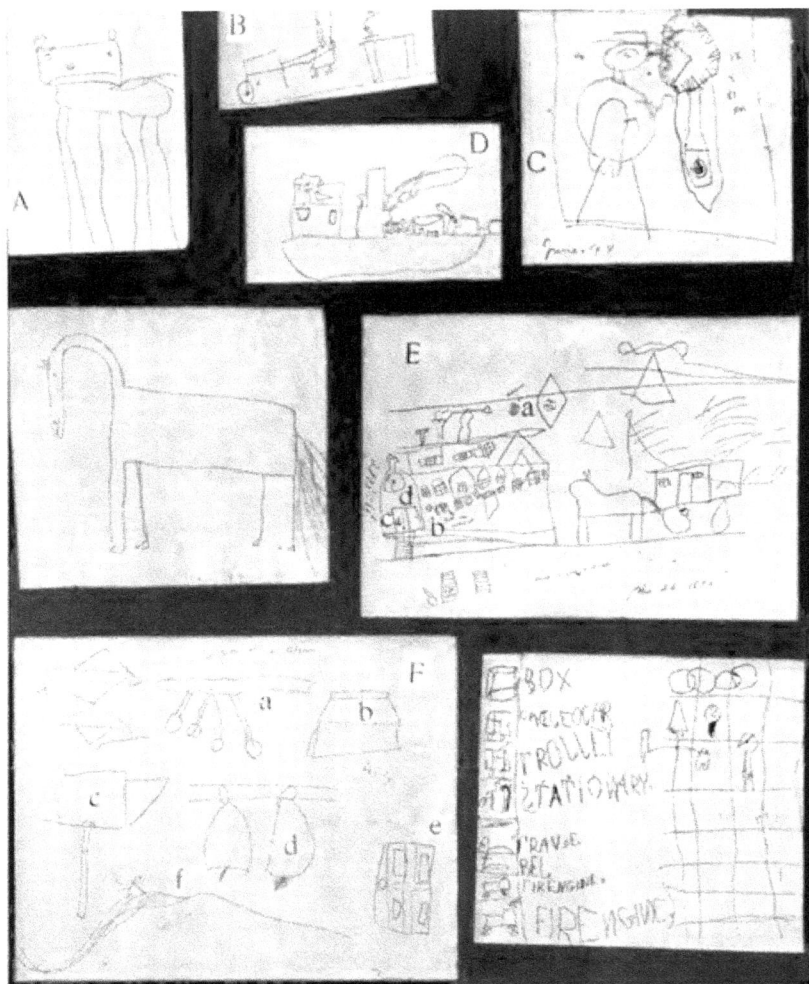

1894 DRAWINGS—FOUR YEARS OLD

A, cat ; B, man with wheelbarrow ; C, man to wind clock ; D, New York fire boat ; E, house, horse, and wagon ; a, balloon ; b, little man looking out of the window ; c, "rope to let the heat out or in of the chimney"; d, front door ; F—a, cherries on stem ; b, letter box ; c, mortar carrier ; d, bells ; e, door ; f, hill with somebody looking over it.

upon which they were living at the time. Mice always fall on their feet like cats. Squealy's condition, upon examination, showed that he, too, had received his share in the battle royal that had just taken place, for his ears were covered with blood. I reached out to pick him up, to put him alone for the night, when he bit me, a very sharp little nip, which hurt and brought blood. This sealed his fate. We concluded that he was not of sufficiently gentle mouse-birth to live among gentle-folks, and we returned him next day to the fancier from whom we had bought him.

Since that time there has been peace and quiet, day and night, and Whitey has shown the most delightful habits. She is sitting now, as I write, within two inches of my pen, lifting her nose in the air in the dainty fashion she has, as if she smells cheese, or possibly ink, for I frequently have to rescue her from the fascination of the ink-bottle. She will lift herself up and look into its inky darkness in the most knowing way. Sometimes she comes up to my hand as I write, when everything is very quiet, and puts her little cold nose against my fingers, as if to pet me. Then she scampers away for a run in and out among the books and papers on the table, which is her nightly treat. She spends all her days in a home she has made her own. It is a newspaper-basket on a stand, and is lined with wadding which is covered with red plush. She has been bright enough to nibble a hole in the plush and pull out a large handful of wadding, which she has made soft with her little teeth, making the loveliest bed imaginable, upon and under which she sleeps, having at the same time given herself a hiding-place under the plush, to which she often runs.

Like some human beings, she has a way of making
herself very comfortable. One thing she does that is
rather queer for a white mouse. We often put her up
high, in some place where she feels uncomfortable or
not safe, and she jumps at once, always towards me,
landing upon some part of my body. We found she
would do this by one time placing both mice, heads
down, upon the straight back of a sofa, down which
Squealy would *crawl* every time; but Whitey did it only
once, jumping every time afterwards.

When running about, she is very independent in
her movements, and uses her front feet exactly as a
kangaroo might. I have often seen her hold on with
her hind feet, or stand up on them and reach her head
and forefeet away out, as if to reach something. Then
she will settle back again and scamper along. When
wide awake and running, her body is raised fully half
an inch from the floor; but when lazy, she drags her
body, feet, and tail, along on the same plane, in the lazi-
est possible way, her body touching the surface over
which she is crawling.

Harold frequently gives Whitey a ride upon one of
his toy-engines, or he will put her in a block-house as
he builds it, and in either case, or, for that matter, wherever he puts her, if contented, she will cuddle up into
a little ball and go to sleep. Sometimes she will play
peep with him in a very fascinating way. We took
Whitey with us to our summer home, where she lived
contentedly in my study, exploring every nook and
corner she could reach. Occasionally we would let her
go about the house. One time we found her down-
stairs in the pantry, possibly looking for cheese.

About three weeks after our return she had a family

DINNER FOR TWO

of seven brown mice, which delighted Harold. He fed
the mother every day, and watched the curious movements of the little ones. As they grew they got away.
It was impossible to tame them, and Whitey did not
seem to care for them as Harold expected she would.
She would run away from the nest we made for them,
and would try to keep away. And the little "Brownies,"
as Harold called them, disappeared one by one, to be
caught later, no doubt, in the mouse-trap down-stairs.
Whitey then seemed to become playful, as she had been
at first, but a cruel fate overtook her. One day a young
kitten belonging to Harold got into the study by acci-
dent. We found kitty seated comfortably in the corner
of a closet that mousie favored, and we thought she
looked as if she had been enjoying a very good meal.
But we hoped against hope, and for days we looked
for Whitey to come back. She never came, but we
often find kitty in the same corner of the closet looking very watchful. As Harold cries bitterly whenever
he hears of anything being hurt or killed, we have
let him think that Whitey has gone away on a visit,
from which she will no doubt return.

A white mouse is a dainty little pet, very interesting,
and giving little trouble—that is, if you can find one
that does not bite, as we have done.

The following is a favorite story of Harold's, embody-
ing our experience with training butterflies when he
was four years old, which I wrote and had published in
St. Nicholas:

BUTTERFLY PETS

It may seem very strange to hear of butterflies as
pets, but there is now in New York City a little boy

who had as pets, during September and November of last year, four Archippus butterflies, and the illustrations to this article were taken from these real models.

The Archippus is one of our largest butterflies, measuring from three to four and a half inches across its outspread wings. It appears in the latter part of July, and lives all through September, and sometimes into the early part of October, if the weather is mild and warm. It loves the sunshine, and has a very leisurely and graceful manner of flying about from flower to flower, as if it were enjoying everything to the utmost. Helen Conant tells us truly in her charming little book, *The Butterfly Hunters*, that there is no butterfly that takes such strong hold of one's fingers with its feet as the Archippus. It is not so bright in color as some others, but the wings are tawny orange, and are beautifully bordered with black dotted with white. Fine black veins cross the wings, and on the tip of the fore wing are several yellow and white spots extending up on the front border. The under sides of the wings are a deep yellow, bordered and veined like the upper sides. The head and the thorax, or chest part, are black, spotted with white, and the slender feelers or antennæ end in a long knob.

The little boy referred to above, whose name is Harold, was out in the fields near Bayonne, New Jersey, one sunny morning in September, playing with his usual companion, when they happened to meet two small "butterfly hunters" who had caught three very large Archippus butterflies.

Harold was charmed with the pretty creatures, and stood quite still, gazing eager-eyed and wistful. The older boy suggested that the boy who held the butter-

THE BUTTERFLY'S BATH

flies should give one to him, which was instantly and kindly done, and Harold heartily thanked them and took home his prize very carefully.

The idea then occurred to me to find out how long the butterfly would live if tenderly cared for; as recently a writer, in describing some captured butterflies, spoke of their short life, saying that from ten to fourteen days was the average.

Harold's first butterfly escaped, after a week, through an unnoticed crack in the window; but he had been taught to feed quietly from his finger, a glass, or a flower. He said at once, "We must go to look for another, or I will have to cry!" You must remember that he was only four years old.

He went into the fields again, and though he saw several small butterflies, found no Archippus, and met no boy-hunters. For a week the loss of his pet was mourned, and then a beautiful specimen was spied in a neighboring yard. Harold watched it from a window until it disappeared, and then begged his mother to go with him in search of it. On the way he interested several small boys in his quest, and they found the butterfly, secured him, and gave him to Harold, who brought him home in triumph. At home he found awaiting his return another Archippus, which had been caught by a boy who had heard he wanted one. Evidently all the boys in the neighborhood were interested, for the next day still another was brought. It took only one day to teach one of the new butterflies to eat the sugar syrup with which they were fed. The others waited several days before they seemed to understand what was being done.

In teaching them it was necessary to handle them

very gently, always closing the wings, and holding the butterfly by them near the head, releasing the feet very carefully at the same time with the other hand, as the Archippus clings very tenaciously, the feet having two fork-like claws which take a very strong hold of any rough surface. The butterflies slept on the lace curtains by the windows, and therefore, when lifted, had to be moved very cautiously. By putting a finger in front of the butterfly's antennæ, and touching one of them very lightly (as if to let the little creature know the finger was there), the butterfly would in almost every instance creep upon the extended finger, where, after one or two trials, he would sit contentedly, sipping his sugar-water.

One of Harold's pets used his front feet in a very impatient way, kicking out right and left, as if hunting for the finger which was usually there when he was ready to pay attention to cleaning his wings, body, and feet, after a meal of thick and sticky sugar-water. His washing was done very daintily, in a basin or bowl in which there was about a gill of water. At the same time he alternately projected and drew in the trunk-like proboscis with which he fed—which is altogether a remarkable and very interesting feature. When not in use, this organ is coiled up very closely, and when the butterfly is asleep the coil is so small that it can scarcely be seen. When feeding or taking his bath the butterfly frequently rolled his proboscis up half-way, and then opened it again and went on with what he was doing.

It was very curious to note the degree of intelligence shown by this butterfly during the six weeks of his life as a pet. It was a very pretty sight to see him sit in the bowl of water, now lapping, then picking all over

THE BUTTERFLY ON THE CURTAIN

his coat and wings, again taking a sip, and so on, until he seemed well satisfied with his condition, and flew away. He would alight upon the curtain, over which he crawled slowly, very likely to dry the under side of his body, which had touched the water; then he would close his wings, and take his usual afternoon nap. Before eating he was very active, fluttering about in the sunshine, up and down the curtains and about the room, and occasionally resting upon Harold's shoulder or hand, or on the floor, where he would bask in the sunshine with wide-open wings. Sometimes we would find him on the under side of the head of the sofa.

This butterfly's companion lived with him, feeding from the same glass and sleeping near him, in the same closet or on the curtain, for nearly three weeks, when, through inadvertence, the poor creature was left in a room for a moment where the gas had been lighted, and he sealed his own doom by flying through the blaze. He fell to the floor, apparently unhurt, but we soon learned that he could not live.

The third butterfly brought to Harold escaped through the same space between the windows that gave liberty to the first one. They would flutter up and down the windows in the sunshine, except when resting upon the curtains, and in this way two of them got between the sashes—the lower one having been raised to give room for the window-screen—and escaped. A week after the first three were brought, another boy came with a fine Archippus, which eventually broke his wing. We brought Harold's pets to New York, in a covered and well-ventilated box, where a compassionate druggist etherized the broken-winged butterfly. Harold feared he was suffering, and was glad to see him die. It

was soon after this that the other butterfly flew through
the gas, and then we had only one, and the season was
too far advanced to catch any more.   This butterfly
was fed once a day with honey, and was allowed to fly
about in the sunshine whenever that was possible.   He
was also put away very carefully at night in a dark
closet, where he liked to sleep resting upon some soft
material.   If put down upon the shelf, he would flutter
about in the dark until he found something soft.   At
one place, during their travels, the three butterflies slept
on the window, behind the curtains, and in the morning
they would begin their fluttering as soon as the sunshine came.   The life of the last butterfly was prolonged
for several weeks by great care, but eventually he suc-
cumbed to three days of rain while we were travelling,
and he had no sunny curtain upon which to bask.
Harold mourned the loss of his pet for a long time.

SPONTANEOUS WRITING FROM MEMORY

"TWO TIMES TWO"

MUSIC

A FAMILY PORTRAIT

THE BEGINNINGS OF A NAVY

1895 AND 1896 DRAWINGS

1895—Printed work from memory ; working out the two table ; music from memory ;
free-hand efforts ; two views of a war boat. 1896—The *Valkyrie*.

CHAPTER VI

NUMBER - WORK — COMPOSITION — FANCY — THE STORY
OF HIS STUFFED KITTY — THE ADVENTURES OF A
LADY-BUG

MAY 23, 1895.—Harold is now five years old. He works at numbers in a very curious way. He just sang to himself: "I wonder how many thumbs there are in the world. But *I* know. Mamma doesn't know. She has two and I have two, and that makes four in this room." Then he said, "And that's all *we* know." Then he counted up fourteen thumbs in the house, for seven people.

A few days ago he wanted to find out how many pennies he needed to make a dollar. He had seventy-four cents. He marked on a slip of paper from 70 to 100, and then beginning at 74 as 1, he counted up to 100, putting down each number from 1 to 15, then counting verbally, as if he had found it was not necessary to write out each number (see illustration facing p. 182). He then announced triumphantly that he needed twenty-six pennies to make a dollar. There were two persons in the room to whom he could have applied had he cared to ask, but he seems to prefer to help himself when he can, and we do not interfere. He does not suspect that he is doing anything unusual, therefore he is always ready to explain.

He said the other day, "Is the sun Jesus's light?"

To-day we heard him say, "Six and three are nine; six and four are ten." His aunt asked him how he knew it. He replied, "I know that six and three are nine, and four is one more than three, and ten is next to nine, so it *must* be so." Then he turned to his mother and said, "Mamma, when you get me a rule again, get me a five-inch or a ten-inch rule" (instead of the regular foot-rule, which puzzled him), "because I can count then 5—10—15—20—25."

The following is an effort at composition:

NEW YORK, *November* 26, 1895.
—— West —— Street.

DEAR PAPA,—I am in bed, and mamma is writing this for me because I want to write you a letter. I told her to put the date and all, the place where we are, and to tell you all about what I am doing, so you can know just what your little boy is doing all the time.

Good-bye, dear papa, with my love,

Your dear little boy,

HAROLD.

Some time between October and December we found among his papers the accompanying efforts at numbers (see illustration facing p. 166). He is evidently working out the two table for himself.

He has learned to count to a thousand with very little effort, by simply asking questions. We taught him numbers by direct teaching from one to ten; the rest he reasoned out for himself by asking occasional questions. At first he thought of numbers as meaning only one to nine; then he wanted to know what came next. We counted with him to twenty, and I explained that after he reached ten it was the same thing over again, only he must say ten instead of one and naught, and eleven instead of one and one, and so on. I did this because I

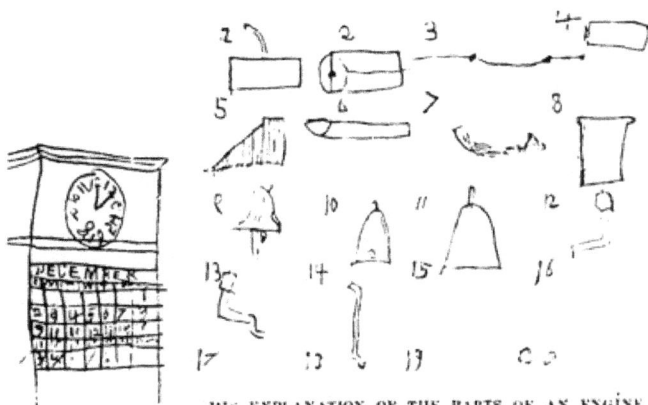

HIS EXPLANATION OF THE PARTS OF AN ENGINE

HIS DEVELOPMENT DURING HIS FIFTH YEAR IN
FREE HAND DRAWING—FROM A COPY

DEAR.PAPA. I.WANT.A.
FOR. MY. REZERVOIR.

EARLY PRINTING—HOW HE ASKED FOR A DERRICK

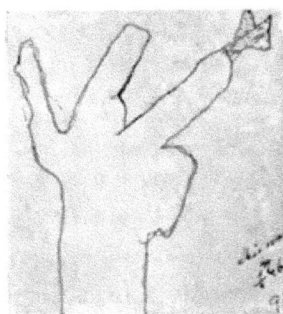

HIS PET BUTTERFLY

A. B. C. went out to tea.
    D. E. F. were reely to har
G. H. I. exclaimed "Oh my"
    J. K. L. didn't feel very well.
M. N. O. didn't want to go
    P. Q. R. SAID. IT WAS too FAR.
2.T.U. HAD. SOME LESSONS. To. DO.
AND. W. SAD, "WE. WON'T. TROUBLE. YOU
X.Y.Z. STAYED. AT. HOME. INSTEAD!

EARLY PRINTING

1895 DRAWINGS

Parts of an engine. Free-hand drawing of clock and ducks from copy. How the child
asked for a derrick. The child's drawing of his pet butterfly feeding. Early printing,
from copy.

feared he was too young to attempt to teach him about units, tens, and hundreds by name. I also told him that when he reached nineteen it began in the same way again, only with two instead of one, saying he must use twenty, then twenty-one, etc. He then asked what came after twenty-nine. I said he should use three, four, and five, and so on in the same way as he had used two in twenty. He then began by himself, counting up to ninety-nine, but saying three-ty and five-ty for thirty and fifty, until I corrected him. For a long time after this he thought only of numbers as consisting of one or two figures—as, for instance, 8 or 24, and he was perfectly satisfied to go no further than ninety-nine when counting for his own amusement. It was at this stage of his number-work that I found him interested in copying printed numbers. He asked me one day for a book that began at page 1. After a long search I found an old paper novel that began with page 1 on the opening page of the story, instead of beginning, as books usually do, with page 5 or 6. This book I gave to him for his own. For two weeks I saw him at various times lying upon the floor with it, a pencil, and also his *Slovenly Peter* book. I did not trouble to look into what he was doing, for he seemed content; and when at the end of this time he came to me and said that *Slovenly Peter* had forty-four pages, I was very much surprised. I thought he might have guessed it, so I turned to page 33 and asked him what page it was. He answered correctly at once. Then I looked into the matter further, and found that he had taken his pencil and had copied from page 1 to 44 in the novel, and had put the numbers at the foot of the page in *Slovenly Peter*. By doing this, counting and comparing with the printed number above, he had learned the appearance of numbers. I said nothing more about the matter at the time, but from this on I noticed that he always knew numbers when he saw them. One day when on the train he saw a passing car with the number 324 on its side. He instantly asked what three numbers together meant. I told him then about hundreds, explaining that after 99 came 100, 101, and so on the same way up. This satisfied him for a long time; but one day, when on the street, he noticed a house numbered 2105, and asked me what four numbers together meant. I then explained about a thousand coming after 999, and so on up to millions, billions, trillions, quadrillions, etc., and about adding three more naughts to each one. These terms seemed to take his fancy, and he often asked about their order; and one day he came to me and exclaimed: "I could count to quadrillions if I had time enough, couldn't I? A quadrillion has fifteen ciphers." This was before he was six years old.

Dr. Preyer thought the child was mistaken in the number of ciphers, and wrote: "If the child exclaims at this age that 'A quadrillion has fifteen ciphers,' this wrong statement should not be mentioned. . . . If he had worked it out by threes, then he would have found twenty-four ciphers; a million having six, a thousand millions nine, a billion twelve, a thousand billions fifteen, a trillion eighteen, a thousand trillions twenty-one, a quadrillion twenty-four. It would have been rather remarkable if he had found this by himself."

Dr. Harris explains, however, that the child was right, for Dr. Preyer counted by the Continental method, and the child referred to in the record had his questions answered according to American counting. (The record

1895 ENGINE DRAWINGS — FIVE YEARS OLD

also shows how at six years of age he found out for himself that he could count to hundreds on the type-writer by using the figures 1 to 9 and the letter o.)

He took up printed letters in the same easy way that he worked out numbers, and thus learned the alphabet, as may be seen from the various illustrations relating to this phase, learning to read and spell, eventually, by the aid of memory and by comparison of the words he knew from memory with the printed words before him. (See illustrations facing p. 166.) His illustrated books of pigs, cats, and dogs, etc., furnished him with sufficient material for this sort of work, and his interest was kept up by the illustrations, and sufficient admixture of out-door play to create a desire for in-door amusement.

His efforts at figure-drawing (free-hand) in his fifth year show steady improvement, as may be seen from illustrations facing p. 168.

His continued interest in mechanical work, boats, etc., may be seen from illustrations facing p. 168. The cut was given just as represented, in response to the request of a playmate of five, who said he did not know the parts of an engine, whereupon he drew the parts and gave the name of each part as noted, giving at the same time a graphic description of how each part worked.

December 10.—This evening Harold was very anxious to use my type-writer. My stenographer cautioned him not to touch it—this was before he had learned to use it — and we heard him say to his playmate, another little boy, "Come away, Leo; when you keep looking at it, it tempts you to touch it, and it is better to go away." We allowed him shortly after to try, and he soon mastered the intricacies of the machine. He asked this evening about seeing faces going up and down when going to sleep; he described one as round, with two dots for eyes, and a straight nose and mouth, that all changed to two marks across each other like this ≠≠, illustrating by crossed fingers. Miss B—— said to him to-day in the basement of a toy-store, "Come, Harold, let us go, it is so close in here." He replied, "Close to what?"

He is full of fancy, and he invests his stuffed kitty with every loving attribute he can think of. To-day he said to her, "Step over yourself, kitty." Then he went on: "There are two ways of walking over yourself. I can step on myself, step one foot on the other, that's touching myself." Then he said that kitty replied, "I can't, unless I put my feet over my head, and that would hurt my nose and eyes." This same kitty was his "darling" for nearly four years (until he was seven years old), and at the end of that time she was not discarded because of lack of love, but because a boy visitor broke her neck and back and she had to go to the hospital. He sent the boy home, and wrote him a note telling him to never come again. On kitty's back I found a handkerchief bandage with a slip of paper pinned to it on which was written the fact that kitty had been hurt (see illustration facing p. 192.)

She was taken to bed with him every night during this entire period of devotion; when in trouble he would go to her, clasp her in his arms, and say, in heart-rending tones, "*Oh*, my kitty!" No one was allowed to speak slightingly to her, and he even begged his mother not to let the boys laugh at her. When the cotton in her neck became displaced he instantly seized upon the idea that the limp condition allowed her to bend her head and say good-morning, which he would cause

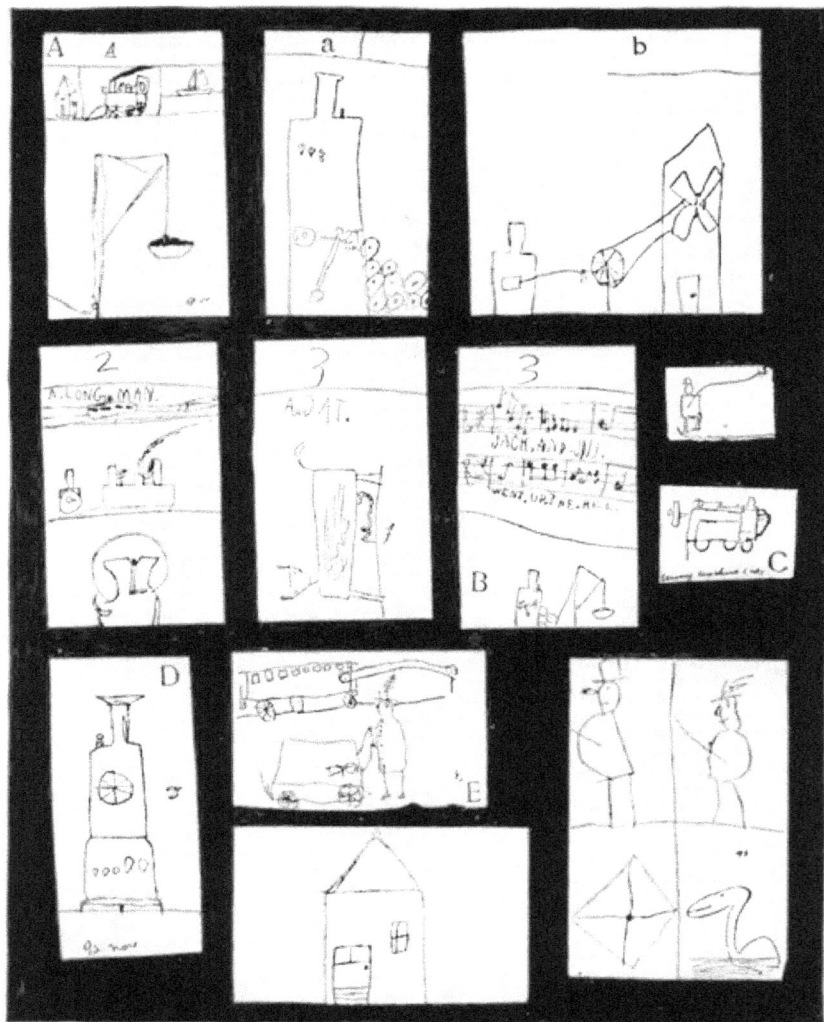

1895 DRAWINGS—FIVE YEARS OLD

a, stationary engine; b, windmill worked by cylinder connecting with a; A, a dredger; B, "stationary engine attached to a dredger"; C, upper part of a sewing-machine; D, alcohol engine; E, man wheeling a baby in coach.

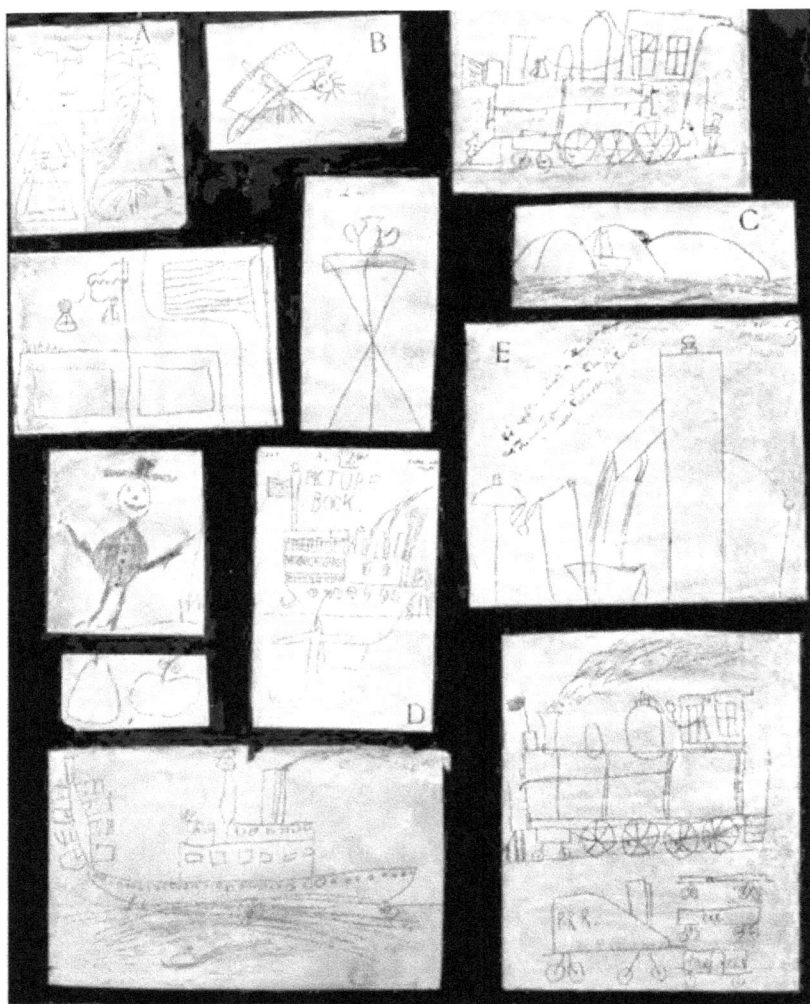

1895 DRAWINGS—FIVE YEARS OLD

A, "the way to hang a bell on an engine"; B, boat going over sand bar; C, boat going between two mountains; D, boat with anchor (note size of anchor); E, "this is a pump, and the water pulls down the weight to make the clapper hit the bell."

her to do every morning. His conversations with her
at night and early morning were frequent and very
charming. He always pretended that she was answering him in a squeaky voice. She grew very dim
about the face from much hugging, and her neck eventually gave way from many "good-mornings;" so in-
numerable "stitches" had to be taken, until at last even
Harold saw that no more could be taken. Then for a
long time he submitted to a great break in her body
from the neck down, about two inches in length; but
even this was for a purpose, for he frequently showed
me through this break how her "heart" would move.
(A piece of the cotton inside did move every time he
made kitty move a certain way.) As the features faded
out, he kept appealing to me to say whether I did not
think she looked "so gentle," "so smiling," and whenever any one of his numerous friends presented him with
a *new* stuffed kitty—no doubt because the old one suggested the gift—he invariably *re*-presented the new kitty
to some one else and clung to his "darling," as he called
her. At last it seemed to dawn upon him that she was
failing, and he suggested that I take him to see some
covers for stuffed kitties, and find out whether he could
get a "smiling" one. I remember he comforted himself afterwards with the thought that if kitties had
nine lives he could use nine covers. We found a cover
that to him seemed smiling. It was in a country store,
where goods are likely to be shop-worn, and this kitty-
cover had seen its best days before he bought it. I prepared to cover the old kitty, but I had to compromise
on closing the lower edges with a large safety-pin in
such a manner that he could uncover his "darling"
whenever she wanted to talk to him. For several weeks

173

he fancied that she couldn't hear him when he talked to her, but I assured him she could; so eventually he uncovered her very seldom, but the safety-pin was a fixture to the end of her existence as a comrade. When we were ready to travel anywhere, kitty always went along, and if there was no room in the travelling-bag, he would kiss her good-bye and place her *on top* in one of the trunks, in order, as he said, that she could breathe and would not be squeezed. Once he carried her in his arms on a long journey and showed her everything he thought of interest. During the day, while he was at play, she was propped up in his crib and told to wait for him, that he would come back again at night, etc. When he wanted to find her for consolation, he knew just where to go every time, and woe betide the person who couldn't find "my kitty." I well remember a trip by candle-light to bring her in from the fence at the extreme end of the garden, where she had been placed during the day to watch Harold "dig at his reservoir," that occupied him three years, and amused not only him but all his numerous playmates. Once it would be a reservoir, another time a cellar to a house, once a sand-pile —for which he bought two loads of sand—again a garden, once even a cemetery, where a funeral over Dollie was held in great state. To us it always seemed to be a great big hole, to be refilled in time. Kitty had to superintend all these operations, and indeed his entire little life seemed divided in its interests between kitty and himself, and no amount of badinage, to which he was often subject from those who were beyond our control, would disturb this loyalty to his " darling kitty."

The following is a favorite story of his that I told to him just before the election of President McKinley,

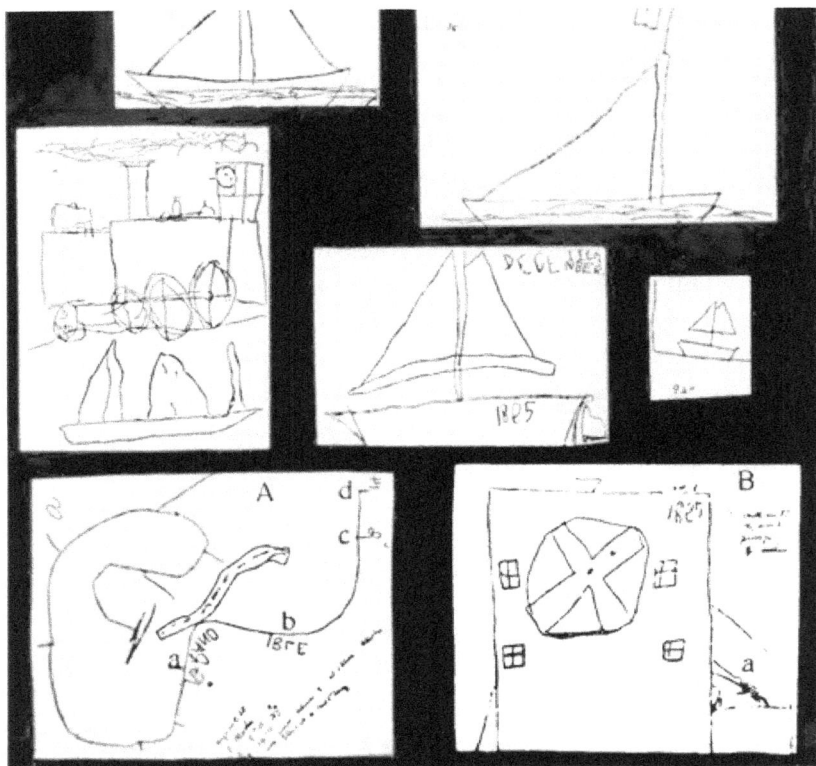

1895 DRAWINGS—FIVE YEARS OLD

A, elevated railroad from South Ferry—a, Grand Street; b, Bleecker Street; c, Eighth Street; d, Fourteenth Street. Note curve between Eighth Street and Bleecker Street, as it should be. When four years old the child could tell all the stations from South Ferry to Fifty-eighth Street from memory; B, windmill to work the pump from which the water, a, is pouring.

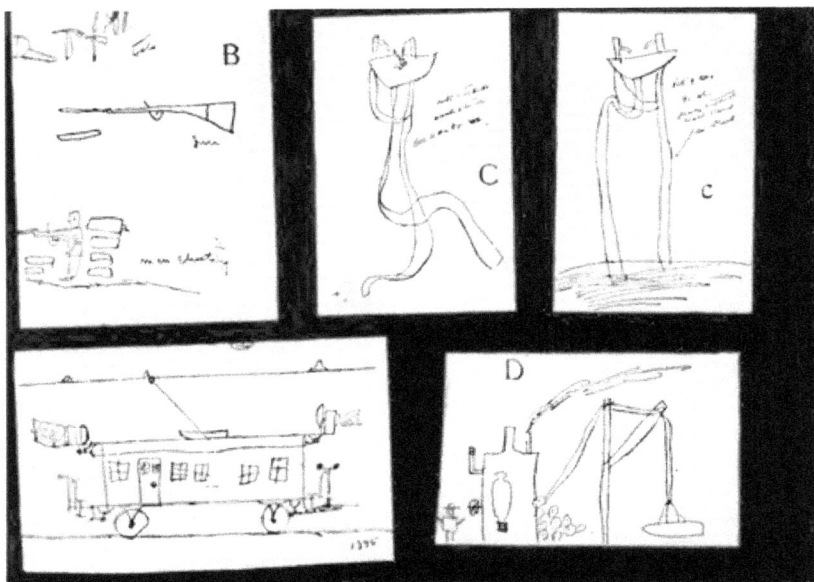

1895 DRAWINGS—FIVE YEARS OLD

A, Market Street car in Philadelphia ; B, tools and a man shooting ; C, well trapped wash stand ; c, poorly trapped wash stand ; D, hoisting-engine for derrick.

when he was very much interested in the remarks he heard so frequently about gold and silver. The story is based upon our experience, and is one of many that I used to interest him when I could not find printed stories that were simple enough to suit my purpose. His constant plea was to read to him stories that he could understand, and to *read* them understandingly, even if they were not printed thus; but he begged me to do so quickly and not stop and explain. He wanted the simple words, but if compelled to choose, preferred to hear the difficult words without a break in his listening, to hearing simple words with explanations.

THE ADVENTURES OF A LADY-BUG

[*Told by herself to Mrs. Fly, on the window-pane*]

I was creeping along the pavement last Friday afternoon, very quietly, and quite intent on my own business, on my way to see Mrs. Gold-bug and her little daughter, when I felt myself lifted, carefully, it is true, but still lifted, away up into the air. It seemed to me as if it might be as high as up to the sky. But it couldn't have been, for after hearing myself admired I was put into a house of some sort that was made of paper, for I know what paper is, having heard it rustle many a time. This paper house had four corners, and one corner was torn off and folded crosswise so as to give me some air. I happen to know this, because while I was being admired I heard what must have been a little boy's voice say, "Oh, mamma, let us keep it and take care of it like we did the butterflies," and I suppose the person who picked me up must have been his mamma, for I

175

heard some one say, "I don't see how we can, for we are going to the park, and what can we do with her, dear little lady-bug. Oh, I see; I will tear off a corner of the envelope of this letter I intended to post, and we can carry her nicely in this until we reach home again. See, Harold, she can get air through this corner even when I hold it shut, this way." So that is how I knew it.

What I thought to be rooms of a paper house was really the folded letter. I do *not* think that I was very foolish in believing this, Mrs. Fly, although you may think so; yet, after all, it was only a letter in a common envelope. What a queer world this is! And then the distance, too, that I supposed I was being carried when I was lifted from the pavement! Instead of its being very, very great, as I supposed, it was only about half the length of one of those queer-looking creatures I used to see walking along the streets every day, and that I heard one day were called men and women. That's what comes of being so little—everything seems so *very* big. Since I am to live here, now, I suppose I will never see many more of those queer creatures; still I may have a happier time of it than I have had lately. I heard voices everywhere, some time ago, talking about silver and gold and about hard times. I'm sure there must be some very queer reason for my trouble in finding the little I need to eat—a thing that has never happened before in my long life of almost a hundred days.

When I was carried to the park to-day (I wonder what park means?), I heard the little boy say to his mother a great many curious things that I could not understand at all. I have a pretty good memory (that is how I know I have lived a hundred days), and I

1895 BOAT DRAWINGS—FIVE YEARS OLD

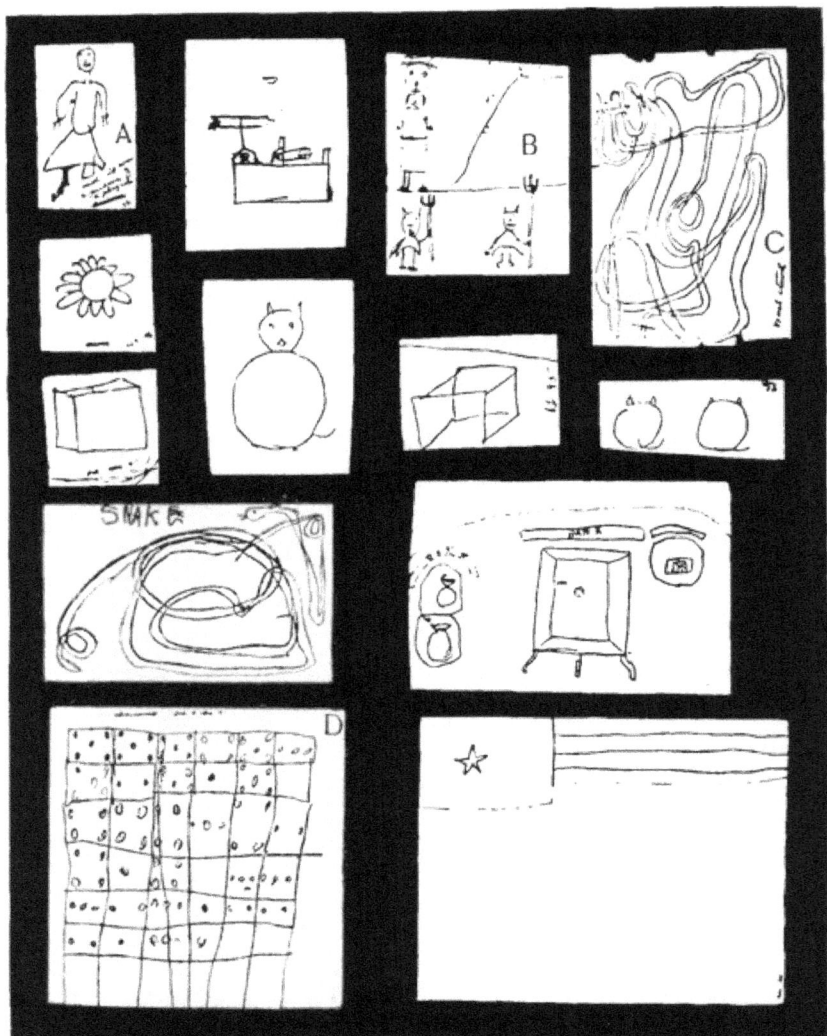

1895 DRAWINGS—FIVE YEARS OLD

A, he said, was a picture of a playmate—I can trace a resemblance in the face ; B, Satan ; C, well trapped wash-stand ; D, dominoes, which he frequently drew and cut out for use in play

think I can tell you some of the sentences he said.
Maybe *you* will know what they mean. He began by saying "Mamma!" with a shriek—so he could be heard, no
doubt, as the noise of the trains and other things was
terrible — "Mamma, *will* we go up in the elevated?
Have you the lady-bug? *Isn't* it a dear little thing?"
(I understood that.) "Oh, mamma, here's Fifty-eighth
Street; *will* we go to see the animals?" (That made me
shudder, for I knew what some animals do who like to
eat insects.) "Oh, mamma, there's the swan-boat; can't
we take a ride? Let me pay. I have money. Can't
we, mamma?" (I wonder what a swan-boat is.) I
heard the mother say, "Yes, dear," and pretty soon I
felt that we were gliding along as gently as I have
often sailed on a leaf on a pond, and it was really delightful. I imagine this was somewhere in the park
spoken of, which the little boy (whose name seemed to
be Harold) once called Central Park. There must have
been a baby sitting beside me, for I heard Harold's
mother tell him to look at a kitten on the bank, and
the mother of the baby said, "Look at the kitty, daughter," and Harold laughed loud because the baby looked
straight up to the sky. I heard him say, laughing loud,
"Kitty isn't up in the sky, mamma." The baby's mamma laughed too, but Harold's mamma said, "Never mind,
baby."

Pretty soon I heard somebody ask to be let off at the
upper end of the lake, as they called it. (What is a
lake?) Some one said, "*If* we can make a landing."
Then we had a good shaking up, and I was a little bit
frightened, for I felt we were getting out of the boat
very cautiously. I happen to know what it means to
be upset in water. One day, when I was sailing on the

pond, the wind turned over the leaf I was on, and I thought I was going to drown. Fortunately I struck a stick of wood in my struggles to save myself, and crawled up on top of it, and stayed there until a big leaf came floating by near enough for me to fly to it, which I did very quickly. When I reached the bank of the pond I made up my mind to stay away from the water—for a while, at any rate, much as I like sailing on a leaf—for I *now* think it is dangerous.

Soon after we landed we heard terrible noises, and Harold said, "Oh, mamma, see the baby hippopotamus! Isn't it a dear little thing?" (I thought they were *big*— *I* am little.) "Isn't it too sweet for anything? See its feet and its eyes. Oh, mamma, see its mother helping it get into the water! Isn't she a *good* mother?" and so he went on. He was talking all the time. I couldn't understand what he meant half of the time, and I wished so much I could see it all. Once he said, "Oh, mamma, see the baby tiger winking to me! Isn't he beautiful?" (I wonder what winking means.)

I heard him talk of polar-bears, grizzly-bears, prairie-dogs, and hyenas, camels, and dromedaries, and I really can't remember what all. I remember he said, "Mamma, don't you think the camel is beautiful? I do. See the way he moves." He seemed to pity the animals that were in cages. He couldn't understand why they had to be brought away from their homes just to let people know what they look like. I heard his mamma say that she didn't believe God meant it to be so, and I believe she is right. I felt sure she would be good to me and feed me after hearing that.

When we came here she let me out very carefully, and I have had a lovely time for several days, going

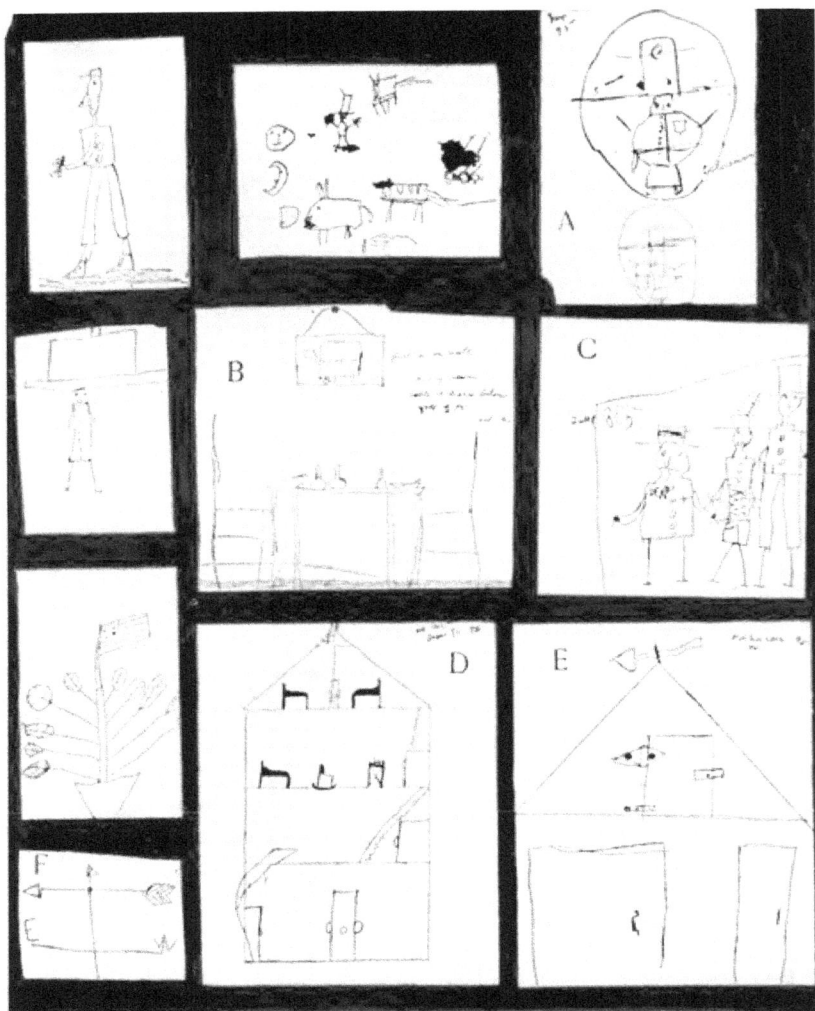

1895 DRAWINGS—FIVE YEARS OLD

A, policeman ; B, dining room, table, dishes, and picture on the wall ; C, inverted 9 in 1895— pictures of papa, mamma, and Harold ; D, inside of a house ; E, outside of a house ; F, weather-vane.

about the rooms. Every day she hunts me up and gives me something to eat and drink. At first I felt afraid she would drown me with the water, but she seemed to know I couldn't take much, for she poured a few drops quite near to me on the window-sill, and I went close and sipped all I needed. The water looked like a wall, almost as high as I was, but it didn't come tumbling over me as I expected it would. I wonder why?

When I was fed she put me on a plate of fruit. I heard her tell Harold it was fruit, and I had the most delicious dinner. I found it inside of a grape-skin. I knew it was that, for I heard her say to Harold, "You should have seen the dear little lady-bug eating her dinner."

He said, "Where did she get it?"

She said, "I put her on a plate of fruit, and I found her eating inside of a skin of a grape that I put there for her."

A little girl was here the other day who must have been very wicked, for she said she would kill me. Harold took me up gently and ran away down-stairs to his mamma and told her all about it. She took me from him carefully and told the little girl how wicked it was to hurt any living thing. The little girl seemed to be sorry, and said she didn't mean it, but I hope she will never come here any more. It isn't nice to have persons like that about one. It makes one frightened.

Harold seems to like to watch me when I clean my feet and wings every morning. To-day I showed him how I reached up on my back with my foot and rubbed off any specks of dust that might happen to be there. I also cleaned my head with what he calls the forks on the ends of my front feet. He likes to watch me get

179

ready to fly, too, which I do sometimes just to please him and to keep in practice. I push my hind wings far out at the back of my body, and he says they look like a little pointed tail before they are spread; then I spread them at the same time that I spread the front ones that make my shell-cover, and away I go. I hear him say every time, "Oh, see, mamma! Isn't that pretty? Isn't she sweet?" He often speaks of the beautiful black spots that I have on the back of my shell wings. He says, "Two on each side, and one where the split is." (I wonder what he means by "split.")

To-morrow I am going to fly up on the window and see the sunshine that I love so much. Yesterday I saw the window was open, and I might have flown away, but I didn't want to do it. There is so much to see and learn here that I like to stay. Maybe to-morrow I will go and ask Mrs. Gold-bug what all the voices talking about silver and gold mean. She ought to know.

1895 CUTTINGS—FIVE YEARS OLD

A bottle in two parts; B violin case—colored green in the original; C, c, two sides of bell—gilded in original; D, d, parts of an engine—cut work to fold and place.

CHAPTER VII

SEVENTH YEAR — LEARNING GERMAN, WRITING, AND
    SPELLING THROUGH PLAY — A BEDTIME QUESTION
    TALK — COMPARISON QUESTIONS AND ANSWERS —
    THE CHILD'S SONG TO HIS COLORS — TWO STORIES
    TOLD BY THE CHILD

July 29, 1896.—His prayer: "Dear God, I want you
to keep the good good, and make the bad good, and I
thank you very much for bringing papa back safely,
and I want you to take care of me in the night-time,
and I thank you very much for letting me pass all the
day so happily."

He was taught the Lord's Prayer by rote, in order that
he might not feel chagrined if he ever had occasion to
join others in saying it in kindergarten schools. The
third time of repetition he had to be helped once only
by supplying "on earth." He insisted on having each
phrase of the Lord's Prayer explained to him.

August 1st.—To-day Harold said, as is usual under
similar circumstances, "The step made me go up." He intended going around the side of the house with a playmate, but from habit he stepped up on the front porch as
he passed it. He instantly stepped down again and went
with her, but she teased him about it, and he replied
in a usual fashion that "it made him do it." I never
understood this remark before, but now I see clearly
what he meant when he said, as he often did, that some-

181

thing *made* him do thus or so—he means his *usual habit* leads him one way when he *wills* another way.

August 7th.—To-day he came in fretting about having no one with whom to play. It was intensely warm. I had been reading about the *Herald* Ice Fund, and I read to him about the sick babies in the slums, and said he should be happy by contrast with his happy home. I inadvertently roused a great storm of sympathy. He cried bitterly, ran crying audibly to the other end of the house, to the nursery, and back again, when he handed me a penny, saying, between his sobs, "Send it to the babies." It was half of all he had at the time. I tried to pacify him, and told him of all the good people who helped take care of the poor children; but he cried for a long time, and wondered pitifully why God let them suffer.

He said to William, a playmate, "You know God, who lives up in heaven; well—part of him is a spirit, called the Holy Ghost. There *is* such a thing as a spirit that isn't a ghost."

September 9th.—He said to me just now, "Plated silver is nickel washed in melted silver, isn't it?"

September 11th. — Harold asked me to-day what "absorb" meant, and how frogs absorbed moisture. I had just been telling him that frogs came out on rainy days for a drink, when they would absorb the rain through little holes in their bodies. He listened intently to my explanation, then said, as he was eating some bread and milk, "See, my bread absorbs the milk."

September 16th.—When going to New York to-day he said, as he stood in the aisle, "Mamma, the faster the train goes the easier it is to stand; it goes over the bumps quicker." Then, pointing to the sign "Drinking-

1896 DRAWINGS

A—When telling me what this was, he said, "I don't like to say that out loud — when I drew it, I used to read fairy stories — it was drawn for a ghost"; B, b, pages of music book; C, horse-car—when drawing it, he asked me whether it wasn't the best horse he had ever drawn; D, "a deaf man who is lame — he is supposed to be listening through ear-trumpets to a and b, and he is standing on c, which helps him move about by machinery inside."

water," he said, "Don't they know it's drinking-water?"
She said, "Yes." Then he said, "Why do they put the
sign up?"

His questions to-day were chiefly about words. He
came to me at different times with the following, asking
what each meant: "saliva," "materials," "natural history," "boast," and "indestructible." He cannot understand why some of his toy-books are called "indestructible" when they can be destroyed. He often asks me
about it.

October 2d.—He said to-night, when in bed, "I put
my hands over my eyes, and I see the loveliest colors;
and I say, colors, please come back until I go to sleep."
Then he began to sing:

> "Dear colors, please come back,
> Until I go to sleep.
> I will never see you again,
> Until I eat a big ben.

> "Dear colors, please come back,
> I'll never disturb you again,
> Until day dawn brings the light.

> "You darling little colors gay,
> Make the prettiest ones you ever had."

Then he fell asleep.

The following is a song of Harold's when falling asleep
after a day of mental pressure in a primary school—
before he was seven—where he was placed against his
mother's better judgment, but in deference to the opinion
of an educational authority, who saw and acknowledged
the error after two days' experience with the child.
At the end of each day he seemed intoxicated with the
charm of learning, and was very much excited — too
much so to fall asleep until several hours after his usual

183

bedtime. The second night he began singing to himself about his colors, as he calls them, as follows, singing every word in a very pretty manner:

"Red, orange, yellow, green, blue, and purple;"

then, in a very unconscious, sleepy way:

"Oh, you darling little colors, come back, come back,
Until I go asleep,
And make another picture.
      Tra-la, la-la, la-la.

"Come red, come orange, come yellow, come green,
Come blue, and purple:
Oh, make another diamond of purple and of blue.

"Oh, colors, come from your little coaches,
You darling little colors! I am sorry to say,
You get in your cabs and drive right home.
I hope you will have happy days.
Good-bye, good-bye, my colors dear, dear, dear, dear."

Between the last two stanzas he sang:

"Tra-la, la-la, la-la,
My pussy-cat lies down by me.
Oh, you dear pussy-cat, I like your hat!
      Tra-la, la-la, la-la."

Then he fell asleep instantly.

Another night, apropos of the color song, he said:

"Black turns to navy-blue; then there came red and light-blue and pink, and now it is so many I can't tell you all, but it is beautiful; now it is red and green, a red spot with green about it; now it is green with red dots in it running through the black; then black; now it is white and brown, gray and white, black with white dots; now it's green, with blue in it; now all green." Then he slept, but first he said, after ceasing his remarks

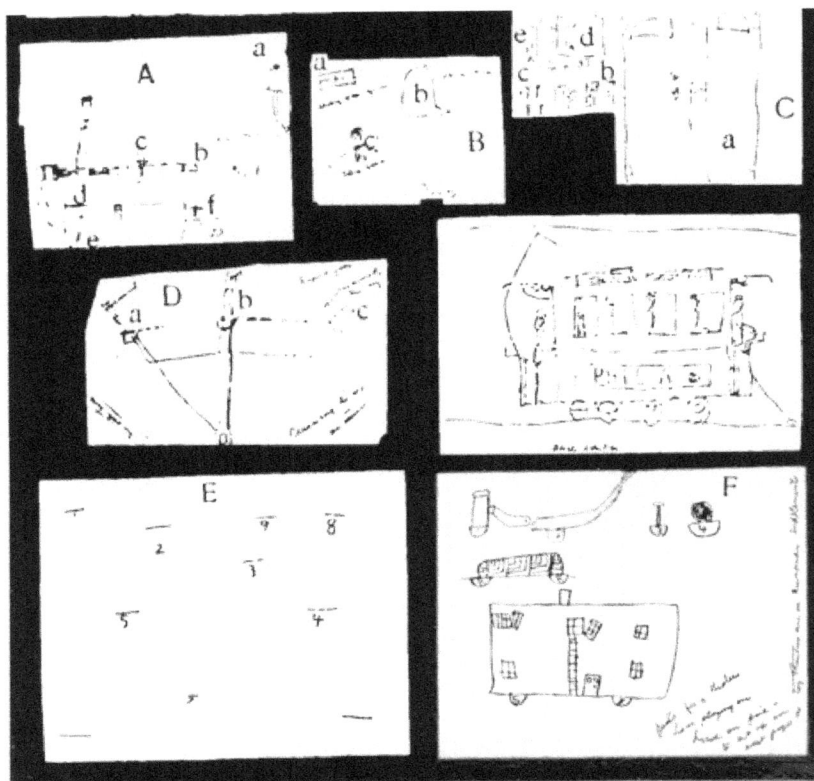

1896 DRAWINGS—SIX YEARS OLD

A, filtering machine; a, pump; b, one of series of filters; c, screws to open or shut off water; d, water-tank to heat and Pasteurize water by lamp e, below; f, faucet to tap water; B, parts of engine; a, sliding of the cylinder; b, steam drum; c, safety valve; C—a, door; b, hinges; c, screws; d, lock; e, key; D, reversing lever on train; a, "engine goes forward"; b, "engine stops"; c, "engine goes backward when this way"; E, plan for theatre stage; F, parts for the theatre—hose playing on house on fire.

about the colors, "Oh, isn't it funny? I saw lots of bubbles when I opened my eyes, and I couldn't see you
through them."

One of his rhymes at this time was, "She gathers the
trees as if they were bees, and takes her ease so good,
so good." Another rhyme I heard the other day
was, "Put the magical corn on your head, and that will
make you dead."

One night, when singing to himself "*Dies' ist die Mut-
ter lieb und gut,*" he sang it in German first, then in English; then he tried to say the words without the music,
and succeeded with the German, but when he reached
the third line of the English words he had to sing it to
get it; then he repeated it again and again until he felt
sure of it. In this way he goes over his day's acquire-
ments while falling asleep—sings, talks, and counts to
himself—and occasionally tries to get me to answer a
question. Not many days ago, when I supposed he was
asleep, we heard him call out, "How much is twice
thirty-four?" I told him. He repeated my answer, and
soon fell asleep. I never knew what led up to the question, but he often asks disconnected questions like the
above, after a period of quiet, during which his brain is
apparently at work over something that puzzles him.
He has taken a fancy lately to have me spell words that
are new to him, without pronouncing them, in order
that he may guess at them by the sound of the letters.

One day I gave him "s-h-o-e," and told him *oe* was pronounced like *oo* in too, and to put the sound *sh* in front.
He tried it several times before he got the word right,
and was then very much pleased to find he could spell
shoe. We then tried "p-l-e-a-s-e" in the same way, which

at first he got as "place." In this way he is learning how to spell many words while he plays, and he now reads a number of short easy sentences. He has a fashion now of spelling all the words he knows how to spell when telling us something—as, for instance, "M-a-m-m-a, come t-o d-i-n-n-e-r." Then she spells "come" for him, and he has one word more. Sometimes I take up a word like "grew," for instance, give him the sounds, and ask him for the word. He first called grew "ga-rew," then tried it faster, and eventually was delighted to find it was a word of which he knew the meaning. This knowledge he gains very easily with play that he enjoys.

Once he asked me what "a-p-e-n" spelled. I said it was no word; then he tried again, and said "a-p-r-n." I said again it was no word, although I knew what he was trying to spell. Then he said, impatiently, "Well, how *do* you spell apron?" Then I told him.

He will take a word like "old," or any simple word he knows, and, beginning with the first letter of the alphabet, he will spell to himself and try to pronounce each combination, thus: *a*-o-l-d, *b*-o-l-d, *c*-o-l-d, *d*-o-l-d, *e*-o-l-d, *f*-o-l-d, etc., all the way through to z. He tells me this is how he is learning all by himself how to spell new words. He often does this before falling asleep, and often asks me some such question as whether "e-o-l-d" makes a word, not recognizing it as such from the sounds of the letters.

October 4th.—"Mamma, you wouldn't say a *Ecke*—but, *das ist ein Ecke*." I heard him saying to himself to-day, "boa-constrictor," then "hug," and "bones," as if he were puzzling about them. He is always inquiring about words, why they are called thus and so. He asked

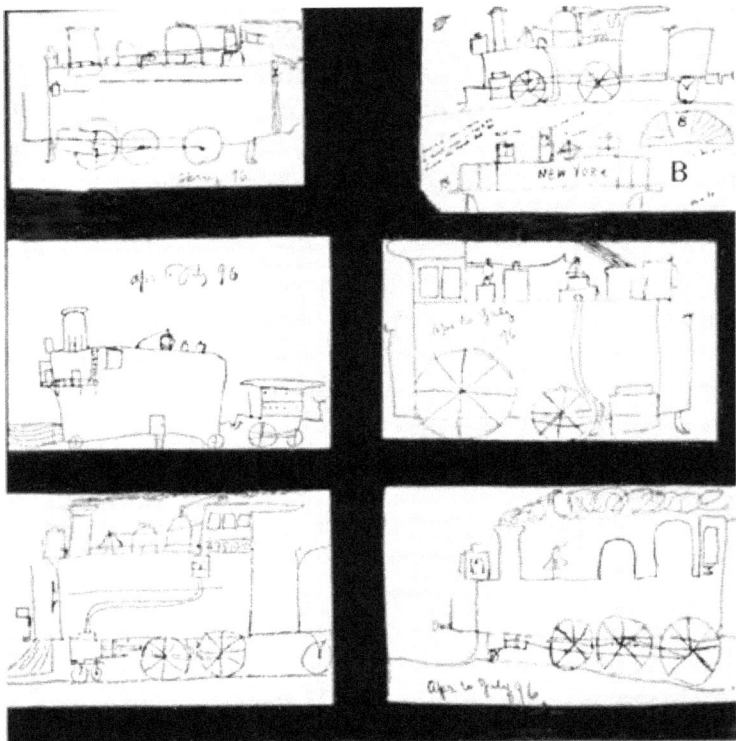

1896 DRAWINGS—SIX YEARS OLD

A. "an engine facing you on the track," with the child's explanations ; B, a key-stone.

to-day, "What does hemisphere mean — half round?" The circle of his engine track suggested it. He set the track upon the edge of two chairs to make an elevated railroad, after having run it contentedly on the table for a long time. He is fertile in invention and adaptation. To-day he repeated the entire story of "The Old Woman and her Crooked Sixpence" without a pause, and when he reached the part where, after the cat had "drinken" the milk (as he said), "the cat began to kill the rat, the rat began to gnaw the rope," etc., etc., he grew breathless and excited and could hardly say it fast enough, it seemed. He called the pig a "piggie wiggie," and omitted the word "yonder," explaining that he feared the little children wouldn't understand what it meant. He always has so much trouble himself to find stories that he can understand from beginning to end that he sympathizes with others in this respect. He has had no phonic lessons, but has had his attention directed to sounds of letters. Many words that are new to him he pronounces correctly from the sound of the letters. I tried him with "s-o-o-n," but it took him some time to get it; first he said "sss-oo-en," then he tried it quickly, and recognized the word. He sometimes reads whole sentences of new words by spelling them and following the sounds, frequently asking me the meaning of the word he may be pronouncing correctly.

In the Andrew Lang Fairy Readers, where the words are divided in syllables all through the reading-matter, he has very little difficulty with words even of three and four syllables.

To-day he spelled saliva from sound, asked its meaning first, then said of some water which he had just used to brush his teeth, "This water has saliva in it, I will throw it away."

He asked me how to spell "Willie"—pronouncing it "Will-lee." When I said "*W-i-l*-l-i-e," he seemed cross, and said "I mean Will-*lee*," then he said, "W-i-l-l spells Will, now spell ee;" so I said "ie," and he was satisfied.

He then said, "P-a-p spells papee." I said "No." He said, "I thought it spelled pa for pa, and the last p was said pee, so it would make papee." He couldn't understand why it should spell pap at first. Then he said, "How do boys spell poppy, when they say it instead of papa?"

October 5th.—I found out yesterday about his so-called April-fool letter to me — sent a short time ago by mail. He really gave it to the postman on Saturday to have it delivered on Monday, and didn't tell me for two days. It came in the usual mail, and he enjoyed my surprise immensely. He addressed me as "Dear Mrs. H——, will you please send me a copy of your book at once?" and signed it "Yours truly, DLORAH." (Here he used his own name reversed, which puzzled me.)

He is learning German in play. This evening, after his first lesson (given yesterday), he gave me a lesson in play. I encouraged it, to find out what he remembered, with the following result: He told me that "No" was *Nein*; "Yes" *Yah*; "Boy" *Knabe*; "Girl" *Madchen*; "Bread" *Brod*; "A" *Ein*; "I" *Ich*; "With" *Mit*; and counted in German up to fifteen.

October 8th.—To-day he asked, "What is meant to die a painful death?" I said, "A wagon running over and killing you would be a painful death." He then said, "And if they *dagged* a sword in you?"

1896 DRAWINGS—SIX YEARS OLD

A, parts for a Brownie ; B, parts of the moon, as it grows ; C, effort at perspective ; D, copy of the block engine he often built ; E—a, cat from model ; b, "This," he said, "is how I used to draw a pussy"; F, f, comparison drawings—F, Harold's ; f, copy by a playmate a year younger than Harold ; G, a gate ; H, two sides to a watch.

He said to me to-day, when I told him that after being dressed he might play in the room in which I was trying to sleep, "You tell God to keep me out of temptation" (alluding to the Lord's Prayer), "but if you dress me and let me play in there while you want to sleep, it will tempt me to talk to you."

October 11th.—When reading to Harold to-day he insisted on having the book about "bones, muscles, and blood." I explained to him with a long tube how water seeks its level, and he busied himself for a long time with the tube and his pump (one that works satisfactorily). He is very quick at contrivances, self-reliant, and self-helpful. He rarely allows or asks us to do anything for him that he can do for himself.

On our way to the park this afternoon he said, "What does b-u-r-n-s spell?" He had caught but a glimpse of the word as we went by on the elevated train. This suggests Catharine Aiken's experiments in "glance-work."

He said, a short time ago, "What does s, f, t, p, o, c, t, a mean?" I asked him where he had heard it. He replied, "Maud sings it; she says, 'If they won't feed the horse good food the s, f, t, p, o, c, t, a will get after them.'" I told him then about the Society for the Prevention of Cruelty to Animals. He is very much interested in the docking of horses' tails. He says he will try to help prevent it, because it is cruel. He explained to me about using a red-hot iron wire to do it. I do not know where he could have heard of this. Some playmate no doubt has told him.

He is now playing that he has a restaurant; he wrote to his father that he was happy because he had one (see illustration facing p. 208.) He brought to a chance visitor, on a tin-box lid for a tray, a little bucket from his pump, filled with water for a drink, making believe the bucket was a glass; a piece of bread, and a round piece of apple that was very thin and had skin on one side; it was the shape and size of a dollar. We were puzzled as to how he cut it in that shape, and asked him about it. He then showed us what he called his knife. It was a circular piece of tin, sharp on the edge, that had covered a bottle, and by turning it a certain way he cut a perfect circle of apple, which gave him great delight.

October 12th.—He said to-day, " How would it feel if I had eyes in the back of my head?" I replied, "I don't know." Then he said, " Well, suppose I cut a rat in two pieces, and then cut one of the pieces in two, would that piece feel it?" I said " No." He wondered why. I said because it was separated from the head. Then he wondered why again. I said there were nerves going to the brain (his "think," as he calls it) telling when anything hurt. I told him also about the sensitiveness of the finger-tips. He experimented, then said, " Are there nerves in the nails, too?" I was not quite sure, but I said " Yes." He looked at them, then said, " How can one see through the nails and not see any nerves?" I was forced to divert him then, and I must study up physiology.

When walking along the street some days later he said to me, "I suppose if we had no nerves, and we shut our eyes, we wouldn't know we are walking."

October 17th.—He evidently puzzles about two, too, and to. I just heard him saying to himself, as he is lying in bed trying to fall asleep, "I am going at *two* o'clock. Are you going *to* town? Yes, I am going, *too*,"

HOW MANY PENNIES HE NEEDED TO MAKE A DOLLAR

ENGINE

ENGINE

A GUNBOAT

HORSE AND WAGON

SPONTANEOUS WRITING FROM MEMORY

1896 DRAWINGS

accenting each one. Then he said, "One, t-w-o" (spelling the words), "one t-o-o, and one t-o," turned over, and began whistling a tune he heard a band play to-day. Afterwards he asked me what a hard *g* and soft *g* meant. I explained; then he asked for a hard *a*, *b*, *c*, and I explained that not all letters had hard sounds and soft sounds; then I said "cake" and "cent" for him, to show the difference in the *c's*. He said, "How about knife? I should think *n* stood for knife." I said, "No, it is *k*, but it is a silent letter." He was satisfied with this, and asked next, "What is whiney or fretty — letting your voice drop down like this?" giving an illustration of it. Then he fell asleep.

To-day he said, "Isn't twice twenty, forty?" I replied, "Yes. How much is twice nineteen?" He said, "I don't know unless I go straight up." I asked, "How do you do it?" He replied, "Why, twice twelve is twenty-four, twice thirteen is twenty-six, twice fourteen is twenty-eight," and he went on until he reached twice nineteen is thirty-eight, evidently having found out that the two-table up to twelve was made by adding two each time; so he experimented up to forty, and asked me as above. This is the way he has experimented, and found out much that he knows about numbers.

The notes opposite p. 192 show how he tried to learn to write. A vertical-writing chart was placed above his little table, and we saw that paper and pencils and his chair were always ready for him, should he want to try it. He wrote a letter to a favorite kindergartner the first day he received it, asking me how to spell the words he did not know, but hunting out the letters for himself by repeating the alphabet as he looked for the letter he wanted. Before six weeks had passed he knew the whole chart from memory, yet he never received direct teaching from it, nor did I tell him to join the letters together when making the words. He did this from the beginning, for the chart he used was carefully prepared to meet this need. One day I saw him slip a cover over some of the letters on the upper row of the chart, by hanging an envelope by its flap on the upper edge of the chart. I asked him why he did it? He replied, "I wanted it so I can learn the letters without seeing them—so," illustrating by first covering *a* and *b* and then writing the letters, and moving the envelope along over *c* and *d*, and so on.

To-day he said, in my hearing, "Vertical-writing chart." I then said, "You should write a letter to your papa." He replied, "You wouldn't have told me to, if I had not said, 'Vertical-writing chart,'" which was true. When speaking of the chart, he said, "Why do they make their letters so decorated? They are more decorated in capitals than below" (meaning the small letters). "You see, they might make the 7 straight at the top—this way: 7." Then looking at 7 on the chart, he said, "I should think it *is* vertical. I know some people who make the 7 this way: ⟋. This is the way it should be: 7. Which way do you think is right? Is this horizontal: ⟍⏌?"

He heard some one say purty for pretty to-day; he came to me and said, "I've always heard of pretty soon; never heard of purty soon."

October 24th.—I said to him when he heard his aunt play Mendelssohn's "Rondo Capriccioso," "Isn't that beautiful that your aunt is playing?" He replied, "Yes, I don't see how she can play such music." I said, "She

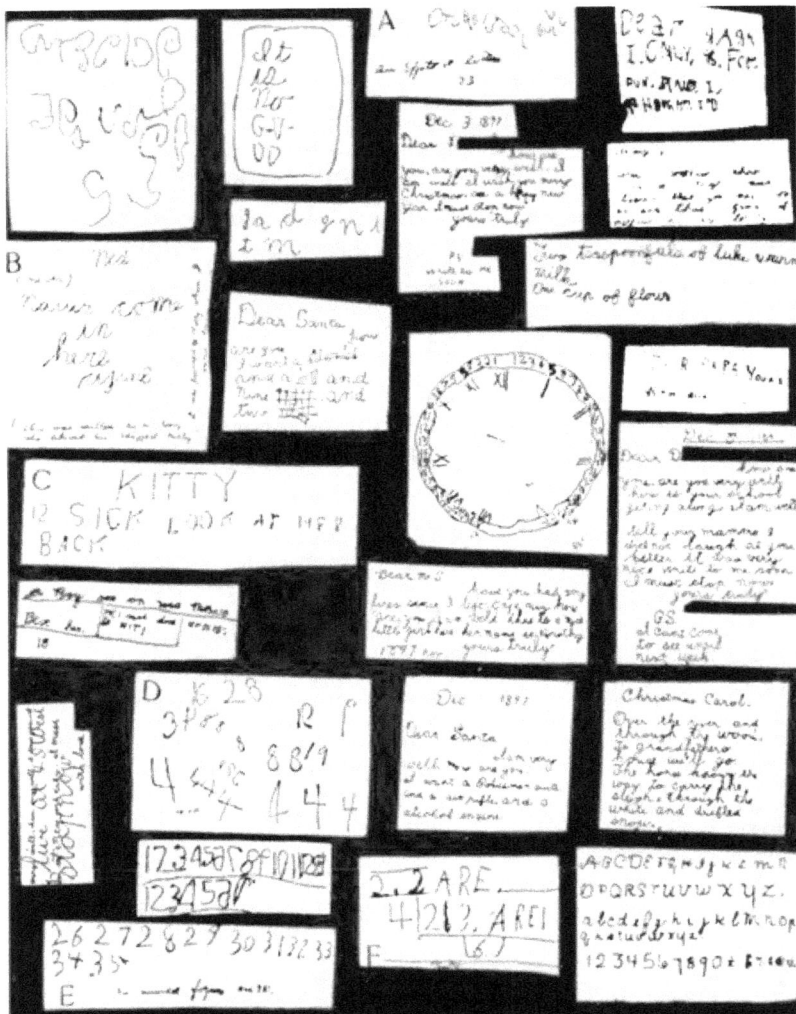

GRADED EFFORT AT WRITING—COMPOSITION AND EARLY EFFORTS AT NUMBERS

is studying it all the time." Then he replied, "I suppose
it isn't hard for her."

October 25th.—He said at tea, to-day, "I like the
raisins in this cake. I don't like them in most cakes. I
like them in Mrs. L——'s cakes too. I wonder why
these are so good. Don't you suppose, mamma, that the
grapes were properly dried to make them so good?
Maybe too the baker used" (then he whispered and
spelled) "c-l-e-a-n hands."

October 28th.—He saw the word "you" upsidedown,
thus—noʎ. He said, "I was puzzled what noʎ meant,
then I saw it was 'you' upsidedown." He has always
been able to read letters from any side presented. To-
night he could not fall asleep easily, because he had too
much excitement just before bedtime. He said, "If
anybody could see the pretty things I am seeing—all
sorts of pretty colors, green, red, purple. I close my
eyes and it gets dark—very dark—and all of a sudden
it *cheers up* and gets *beautiful colors*. I am going to
have one in a minute, I think," were the last words I
heard. When I looked again he was asleep.

I asked him this week to tell me a German sentence,
if he had learned any. He promptly said, "*Zwei augen
hab eich.*"

When he sings, "Good-morning, Merry Sunshine," the
kindergarten song which he learned after hearing it
twice, he always prefaces the last verse with the words,
"This is what the sunshine says now, mamma, that I
am going to tell you."

As we neared Hanover Square, on the Third Avenue
Elevated, *after an absence of a year*, he turned at a certain place and said, "Let me see—this is the place we
saw the cannons," and he showed one to me. He then

amused himself all the way to Thirty-fourth Street with making and pulling a slip-knot—with a string he found on the floor—saying at last, "This is the way to hang a man," putting my purse in the loop. Some one must have indiscreetly told him about it.

October 29th.—A "question talk" to-day with pussy. "Did there be, a long time ago, an idol—an ugly thing made of stone—that little boys prayed to—do they?" He said this as if he thought it couldn't be so. He then told me he heard it in a Sunday-school he visited once. He then began talking about the matter to his stuffed kitty. Saying, "You wouldn't pray to idols, would you?" Then he turned to me and said, "Did you hear what pussy said?" I said, "No." He replied, "Why, she said, 'No, I wouldn't do it for the world.'" Then he went on, "You precious little pussy, you precious pussy darling, you're the sweetest little pussy in the world; no, you're not little, you're big—only not so big as me. I wish you'd grow—don't you?" Then he changed his voice to represent kitty speaking, and said, "Yes, I does, I does, I does," turning to me at the same time and saying, "Do you hear her?" "You wouldn't pray to idols, would you, kitty?" Then the changed voice came again in reply, "No, I'll kill every one I get near." Then Harold said in a very wise way, "But, pussy, they are not alive, they are made of stone." Then he turned to his mother and said, "Mamma, I know what dragons are; they are idols. Don't you believe it? Maybe a one-headed dragon is an idol in Africa—*but it couldn't breathe and spit fire.*" The above is a fair sample of his conversations with pussy before he falls asleep. He is now singing to himself:

> "The diddy pawn lies on the dry land there,
> Sitting there, sitting there, sitting there.
> He sits there and eats a pear,
> Tra-la-la-la, tra-la-la-la, tra-la-la-la."

November 1st.—I placed some books on a shelf above his bed, and he asked me not to put them so near the edge, for fear they might fall on him in the night-time. He has always shown forethought and caution—yet is reckless in play.

November 3d.—He has taken to German very kindly. He has had, in play with Fräulein, a half-hour lesson, for three weeks, five days each week. He comes to me at times to teach me his lesson. His second lesson was as follows—he first said:

> "Zwei Augen hab eich—two eyes have I."

Then he repeated from memory:

> "Die Uhren, liebe Kinder,
> Sie haben keine Ruh'
> Im Sommer wie im Winter,
> Sie gehen immer zu—
> Tic-toc, tic-toc, tic-toc."

Then he said, "I don't know what this means, but *die Uhren* means the clock." Then I said, "It means that it goes winter and summer," and he replied, "Oh yes, it says tic-toc, tic-toc, and it means that the clock always goes—in winter and in summer."

Then he repeated from memory:

> "Dies' ist die Mutter lieb und gut,
> Dies' ist der Vater mit frohen Muth;
> Dies' ist der Bruder lang und gross,
> Dies' ist die Schwester mit Püpchen im Schoss;
> Dies' ist das Kindchen, klein und zart,
> Und dies' die Familie von guter Art."

195

Then he repeated it in English.

Another lesson was as follows:

"Mamma, how do you say soldiers in German?" She replied, "*Soldaten.*" He smiled, and said, "Yes. How did you know it?"

Then he counted to one hundred in German correctly; then said each hundred to a thousand, calling that "*zehn hundert*" first, because he didn't know the word thousand in German. The only question he asked while doing it was when he reached twenty-five. He then asked if "*fünf*" was five. At thirty he said first "*zehn und zwanzig,*" then corrected himself, and said, "*dreizig.*"

When singing to himself to-day, in spite of a cold, and keeping time and showing expression, he sang first the song, "Good-morning, Merry Sunshine," which is a favorite; then he began:

> "Good-morning, good-morning, kind teacher so dear,
> How gladly we greet you, till all doth appear;
> Our playmates we welcome, each one with delight—"

(Here I asked him what delight meant. He said, "With happiness—very glad.") Then he went on—

> "Our hearts are so happy, because we do right."

(Here he turned to me and said, "It isn't *write,* but because we do right—do the right thing.") Then he completed the song—

> "Good-morning, good-morning, our dear little school,
> How happy we are in obeying each rule;
> For love is our motto in work and in play,
> So let us be thankful for each happy day."

We *followed* nature-work and science stories with fairy stories at six, instead of giving fairy stories first.

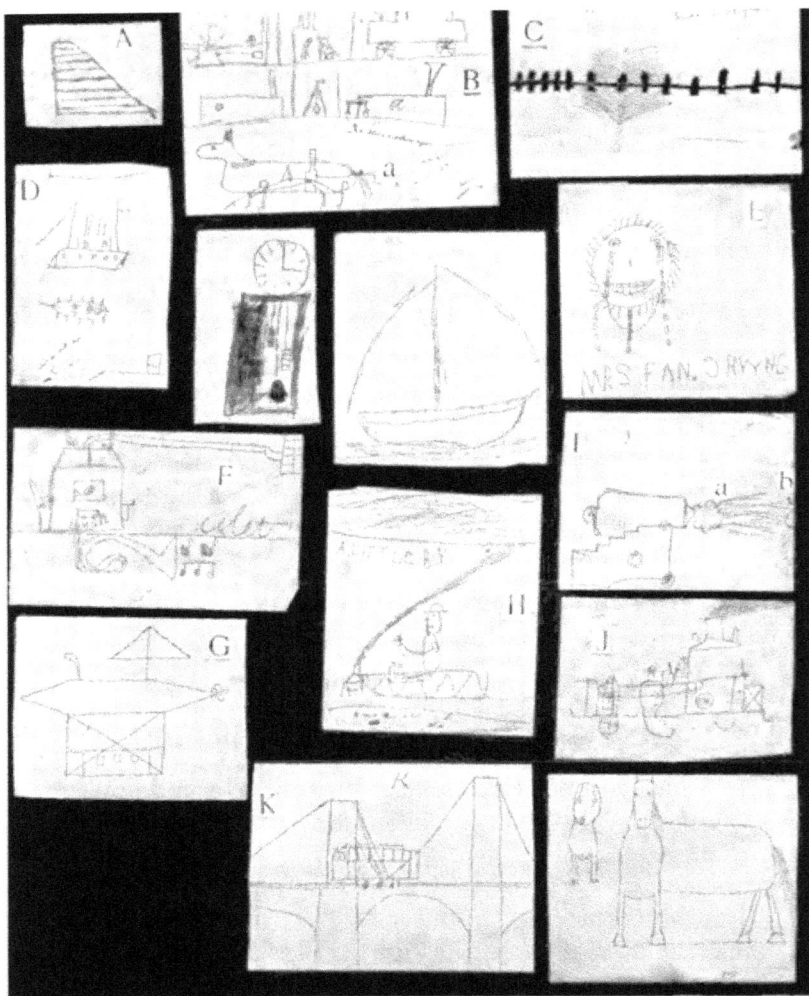

1896 DRAWINGS—SIX YEARS OLD

A, harp; B, stationary, drilling, and stone cracking engines, and a horse with a steam engine inside with a handle, a, to make his legs work; C, birds on a telegraph wire; D, "side and top of a war boat"; E, "Mrs. Fan crying"; F, heater; G, "This is the way a flying ship looks, mamma"; H, "a little boy on his sled—he is lost and so far away from his house that you can hardly see it"; I, shell thrower—a, "here's the explosion"—b, "here's the end of the shell"; J, electric fire engine—"the wheels are turning so fast that you can't see them"; K, cable car on bridge.

I find he has therefore no fear of goblins, because he knows they are myths; yet he loves the make-believe part, and, for so young a child, he has developed great power in creating fairy stories.

November 6th.—He said to-day, "Mamma, what does atmosphere mean?" She said, "The air around us." Then he said, "Does the air mean atmosphere, or does atmosphere mean air? I thought atmosphere meant a kind of sickness. Oh, it's esterics (hysterics) I meant what I was thinking of, mamma. Why do they call it 'esterics'? They might call it 'Can't stop it.'" (He had asked before this for the meaning of hysterics, and evidently deduced his own explanation of "Can't stop it.")

I heard him say to-day to a little girl whose word he doubted, "Honest and truthly?"

November 10th.—To-day he told me that Miss H—— had given them copy for writing in the kindergarten, and it was a little bit slanting. He said in great surprise, "When mine was done, I saw it was *vertical*." I replied, "So it should be." He is being taught the vertical hand, but he evidently tried to write slanting, after the copy, and was surprised to find he had not done it.

November 24th.—To-day he asked his mother whether the germs of whooping-cough got it themselves (meaning the cough by "it"). She said, "No." He said, "Then how do they give it to us?"

We have been reading a story in which the giants that were killed were a number of bad habits and character-istics, and those who helped to kill them were the good fairies. The questions are mine, and the answers his —and his understanding of his own nature is pretty accurate:

Bad temper ?................	Half dead.
Carelessness ?...............	Nearly dead.
Selfishness ?................	Half dead.
Laziness ?..................	Dead.
Disobedience ?..............	Dead.
Lies ?.....................	Dead.
Untidiness ?................	Half dead.
Exaggeration ?.............	Pretty nearly dead.
Fear ?.....................	Half dead.
Love of praise ?............	$\frac{1}{18}$ left to kill.
Boastfulness ?..............	Dead.
Concealment (which he called Sneakfulness).............	$\frac{1}{100}$ to kill; nearly dead.
Bitter words ?..............	$\frac{1}{1000}$ to kill.
Hate ?.................	Quite dead.
Anger ?....................	$\frac{1}{10}$ to kill.
Cruelty ?..................	Dead.
I can't ?...................	$\frac{1}{100000000}$ to kill.
Delay not ?................	Pretty nearly dead; half to be killed.
Bashfulness ?..............	Nearly dead.
Proudfulness (his own term) ?	Dead.

He said, from memory, that the fairies to help you kill the giants were lovefulness, courage, self-control, obedience, honesty, patience, good-temper, kindness, diligence, courtesy, gratitude, and perseverance, which he said meant "Try, try again."

November 28th.—Harold's prayer. After saying the Lord's Prayer, he added as usual his voluntary prayer, this time saying, "God bless me, all the animals, insects, birds, and everything. Bless me, and make me a good boy. Good-night. *Ah*-men." Then he got up, and as I began brushing his hair he suddenly dropped on his knees, and said, "Dear God: I'm going to bed now. Excuse me a minute until I see what time it is." Then he turned his head, looked at a clock in the hall, put down his head again, and said, "It's just ten minutes past eight, and I think I'd better go to sleep now. So good‑night, dear God. *Ah*-men." As he started for his bed I said, "Wait, let me brush your hair." He replied, "But I told God I would go to sleep right away." So I said, "Well, run along then," and he was asleep before I could write this down. It is curious to note that he has said "*ah*-men" ever since he heard it the first time when visiting a kindergarten, although he originally heard it pronounced āmen. It must be from choice, for he still says "forgive us our trespasses as we forgive those who trespass against us," although he heard during the same visit, "forgive us our debts as we forgive our debtors," and told me of it, asking me which I liked best.

I just discovered that he has for some time thought the words "Jesus, Saviour, Son of God," in a little prayer he says, meant "Jesus, save your Son of God." He said, "Oh, it was the Son of God's Jesus, Saviour." First he asked what it meant, and that was how I discovered his error.

November 29th.—When going up the Sixth Avenue Elevated one day recently he saw the girders, and was very much excited, as he was once before, when I told him what they were. He told me that he used to think they were derricks. I asked him how he found out his mistake. He said, "I think you told me girders were to hold up things. I know it by this time. I don't know how I found it out." Then he said, "See how the train curves slowly."

A BEDTIME TALK

"Doesn't w-o-l-d spell world?" (He was thinking of the sentence, "God so loved the world," which he had learned that day from a calendar, in his usual questioning fashion of saying, "Mamma, what does that read?")

I said, "Isn't there a sound of *r* in world?"

H. "Oh yes; w-o-r-l-d, world; doesn't w-o-r-d spell word?"

I said, "Yes, and w-o-l-d spells wold — a word not used very often, and I am not quite certain of its exact meaning."

H. "Can't you tell me what you *think* it means?"

"Yes, but I will look it up and tell you to-morrow night. See how easy it is to learn a word every day, and soon you will know enough words to read."

H. "I can read now a little. I can tell you three ways to spell too—t-w-o, t-o-o, and t-o."

I said, "Can you tell me what they mean?"

H. "I don't know—oh yes, t-w-o means one, two, three. I don't know the others."

Then I said, "Well, if you go *to* bed, will mamma go *too*?"

H. "Oh, *too* means that?"

I said, "Yes." Harold said then, "Now what is t-o?" I said, "To bed?"

H. "Oh, is that it? I can tell you something without the book."

Then he repeated, "A, B, C went out to tea, D, E, F didn't feel very well," etc., to the end of the nursery rhyme. Then he said, "I can tell you something else: 'Here's fun — a little fat piggy-wig trying to run.' Doesn't t-i-c spell something like tick?" I said, "Yes, and t-i-c-k spells it also." Then he said, "Is t-i-c tic of tic-a-toc?" I said, "Yes; and what sound makes toc? What sound is in God and dog?" (words he knew). He said "wait" (whispering d-o-g, t-o-c); then he said

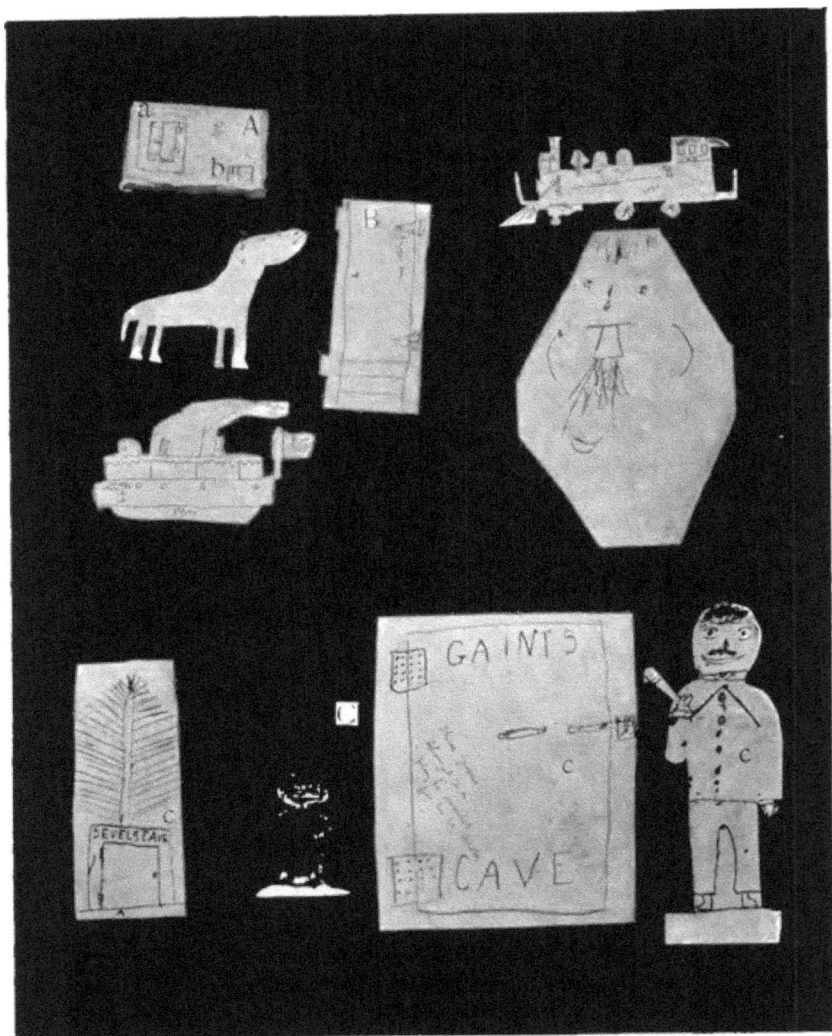

1896 CUTTINGS AND DRAWINGS—SIX YEARS OLD

A, cut and folding work—a kitchen with closet, a, and stove, b ; B, door and hinges ; C—c, c, c, c, parts for toy theatre—a, Devil's cave ; b, Satan ; c, giant's cave (note spelling); d, giant holding a club

"now" (as if he had it), and began to spell, in great delight, "t-i-c tic, a, t-o-c toc," three times over. Then I said, "Now, dear, go to sleep, for I must write to finish this book for the publisher." He said, "Why?" at once. I replied, "It must be finished this week." He said, "Can't he write it himself?" I said, "No. He didn't know how, so that was why I had to do it." "Can't you tell him how?" I said, "That is what I am doing by writing it."

H. "What is it about?"

I replied, "About how to fix milk for babies"—thinking to give him a familiar subject, for I was writing about Pasteurization.

H. (expectantly). "Mr. ——" (mentioning the publisher) "is going to send one to every mamma who has a sterilizer."

I said, "Yes; but how did you know it?"

H. "Why, I know they sell sterilizers, and I know babies' milk must be sterilized, and I know what you are writing tells how to fix milk for babies, and it is for Mr. ——, so I think it *must* be the *directions*." (The last word he said in tones of triumph.)

I said, "You have a busy little head."

H. "Yes, and I told you this morning the plate was a picture of a baby's stomach." (He saw a cut of one in a medical book.)

I said, "Yes; go to sleep now, dear."

H. "Couldn't the pipes" (he always calls intestines pipes) "go straight, instead of being all around?"

I said, "No; they are too long."

He then asked, "How could I measure yours?"

I said, "You couldn't unless I were dead and you would do like they do in hospitals, where they teach

201

doctors how to help live people, by learning the parts of
the body from dead bodies, that might as well be used
as go to dust." (I gave the suggestive answer for the
purpose of familiarizing him with the idea of the importance of the soul and the indifference to be felt for the
lifeless body, to which he has been carefully trained,
and also for the purpose of doing away with any idea
of cruelty he might gain in the future from indiscreet
remarks about hospital-work that might inadvertently
reach him. Many unnecessary things *must* be told to
a child to prepare him for what he will inevitably meet,
or he will be unfitted for the world as he will invariably find it.)

H. " Do our bodies go to dust ?"

I said, " Yes, after the ' think '" (his idea of soul) " has
gone to God. Don't you think they might as well ?"

H. " Yes; and do crabs go to dust too when they
are dead?" (Probably thinking of their hard shells,
with which he often plays.)

I replied, inadvertently, " Yes—dust, gas, etc."

H. " *What is gas ?*"

" Something that you can smell." (A poor answer,
but the best I could think of at the time.) " Everything
goes into something else. God made the world so when
he made Adam and Eve out of dust."

H. " *Who's that ?*"

I replied, " Adam the first man and Eve the first
woman. God made them out of dust—you know he can
do anything if he sees fit—and put life into them. God
made the world and tried to keep it good."

H. " How can the dust go into something else ?"

I replied, " By being the earth, to help wheat grow to
be made into flour to make bread, etc."

H. *"And then bodies can be made over into other bodies?"* (Thinking of eating to make tissue, blood, etc., in which he has always been greatly interested.)

I then said, "Good-night, dear. You have enough to think of now to go to sleep pleasantly," and he fell asleep in a few minutes. If indulged, this would be a daily, or rather a nightly, occurrence, or whenever the notion seizes him to begin asking questions, and it could be kept up for hours without apparently tiring the little fellow; but effort, as a rule, is made to keep all suggestion from him that has a tendency to excite his brain. It is sufficiently perplexing to answer his ordinary questions, without giving him more food for thought. The above answers were more than usually suggestive, because he was wide-awake, and it was necessary to tire him a little to get him asleep quietly. We answer his questions truthfully but restrainingly—to keep physical poise.

One night when ready for bed he begged for a romp. While jumping up and down on a spring-bed he began banging his beloved stuffed kitty—something very unusual, for he has always treated her with tenderness. I couldn't understand his action, but said nothing; at last I heard him say to his nurse as he banged her again:

"That's Jesus in the hard times of 1896 years ago." Then I remembered that in 1895 he had been told a story, during my absence, about Jesus and his crucifixion, his cruel treatment, and other unnecessary details that are beyond a child's comprehension and should never be told to them. He came to me for an explanation of the cruelty, and it took a long time for me to undo the impression that had been created. I did it at last by giving him a loving story of how God in his goodness sent Jesus, but he often said afterwards, when reverting to the story, that whenever he thought of Jesus it made him "so sad."

When I asked him what he was doing to kitty, he said, "Banging kitty." Then I said, "Poor kitty!" He replied, "Well, wasn't Jesus banged by the wicked people?" Then he suddenly changed and said, "Poor kitty!" petted and kissed her, and took her to bed with him.

One day he said, "Won't you tell me that story that you told me last year, about some one, I don't know whether it begins with a J or a G" (meaning Jesus), "but he is way up in heaven, you know?" He has always shown a great desire for any story about God or Jesus.

Professor Barnes of Leland Stanford University directed attention some time last year to the value of records of different children's replies to the same set of questions, in regard to what certain words meant. I selected three boys of very different temperament and environment—playmates of Harold's—and asked each one, also Harold, the meaning of the same set of words, as follows—I did it in such a way that none of them knew what was being done. It took me several days to divide and ask the questions, in order not to arouse consciousness:

E——'s LIST

A boy with a kind step-mother. He was a little over Harold's age:

Arm-chair—Wood.
Hat—Some are cloth.
Garden—Vegetables.
Mamma—A person.

204

1896 CUTTINGS—SIX YEARS OLD

A, a, doll and dress; B, fairy godmother in Cinderella toy theatre; C, calendar made to slide up and down to show dates; D, kindergarten weaving—materials made and colored by the child; E, design by folding and cutting

Potatoes—Vegetables.
Bottle—Glass.
Flower—Something pretty.
Snail—Little animal.
Mouth—Something to chew with.
Lamp—Something to make a light.
Earthworm—Something to dig the earth.
Shoes—Something to wear on your feet.
Finger—Something to take hold of things with.
Clock—Something to tell time.
House—Something to live in.
Wolf—Something to eat you up.
Omnibus—Something to take your rides in.
Piece of Sugar—Something to eat, put in tea or coffee.
Thread—Something to sew with.
Horse—Something to give you rides.
Table—Something to eat off.
Bird—Something to sing.
Dog—Something to bark.
Carriage—Something to ride in.
Pencil—Something to write with.
Balloon—Something to sail in the air.
Village—Something to live in.
Box—Something to put things in.
Handkerchief—Something to blow your nose on.

B——'s LIST

Same age as Harold, but a very nervous child, and subject to very variable training:

Arm-chair—To sit in.
Hat—To wear on your head.
Garden—To grow things in.
Mamma—To *whip* the naughty boys.

Potatoes—To eat.

Bottle—To put medicine, water, or anything in.

Flower—It looks pretty.

Snail—I don't know—oh yes, I know now—oh no, I don't; oh, don't I forget quick! Oh, I got it again—to crawl up things. *I got that.*

Mouth—To eat with.

Lamp—To light.

Earthworm—To crawl.

Shoes—To wear. My! these are easy lessons.

Finger—To touch things with.

Clock—To tell time.

House—So people can live in it.

Wolf—To bite people.

Omnibus—To get a ride in.

Piece of Sugar—To make milk and everything sweet.

Thread—To sew.

Horse—To take out riding with.

Table—To stand things on.

Bird—To fly.

Dog—To bark.

Carriage—For people to get in.

Pencil—To write with.

Balloon—To take people up in the air with.

Village—So people can live in it.

Lamb—To give you nice wool to wear.

Handkerchief—To wipe your nose on.

W——'s LIST

A year younger than Harold—His mother is dead:

Arm-chair—To sit in.

Hat—To put on.

Garden—To make things grow.

Mamma—I don't know.

Potatoes—To eat.

Bottle—Put things in.

Flower—To smell.

Snail—To look at.

Mouth—To eat out of.

Lamp—To walk along with.

Earthworm—To look at.

Shoes—To put on.

Finger—To get a hold of things.

Clock—To hear of.

House—To live in.

Wolf—I don't know what that is. I've heard of story ones, but I've forgot.

Omnibus—To get a ride in.

Piece of Sugar—To put in things.

Thread—To sew with.

Horse—To pull you with.

Table—To eat off of. Didn't I tell you that once? (Yes.) Then why did you ask again?

Bird—Tell it was nice—to bite you. (He had an idea that a bird once tried to bite him.)

Dog—To look at.

Carriage—To sit in. I told you once.

Pencil—To write.

Balloon—To look at.

Village—To look at.

Box—To put things in.

Handkerchief—To wipe your nose on.

HAROLD'S LIST

Arm-chair—Something to sit in, chair with place to put your arms on.

Hat—To put on your head.

Garden—To plant things in.

Mamma—Somebody to take care of you.

Potatoes—Something to eat.

Bottle—Something to put things in.

Flower—Something to look pretty, smell nice, and to pick.

Snail—To dig up the garden.

Mouth—To eat with, talk with, open with to get things in to eat.

Lamp—Something to make light.

Earthworm—To dig up the earth, to make holes, to make flowers grow. I asked " How?" He said, " Keeps the earth soft for them by going through it."

Shoes—To wear. Why? To keep your feet from treading on tacks and everything.

Finger—Something to point with—depends on which finger it is—to help pick up things.

Clock—To tell you what time it is.

House—To live in. Why? So you can live. Couldn't you live in air? You have houses to keep you from all animals and things—to live in, sleep in, eat in.

Wolf—Something tries to eat you, get after you; kills goats, kills people.

Omnibus—Something to carry you in.

Piece of Sugar—Something to eat, to put in your coffee. Why? To make it taste sweet.

Thread—To sew with; to make cloth with.

Horse—To pull carriages and to ride in—to pull old wagons.

Table—Something to eat from, to lay things on.

Bird—Something that lays eggs and sings.

Dog—Something that chases cats, barks, chases peo-

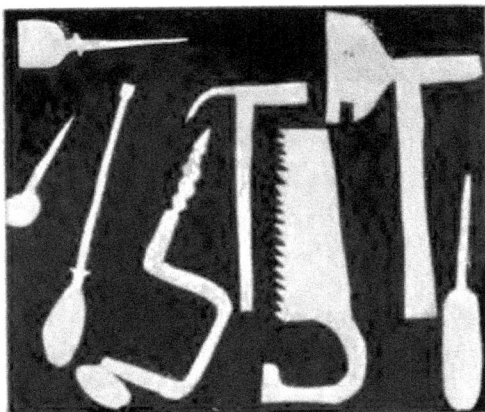

EARLY CUTTINGS— TOOLS

VARIOUS POSITIONS OF AN ENGINE-
BELL RINGING

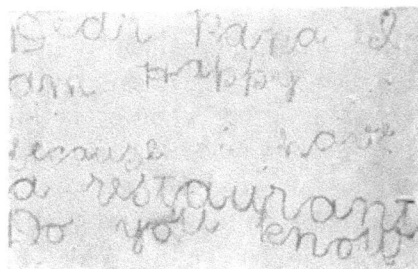

SPONTANEOUS WRITING FROM MEMORY

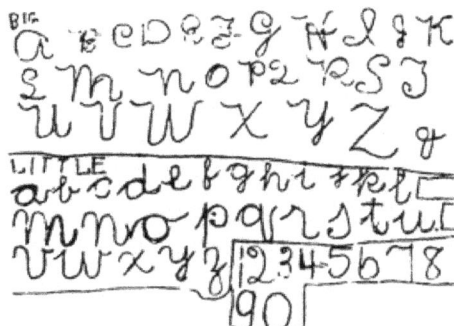

WRITTEN SPONTANEOUSLY FROM MEMORY, AFTER
SIX WEEKS' STUDY AND PRACTICE

Various positions of an engine bell ringing. 1896 cuttings, writing, and drawing from memory. A sketch of "Tommy," which was drawn in 1897

ple away from houses, plays with you, shakes hands, and whatever you train him to do—does lots of things.

Carriage—Something to take rides in.

Pencil—To write.

Balloon—To sail up in the air.

Village—A little place to live in, a little kind of a street up in the mountains.

Box—Something to put things in.

Handkerchief—Something to wipe your nose with and to do lots of things. What? To keep in your pocket, and I don't know all of them.

"The Haunted Castle" is a fairy story that he told me, so that little children could, as he said, understand it. He was six years old at the time. He selected the title, printed it, began to write, then said to me, "You write the rest." He sat before me and told the story as fast as I could write it. It was just before his bedtime, when his brain seems always to be unusually active— an inherited characteristic that can be readily traced. His idea in trying to tell fairy stories is always to tell the stories he has heard in more simple language for his playmates, remembering how I must "read them down" to him. He would beg me to "say the meaning quickly" as I read along, so as not to interrupt his enjoyment of listening to an unbroken story.

THE HAUNTED CASTLE

PART I

Once there was a king who had but one daughter, and there was a castle which ghosts lived in, and the king offered his only daughter in marriage to whoever would stay in the castle three nights; and there was a house in the forest, and there was a youth there that wished very much to learn what it was to be afraid. One day he was walking along the street, saying, " Oh, how I wish I knew what it was to be afraid!" And a wagoner came by, and he heard the boy saying to himself, " How I wish I knew what it was to be afraid!" So the wagoner (I suppose they might not know what a wagoner is, but they will ask their mamma, and she will tell them it is a man who drives a wagon—isn't that what it is?) said to him, " Do you wish to learn to be afraid?" And he said, " If you want to learn to be afraid, come with me." So he took him and led him to a gallows, and said, " Stay here till midnight, and you'll soon learn to be afraid. The rope-maker has married seven men; sit under this tree till midnight, and watch under it. You will soon learn to be afraid." So the boy said, " You come to me early to-morrow morning," and said, " You will get a fine cow that gives golden milk and golden butter," and then the wagoner left the boy. And then he sat down under the tree and waited till midnight, and he saw just at midnight six black dogs come running around the tree barking, and then each dog settled around him and could speak our talk. So then they had a good talk with him, and then there came afterwards two ugly black men with dirty eyes and crooked toes as crooked as a spring, and their ears went like cat's ears, and they had tails with points on them, and the seven black dogs jumped up at them; one pulled out its tail, one pulled out its eyes, and one (how many black dogs did I say?) pulled out his teeth, and one his tongue, and the other took care of the boy. In the morning the man came to

the boy and said, "Now I hope you have learned what
it is to be afraid." The boy said nothing came but
seven black dogs that could talk, and two men with
pointed tails, cat's ears, and curly toes. So the man
went off and didn't get the cow after all. So he went
to a tower, and the landlord heard him say, "Oh, how
I wish I knew what it was to be afraid!" and he said,
"Go to the castle two blocks away, and there you will
soon learn to be afraid." So he went to the king and
said, "I will sleep in the castle for three nights," and
the king said, "You may ask for three things without
life to take with you." He said, "All I want is a turning-lathe, a fire, and knife." So the king had these
articles taken in at the day, so the youth went right in
and slept in the castle. Just as the clock struck twelve
he saw the devil, or Satan, coming in with a pitchfork
in his hand, and the boy had a shield on or a armor.
So when Satan went to hit him with the pitchfork it
didn't hurt him. So he began to throw fire at the boy,
and the iron only sent it back into his own face, which
made him very angry, and he said, "Be off with you,
boy!" And then the cock crowed and Satan vanished
from his eyes. (Do you think they know what vanished
is? It means disappeared.) Aren't you writing more
than I say?—you write so long. He asked this when I
put in his interpolations. And then the king came and
found him sitting on the floor by his fire. So then the
boy went to go away, and then the next night he came
and sat down again by his old fire, and just as the
clock struck twelve he heard a rumbling, crumbling,
squeaking noise in the corner of his room, and he saw
a black cat coming with a little yellow dwarf on its
back, and the yellow dwarf said, "I will do you no

harm, but come every evening at ten o'clock while you
are here, and keep everything away." And then he rode
around the room six times on his black cat and then
vanished. But the little yellow dwarf was telling
stories. He wasn't coming every night. So then he
fell asleep on the floor, and then the king came, and
then he went away and came back to his old fire once
more, and then seven little men came tumbling down
the chimney with leg-bones in their hands and skulls
for balls. They stood the leg-bones up for tenpins, and
began to play tenpins. And then the boy said, "Can I
play with you?" and he said, "Yes, if you've got any
money." And he said, "I've got money enough, but
your balls are not round enough." So he took the skulls
and put them in his turning-lathe until they were quite
round, and "Now," he said, "they will roll better."
Then he began to play with the funny little men; so
then the cock crew and they all vanished from his eyes.
Then the king came for the last time and said, "I hope
you have learned what it is to be afraid now," and he
said, "I haven't learned such a thing." Then the king
said, "Everybody that has come here has been killed by
the ghosts, and you have lived, and you shall have my
daughter in marriage." So he was not quite happy,
because he did not know what it was to be afraid. So
her chambermaid said, "I will help you out in this matter if you give me a cup." So she went to the brook
and filled the cup with water with little minnows in it
(first he said gudgeon), and then she brought the cup up
to the house and gave it to the king's daughter and said,
"To-night when he is in bed you must throw this over
him." So that night when the youth was sleeping she
threw the water over him, and the little gudgeon wig-

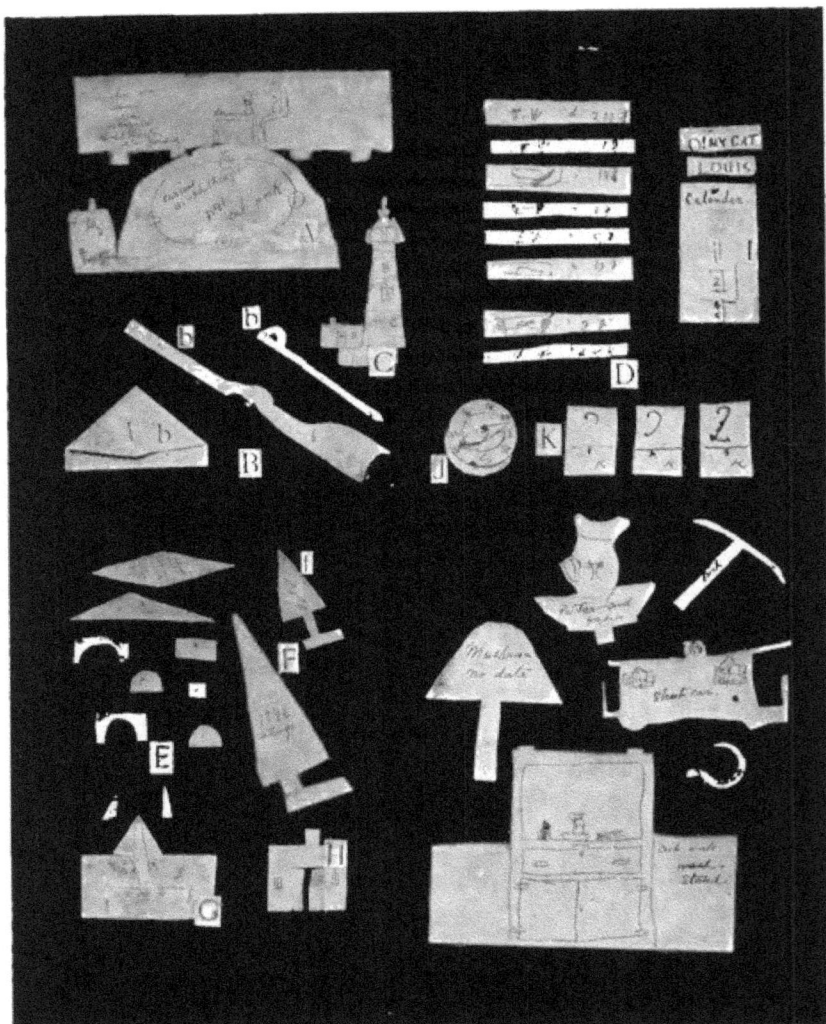

1896 CUTTINGS AND DRAWINGS

A, cut work—circus amphitheatre and box office ; B—b, b, b, pussy's soldier set ; C, light house ; D, eight different kinds of hats with prices, for playing store ; E, mental pictures of kindergarten models ; F, f, large and small umbrella, half closed ; G, toad stool ; H, house with screen doors ; I, calendar ; J, compass ; K—k, k, k, parts of figure 2 for kinetoscope.

gled about. He awoke and said, "Oh, how I am afraid! Oh, how I am afraid!" And then they lived happily all the time afterwards.

The following story he told me at bedtime, without effort, as rapidly as it could be written, when he was six years and a half old. It is entirely original:

THE SAILOR AND HIS MONKEY

There was once upon a time a sailor who was working on a ship, and he had a monkey that did all sorts of tricks. The monkey would stand on its head and turn a somersault and dance so high that you wouldn't know what he was doing. The monkey's name was Tommy, and the sailor was very fond of this funny, mischievous monkey.

This was a very large ship, and they had an organ in the dining-room, and the monkey was tied to the organ. At every meal the sailor would come in with his monkey, put a little cushion on the floor, and put the little monkey's clothes on. The clothes for the monkey were two little black shoes, a little hat, and a little coat with two little pockets in it; and so the sailor would tie his monkey to the organ and begin to play. The monkey would run over to the little cushion and begin to dance all around the little cushion. It would dance, and in the middle of every tune that he played on the organ the monkey would turn a somersault, and at the end of every tune the monkey would take off his little hat, and then when everybody had finished their meals the sailor would stop playing on the organ. The monkey would get off of the cushion, take it up in its mouth, and bring

it over to the sailor, and the sailor would unfasten the
monkey from the organ, and then the monkey would
jump up on the sailor's shoulder, and he would go out
of the dining-room of the ship. One day when the
sailor had finished playing on his organ they heard a
loud noise—bang! (he told me to "use" an exclamation
mark)—right under the ship, and what do you suppose
happened?—the ship shook like everything. So the sail-
or and his monkey heard another noise—bang! so they
heard that same noise bang! again, three more times,
and at the last time the ship went crang!—right over on
its side. So the sailor got a tub, put his monkey in it,
and got in himself—a wash-tub. So he took two brooms
and stuck them through the holes in the handles on the
wash-tub and began using the brooms like oars, and the
monkey and the sailor went spinning through the water;
but at last the tub tipped over and they went ploom!—
right down to the bottom of the sea, and said, "Oh,
dear me!"

CHAPTER VIII

EIGHTH YEAR — EFFORTS AT ARITHMETIC — "A STORY
ALL UPSIDEDOWN" AND "A WONDERFUL DREAM"
TOLD BY THE CHILD—MEMORY-WORK—CONCEPTION
OF FRACTIONS — EIGHTH - YEAR DEVELOPMENT IN
DRAWING AND DESIGNING

APRIL 23, 1897. — He said to his mother to - day:
"Mamma, I am like a little tree growing: bad boys
pull me over crooked, and you straighten me. If mothers didn't do this the boys couldn't grow straight when
they get older, but would be crooked." He asked me
repeatedly last night what I
wanted, so he might pray
for it for me. When I told
him I intended going to sleep
when he did, he said, "Oh,
won't that be lovely!"

April 24th. — To - day he
wanted to know what adding
meant. I wrote some num-
bers (as shown in the accompanying illustrations, *a* and *b*)
and explained to him how to
carry 1, by placing a figure 1 over the next column to
the left when he had counted beyond 10, and put down
the remaining number underneath the column he had
just added. He needed but one telling, and the figures

A LESSON IN ADDITION.

215

underneath with the 1's are his own. The illustration marked *b* is his own altogether.

July 21st.—The illustration *c* is one of his efforts to understand the principle underlying addition, subtrac-

b

tion, multiplication, and division, after I had explained to him with the aid of the following figures:

$$\begin{array}{r} 234 \\ 234 \\ \hline 468 \text{ addition.} \end{array} \qquad \begin{array}{r} 468 \\ 234 \\ \hline 234 \text{ subtraction.} \end{array}$$

$$\begin{array}{r} 234 \\ 2 \\ \hline 468 \text{ multiplication.} \end{array}$$

$$2)\ 468$$
$$\overline{234}\ \text{division.}$$

He experimented then for himself for a long time, using his own numbers, and using them correctly, as indicated:

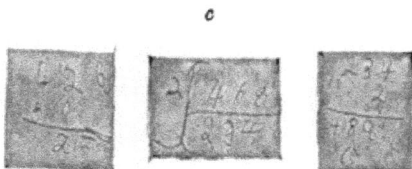

c

A LESSON AND ITS RESULT: EARLY ATTEMPTS AT
SUBTRACTION, DIVISION, AND MULTIPLICATION.

1897 DRAWINGS—SEVEN YEARS OLD

A, a, c, gold-backs; B, b, copy, with pen, from printed T; C, c, line work from memory of kindergarten lessons; D, train on grade; E, efforts at drawing a glass—the one not numbered was his
copy; F, engine and coupler—a, b; G, plan for a school—p. r., dining room; p. g., playground;
s. s., theatre for amateur work; b to n, bedrooms; H, plan for a comfortable Pullman car which
he proposes to build when he is big—he still uses inverted letters; I, mechanical work—plans for
a locomotive he was trying to make.

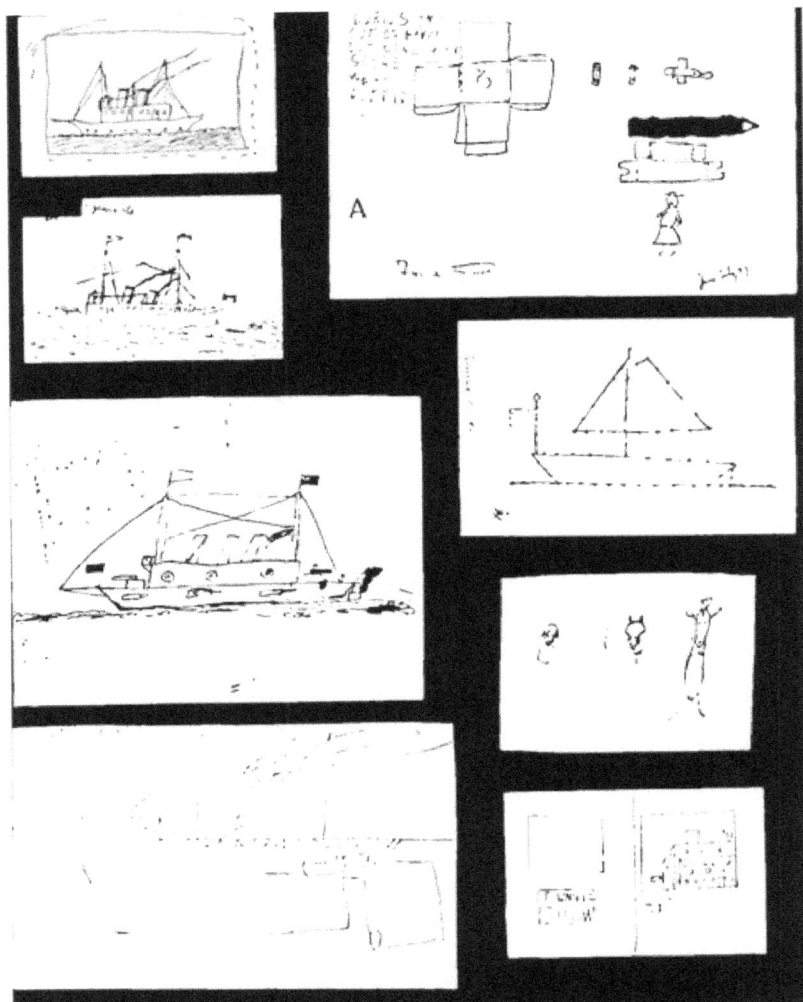

1897 DRAWINGS—SEVEN YEARS OLD

A. For a theatre. Note spelling of "directions." The child learned all his spelling from observation or sound. He was never told when he spelled a word wrong, but if he asked how to spell a word, he was told correctly.

I heard him say to himself the other day:

> "This is the mighty dragon,
> His home is in a cave,
> And still he does not
> Know how to behave."

February 23d.—The following original story was told very rapidly by the child, when seven, to his mother, just before going to sleep. He called it—

A STORY ALL UPSIDEDOWN

CHAPTER I

Once upon a time, in olden days, they had men turned into monkeys, and fishes were turned into dragons, and elephants were turned into fishes, and people walked on the sky. All the rocks and stones and pebbles were alive, and everything was turned upsidedown — everybody walked on their hands, and curtains were turned into people's coats; so there was a boy that wasn't changed into anything.

CHAPTER II

And this boy will tell you where he was. He was once living in a little cottage in a dark woods (wood—his correction); so one day he went out of his cottage, dressed up as a soldier, and locked up his cottage; so he went and walked and walked and walked until he came to a mountain, and he saw two little men fighting; so he went up to them and said, "What's that ring lying down there?" So they said, "That is a wishing-ring, and we are fighting to get it." So he went off about a quarter of a mile and stuck a spear into the ground, and then went

217

back to them and said, " Whoever gets that spear first
shall have the ring." So off went the little men at full
tilt, and he picked up the ring while they were running,
and then called to them and said, "Now neither of you
have got the ring; I have got it myself." So he wished
himself up at the top of the mountain he had come to,
because he could not climb up it; and when he was up
at the top of the mountain he saw a man that had don-
key's ears and a cat's tail, and crooked toes, as crooked
as sprigs; and so the funny man said to the soldier with
the wishing-ring, " Now I will kill you." So they are
fighting yet, I suppose.

The following was told by Harold without a pause,
September 17, 1897, when seven and a half years old:

A WONDERFUL DREAM

Once upon a time there was a little girl and a little
boy who lived all alone in a tree, and somebody found
them and took them home to his house and gave them
a little room, and they got in bed and went to sleep, and
at night-time the man came in and looked at them and
said, " Those children look as if they were going to sleep
nicely." And they went asleep so coseyly and slept so
snug and warm that he didn't disturb them. And one
night the children heard him saying in the other room,
"If you are not out of this house by to-morrow morning you will have to go away and live out in the woods."
And they didn't hear him at first, and so they got up
and got dressed and went down-stairs and took their
fishing hook and line, and went out to fish. They found

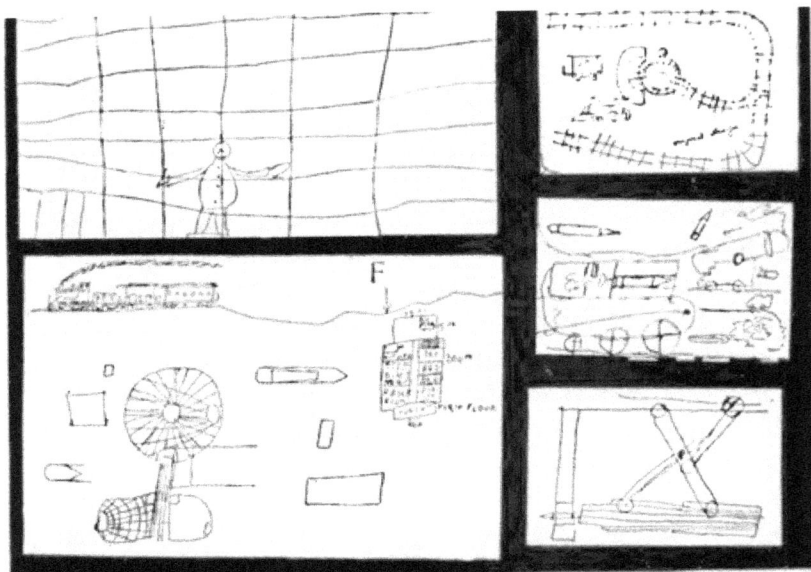

1897 DRAWINGS

A. Washington car on Fourteenth street; B, disappearing cannon; C, curved track; D, d, original designs of track for his engine; E, jail; F, plan for first floor of a house.

1897 DRAWINGS—SEVEN YEARS OLD

A, two boys on sleds going to the opening in the ground leading to the fairy's home underneath; a, chairs for the king and queen of the fairies; B, cut work for toy theatre.

1897 AND 1898 DRAWINGS

A, boats and war boats; B, American flag; C, "Spain getting licked," the child said; a, U. S. shells hit; b, "Spain shells have no force and fall to c"; D, memory work; E, concept of fraction work; F, writing from memory; G, Disappearing cannon; H, b, giant and the beanstalk.

some clams lying along the side on the sand in their shells, and they found a nice new penknife lying in the grass, and they took that and opened the clam-shell, and put a piece of clam on their fishing-hook; they threw the line in, and by-and-by they had a great big fish on the end of their line, and they pulled and pulled and pulled and they couldn't get it up; but at last they got it up, and then it was only a little bit of a fish about as big as a small alarm-clock. There it was on the line, and it began talking, and all of a sudden it jumped and went back into the water, and they went off and went asleep near a tree, and when they awoke they saw they were close by a deep pit, and all of a sudden it began to rain dirt right over the pit until the pit got filled up, and then they saw a beautiful fairy with a long train on her skirt, and a thousand little brownies were lifting it up in their hands, walking along behind her, a foot away from each other, and so they walked after the pretty fairy right straight up to the little girl and boy. The boy's name was Tommy, and the little girl's name was Jennie, and the fairy said, " Here's a ring," and she pulled two pieces of grass up out of the field (wood), and tied it together and touched it with her wand and said, "Here's a ring, Tommy, and here's a ring for you too, Jennie;" and she said, "Just turn this ring around on your finger for what you want and you will have it immediately before you." And so Jennie and Tommy said "Thank you" to the fairy, and they wished for a house and things to eat in it, and they got it, and a river was in front of the house, about one-eighth of a mile away from it, and a little dock-place, with a naphtha-launch outside tied fast, and five cans of naphtha in a little room in the dock, and they got in this little naphtha-launch and went sailing up and down, and at night a great big castle grew up out of a hole, and the naphtha-launch and everything burned up, and the little girl got awake and found herself in bed, and it was only a dream.

The record above shows clearly how the child's spontaneously developed *self*-activity is enlarging the boundaries of his knowledge; and the more he acquires, the greater is his desire for study. He is keen to observe, quick to comprehend, and has an excellent memory, which, with his indicated *self-control*, will make all future work easy. He shows no sign of physical strain; he is only a romping, hearty, obedient boy, and full of fun, when not repressed by unsympathetic surroundings; and instead of thinking of lessons as a task, he is always more eager to learn than his parents are willing to have him taught. His mind is thus rapidly expanding without endangering his physical equilibrium.

THE END

www.ingramcontent.com/pod-product-compliance
Lightning Source LLC
Chambersburg PA
CBHW021118270326
41929CB00009B/943